The Archers
Archives

The Archers
Archives

60 YEARS OF LIFE, LOVE
AND STORIES FROM AMBRIDGE

SIMON FRITH
AND CHRIS ARNOT

This book is published to accompany the BBC Radio 4 series *The Archers*.

The editor of *The Archers* is Vanessa Whitburn.

1 3 5 7 9 10 8 6 4 2

Published in 2010 by BBC Books, an imprint of Ebury Publishing.
A Random House Group Company

Script extracts written by: Edward J. Mason, Geoffrey Webb, Bruno Milna – pg10, 19, 22, 25, 28, 34, 41, 48, 56, 66;
Brian Hayles – pg59; Keith Miles – pg70; Helen Leadbetter – pg85; Margaret Phelan – pg108; Brendan Martin – pg122;
Sally Wainwright – pg133; Mick Martin – pg136; Louise Page – pg153; Joanna Toye – pg168, 200, 210;
Mary Cutler – pg180; Adrian Flynn – pg202; Graham Harvey – pg223.

The Random House Group Limited Reg. No. 954009

Addresses for companies within the Random House Group can be found at
www.randomhouse.co.uk

A CIP catalogue record for this book is available from the British Library.

ISBN 978 1 84990013 3

The Random House Group Limited supports the Forest Stewardship Council (FSC), the leading international
forest certification organisation. All our titles that are printed on Greenpeace approved FSC certified paper
carry the FSC logo. Our paper procurement policy can be found at www.rbooks.co.uk/environment

Commissioning editor: Albert DePetrillo
Project editor: Nicholas Payne
Copy-editor: Steve Tribe
Designer: O'Leary & Cooper
Production: Phil Spencer

Printed and bound by Firmengruppe APPL, aprinta druck, Wemding, Germany.

To buy books by your favourite authors and register for offers, visit www.rbooks.co.uk

ACKNOWLEDGEMENTS

Special thanks to the Editor of *The Archers*, Vanessa Whitburn, and her production team, especially *Archers* Archivist Camilla Fisher, who worked so hard to provide facts and photos. The book wouldn't exist without Joanna Toye and past production staff, along with the many dedicated writers and performers whose creative input has shaped the programme throughout its sixty years. Thanks also to Nick Payne and Albert DePetrillo for their encouragement and editorial support; also to Dr Roy Brigden, keeper of the Museum of English Rural Life at the University of Reading for his insight into the history of post-war agriculture.

No one book can hope to provide a wholly comprehensive picture of such a long-running and wide-ranging drama, and apologies are due to any whose favourite story or character has been inadvertently missed. Those wishing for more should read Joanna Toye's entertaining and informative Archers Trilogy – *Family Ties*, *Looking for Love* and *Back to the Land*, which were an invaluable help in the reconstruction of the earlier years of the series.

FOREWORD

I will have been running *The Archers* for twenty years in 2011, and the team has created some fantastic storylines in that time.

The first under my editorship was Elizabeth's heartbreaking affair with fraudster Cameron Fraser, which led to her decision to have an abortion, against her mum's wishes. This provoked a huge debate in the real world as listeners on both sides lined up for Elizabeth or for Jill. I always enjoy storylines that ripple out into the real world in that way.

Another was the raid on the village shop which led to the imprisonment of Susan Carter and the 'Free the Ambridge One' campaign. Started by a listener, it ended up with badges, comments from MPs in Parliament and a petition in the *Daily Mail* for the Editor to stop the sentence!

Then there was the death of Mark, Shula's grief and the birth of Daniel, the child Mark never saw; the Grundys' bankruptcy and the loss of their farm; the inheritance battle at Brookfield leading to the long-term feud between David and Elizabeth, and 'Who's the daddy?' as the press labelled the story of Emma. She married Will yet thought she was pregnant by his brother. And, of course, there was Brian's affair with Siobhan. But there were many others, just as there were during the forty years before I took the helm.

The death of Grace after the fire at the Stables in 1955 has become an iconic moment in broadcasting history, and when Tom was arrested and charged with manslaughter in 1957 the nation held its collective breath until he was released. Then there was poor Dan's battle with foot-and-mouth at Brookfield, echoes of which swept through the family when David had to face a possible outbreak in 2001. In the middle of the Swinging Sixties, Jennifer scandalised Ambridge by announcing she was pregnant and refusing to tell her parents the identity of the father. Then Shula caused an outcry in the 1970s when she rolled over in the hay with reckless journalist Simon Parker. The 1980s saw the introduction of organic farming when Tony and Pat took Bridge Farm down a route that felt outlandish to some at the time, but which has now proved itself in the farming mainstream.

In the pages of this book you can relive these stories if, like me, you heard many of them at the time. For newer listeners it's a chance to catch up with the history of a unique and often ground-breaking drama. Beautifully told by Simon Frith, one of the leading writers on the *Archers* script team and augmented with interviews conducted with members of the cast and production team by Chris Arnot, the book also gives you a behind-the-scenes peek into the way the programme is put together and an insight into the lives of our clever team of actors.

Enjoy it and, above all, keep listening as we head towards our centenary.

Vanessa Whitburn
Editor, *The Archers*

Chapter One 1950s

Decades are not neatly tied up at each end like links of Tom Archer sausages. Trends that began in the 1950s gathered pace in the 1960s, while farmers in the 1950s could only begin to invest in the mechanisation that would increase efficiency in subsequent decades because of the security that flowed from the 1947 Agriculture Act. Representatives of the post-war Labour government agreed to meet with the National Farmers Union every February to set a guaranteed figure below which the price of grain in particular would not be allowed to fall.

Farmers have long memories and those, like Dan Archer, who had fought in the First World War, remembered the 'great betrayal' that followed when the government of the day reneged on a similar promise to underwrite losses. Result: swathes of the countryside became inter-war wastelands.

This time, it seems, the government meant what it said, and subsequent administrations stood by the pledge. As the 1950s wore on, the process of mechanisation gathered pace. Some farmers, such as Dan's friend Walter Gabriel, remained resistant to change. Indeed Walter was prepared to buy his 'old pal' and 'old beauty's' plodding plough-puller Boxer when, in 1951, Dan invested in a different kind of horse power. He was not alone.

On the Land...

- By the end of the 1950s, tractors had replaced horses on most British farms.
- The number of combine harvesters, binding and threshing in one operation, quintupled from roughly 10,000 in 1950 to around 50,000 by 1960. In 1955, haymaking at Brookfield was still un-mechanised – but not for much longer.
- Frozen fingers squeezing a cow's udder were gradually being replaced by milking machines. Brookfield acquired its first egg-washing machine in 1952.
- In 1953, myxomatosis was introduced to the UK as a way of controlling the damage caused to crops by rampant rabbits. The disease visited a prolonged and agonising death on 95 per cent of the rabbit population within two years.
- Shorthorn cattle were slowly but surely being replaced by Fresians with higher milk yields. The big switch in Ambridge happened in 1956 after the Brookfield herd was devastated by foot-and-mouth disease.

... And in the Land Beyond the Farm Gate

- A few months after the launch of *The Archers* in 1951, the Festival of Britain opened on London's South Bank, offering a vision of a brighter, modernist future in grey, pinched post-war days.
- Rationing continued well into the 1950s and was only lifted on meat and bacon in 1954. Petrol rationing briefly resumed during the Suez crisis of 1956.
- ITV's launch on 22 September 1955 was rather scuppered by the death of Grace Archer, which had over 20 million listeners anchored to the 'wireless'.
- Teddy boys ran amok in cinemas during *The Blackboard Jungle* (1956) and Elvis Presley's *Jailhouse Rock* (1957).
- Novelists like Alan Sillitoe and John Braine wrote about mean streets and factories they knew, laying the foundations for a new wave of British cinema known as 'kitchen sink dramas'.
- Harold Macmillan told the nation that they'd never had it so good.
- Ownership of TV sets went up from 53 per cent of households to 78 per cent between 1957 and 1960.

1950s

NEW YEAR'S EVE, 1950: a little over five years after the end of the Second World War and almost thirty years since Dan and Doris Archer had begun their life together as tenants of Brookfield Farm, Ambridge. Doubtless many of those years had brought their share of long winters, cold springs, wet Junes and storms at harvest time; but as the Archer family gathered in the Brookfield kitchen to welcome in the New Year, Dan and Doris could reflect that they had much to be grateful for. Hard work, sound management and government subsidies had earned them a modest prosperity. Their youngest child, 20-year-old Christine, had won a grammar-school scholarship and now had a job at Borchester dairies. Phil, 22, had trained at the Farm Institute and looked set to have a successful farming career ahead of him. True, their eldest son Jack wasn't making quite such a success of running his smallholding, but he and his wife Peggy had already given them two lively granddaughters, and Peggy was now expecting a third child. Also invited to share their New Year celebrations was Phil's girlfriend, Grace Fairbrother, who (in spite of Doris's hopes) wasn't quite ready to become one of the family.

FADE IN ON FAMILY INFORMALLY
SINGING AULD LANG SYNE

DAN — And a Happy New Year to all!

GENERAL EXCHANGE OF GREETINGS

DORIS — (QUIETLY) A very happy New Year, Dan.

DAN — Thanks, mother. If it's as good as the last 'un I'll be satisfied.

JACK — How about some more of that rich and ripe old cooking port, Dad?

DAN — That's no cooking port, Jack. You've got no palate on you. Your mother bought that at old Mrs Benson's sale two years ago, and goodness only knows how long it had been lay down in her cellar.

JACK — Doesn't seem to have been lying down with very good company.

DORIS — Really, Jack!

DAN — Never mind Jack, mother. It's good enough for me. And now we've all got our glasses filled, here's a toast.

PHILIP — (POMPOUS) Pray silence for the lord and master of Brookfield Farm and Sire of the illustrious Family of Archer and – and –

CHRISTINE — Shut up, Philip.

DAN — (SERIOUS) Doris, Christine, Jack, Philip, Peggy – and that includes your two youngsters, me dear, and the one on the way – I – Oh, and I mustn't forget you, Miss Fairbrother.
Well – all of you – I haven't got much to say, but – somehow –

PHILIP — You're going to take a long time saying it.

DAN — (GOOD NATURED) Shut up, Philip, you're putting me off. All I want to say is – here's to the coming year and may we all get what we're after, may we go on being as happy and united a family as we've been up to now – and may the weather be a bit kinder to all farmers.

HEAR HEARS AND LAUGHTER

Young Love ❧

Phil Archer was a hard-working and headstrong young countryman, determined to make his own way in the farming business. Grace (the daughter of well-to-do widower and neighbour George Fairbrother) was a stunning, sophisticated girl, more used to the city life, who could be both passionate and wilful. So perhaps it was inevitable that their courtship soon ran into complications.

(Opposite)
Dan and Doris Archer
(Harry Oakes and
Gwen Berryman)
at Brookfield Farm

The year had hardly begun when Phil got into trouble after crashing Grace's car while taking Rita Flynn, the flirtatious Bull barmaid, to the station. Grace forgave him when she realised that his intentions were strictly honourable, but then it was Phil's turn to become jealous of Grace's involvement with dashing Korean War veteran, Lt. Alan Carey. What threatened to become a love triangle soon took on a more complicated geometry when Phil became farm manager to Grace's father, George. Phil quickly forged a close working relationship with Jane Maxwell, a tall blonde with well-to-do parents, who was in charge of Fairbrother's poultry flock. Grace soon became suspicious of their friendship, and not – or so it would appear – without some reason. She came across the pair out rabbiting together, and swimming al fresco

Grace (Monica Grey)
flirts with Phil (Norman
Painting) watched by
George Fairbrother
(Leslie Bowmar)

in a local pond. But the real crisis came when she discovered them in what seemed to be a romantic embrace in the farm office. Deeply hurt, this time she wasn't convinced by Phil's excuses, and began to think that she'd lost him for good. Then, later in the year, George Fairbrother announced that he and Grace would be leaving the area, following the collapse of his scheme to turn much of his land into an ironstone mine. Doris must have despaired of ever seeing Phil and Grace walk down the aisle together.

Family and Friends ❧

There was cause for much celebration when Peggy gave birth to a son, Anthony William Daniel, a young brother to 6-year-old Jennifer and 4-year-old Lilian. The birth heralded another arrival in the short but formidable form of Peggy's mother, Mrs Perkins, better known as Mrs P. It wasn't long before she was befriended by Walter Gabriel, who gave her a Siamese kitten. This was to be the start of a long if intermittent campaign by Walter to win her affections, stoutly resisted (on the whole) by Mrs P.

Say it with a cabbage:
Walter woos Mrs P
(Chriss Gittins and
Pauline Seville)

Christine, meanwhile, became friendly with Dick Raymond, reporter on the *Borchester Echo*. At the same time – perhaps feeling the need to keep up with her elder brother – she also began seeing visiting mineralogist Keith Latimer.

The Archer family at tea. Phil, Doris, Dan and Christine (Lesley Saweard)

Hearts and Mines

The reason for Latimer's presence in the area became clear when George Fairbrother revealed that he intended to mine the large ironstone deposits beneath his land. Although Phil naturally hated the prospect of the loss of hundreds of acres of good farmland, he found his loyalties divided, as Fairbrother was his employer as well the father of the girl he loved. The opposition campaign soon turned ugly when drilling equipment was sabotaged. Duty-bound, Phil organised a small group of vigilantes, including Dick Raymond and Jane Maxwell, but after a daring night-time skirmish they failed to catch the mysterious culprits. Soon after that, Mrs P's landlord Bill Slater died after a brawl in The Bull and stolen drilling equipment was found in his shed. Fairbrother's plans were ultimately doomed, however. Although accepted by a public enquiry, there were technical problems, and he also confessed himself deeply affected by Bill Slater's death. He eventually abandoned the scheme and took Grace off to the French Riviera, hinting that he might never come back. Most of Ambridge breathed a long sigh of relief.

Lovers and Rivals ✑

1952

If Jane had hoped that Grace's departure would leave the field clear for her to pursue Phil, she was to be sorely disappointed, as Grace's absence only served to remind Phil where his true affections lay. Eventually a disheartened Jane conceded defeat, gave Phil a week's notice and went back to live with her parents. This left the estate poultry without a keeper, a vacancy promptly filled by Grace when her father decided to return to live in Ambridge after all. Her romance with Phil looked set to be on course again, to the satisfaction of Dan and Doris; on one of her frequent visits to Brookfield they entertained her by singing a duet of 'Down The Vale'.

However – as Phil suspected – Grace wasn't such a natural in the art of poultry care. After the untimely death of some day-old chicks she decided that she was happier working with horses and would use some of her mother's legacy to open a riding stable at Grey Gables. She managed to recruit Christine for her practical skills, and the two girls set up a partnership. Perhaps prompted by this show of independence, Phil decided it was time to take the initiative and attempted a man-to-man talk with Fairbrother about his prospects of marrying Grace. When he discovered that she was far wealthier than he'd assumed, he told her that he would only marry her when he'd saved £2,000 of his own money – no more, no less. She was dismayed at the prospect of what might be several years' wait. This wasn't just out of a desire to share her life with the man she loved; her father had remarried, and she found her role at home usurped by her new stepmother, Helen, who soon announced her pregnancy. In spite of all this, Phil's strong sense of self-respect – and obstinacy – led him to stick doggedly to his guns. Grace's patience was quickly put to the test by the arrival of the Squire's nephew, Clive Lawson-Hope, who'd come to Ambridge to help manage his father's estate. He gave her first aid after a minor car crash, and then asked her out to the pictures. It began to look as if Phil had a serious rival.

Grace (Ysanne Churchman) and Phil

Family and Friends ✑

Christine's relationship with Dick Raymond faltered when he accepted a newspaper job in London, and then, soon after, in Malaya. She continued writing him fond letters but his replies became steadily fewer. The final blow for Chris came when she heard from a chance visitor that Dick was engaged

Dan at home with daughter Christine

Profile
PHIL ARCHER

T HE VOICE THAT BECAME familiar to millions as Phil Archer was 'glorious, comforting and warm, like fruit chutney' as one obituary put it. This was a man of 85 who had survived cancer only to be brought low by one heart attack after another. But he was also an old trouper who wanted to carry on working until the end. He was driven up to the studios in Birmingham from his home in an idyllic Warwickshire village two days before his death. Only the week before, he had levered himself upright, handed the key through the kitchen window and sat down to reminisce and reflect when he would rather have stayed in bed.

By then *The Archers* was not too far off its 60th anniversary. Yet Norman Painting had hardly expected the series to last six weeks. Nor, it seems, did the fellow cast members with whom he gathered for a characteristically meagre lunch at the old Broad Street studios' canteen late in 1950. 'Harry Oakes, who played Dan remarked that the £12 a week that he was getting wasn't a sum to be sneezed at,' Dan's fictional son recalled.

There was a stunned silence as what Oakes had just said sank in. The actors had

been assured by *Archers* founder Godfrey Baseley that they were all being paid the same. 'It transpired from the conversation around that lunch table that we were on different rates and that I was being paid not much more than half what Harry was getting,' Norman remembered.

There followed a noisy confrontation between himself and Godfrey – or 'God', as he was known in the studio. It took place in the music room and the shouting was punctuated by the discordant accompaniment of clenched fists slamming into keyboards. 'I've never had such a row in my life,' sighed the actor.

Baseley was not used to being queried. His last words to the angry young man confronting him were: 'If I ever hear that a member of this cast has discussed his or her fee with another, there'll be trouble.' Norman smiled wanly. 'It was an empty threat. But after that row we became good friends. I saw another side of Godfrey – the first-rate poetry reader on the old Third Programme.' And Godfrey saw another side of Norman as one who could write as well as act.

At Baseley's insistence, he eventually turned out 1,198 *Archers* scripts under his nom de plume of Bruno Milna. He wrote here, in the heart of rural England, one ear tuned for the rhythms of village life ('It matters that we get it right'). After a day at the typewriter, he would plunge into his swimming pool and do twenty lengths before supper. The pool is empty now and his study long mothballed. It was lined with books and oak panelling, rather like his rooms at Christ Church College.

He lectured on Anglo-Saxon, having won a scholarship to Oxford through a first-class honours degree in English from Birmingham University – no mean achievement for a railway signaller's son in those days. His undergraduate production of *King Lear* at Birmingham is still talked about by those old enough to remember.

> '... there was no possibility of *The Archers* being labelled predictable.'

It was a different kind of dramatic tragedy, however, that made Phil Archer a household name. Some 20 million listeners tuned in on 22 September 1955, when Phil's first wife Grace was killed in a barn fire. The episode has passed into broadcasting folklore. For that week only, episodes were recorded on the day of transmission – in London, not Birmingham. Norman remembered meeting Ysanne Churchman (Grace) in a corridor shortly before recording. 'She was white-faced. "They've done it," she said. "They've killed me off." I didn't know quite what to say. Part of me could see that it was a very clever idea for the programme. After that, there was no possibility of *The Archers* being labelled predictable.' Another part of him was sympathetic to a fellow actor. Norman, Ysanne and her husband Tony used to gather for what they called the Grace Archer Memorial Lunch every 22 September.

And Norman Painting, OBE? He will never be forgotten. Apart from anything else, his name is engraved on a paving stone outside the site of the old Broad Street studios. 'I'm quite touched,' he said, just before recording that last episode, 'that the younger actors seem quite anxious to talk to me.' And why not? The name Phil Archer resonated with the listening public for nigh-on sixty years.

Six weeks indeed!

Profile
PEGGY WOOLLEY

PEGGY RATHER THAN GRACE could have been the Archer sacrificed on the altar of a great storyline. Godfrey Baseley, the programme's first editor, considered bumping her off as early as 1953. The actress, June Spencer, was leaving the programme anyway because she and her husband were about to adopt the first of their two children. 'Godfrey was also cross because I'd refused to go to a cast party one Friday evening,' June confides. 'I'd already been up to Birmingham [from London] twice that week.'

She was never one to be intimidated by the formidable Baseley. 'Anyway the powers-that-be [H. Rooney Pelletier, no less, Controller of the old BBC Light Programme] said "no" to his plans. Quite right too,' she adds. 'Peggy was a key character, married to Dan and Doris's oldest son.'

Another actress, Thelma Rodgers, took over and became landlady of The Bull until June returned to the role in 1962. 'God' had obviously forgiven her. Baseley knew acting talent when he heard it. He even allowed her to come back to the studio during the intervening

years in the less time-consuming part of the flighty Flynn – Rita Flynn, that is, who worked in Doughy Hood's bakery and spent much of her spare time on the other side of the bar from Peggy. 'I modelled her Irish accent on my old landlady in London,' she recalls, stirring sweeteners into her coffee.

We're sitting in the lobby of the BBC's Mailbox studios. Igglepiggle, Upsy Daisy and other CBeebies characters cavort silently across the TV screen behind her while June is waiting to record yet another episode of The Archers. She's the only surviving cast member who was in the programme for the very first pilot of what was billed as a 'farming Dick Barton'. Ah, yes, *Dick Barton*, Special Agent. You'd have to be getting on a bit to remember that radio thriller. Well, June is 91 and she doesn't just remember it; she was in it. 'I played assorted heroines, locked in cupboards or tied up in cellars with the water rising,' she says nonchalantly.

It's difficult to believe that this poised and wryly humorous woman was born a year or so after the end of the First World War. By 1943, four years into the next war, she was a professional actress, having cut her teeth doing after-dinner sketches at Masonic lodges in her native Nottingham. She wrote them too. 'I did Joyce Grenfell-type monologues,' she smiles. 'I used various characters, like a dizzy blonde and a north country Cinderella. Oh yes, and a Cockney woman from the ATS.' Not unlike Peggy, who was in the Auxiliary Territorial Service before she left the East End for Ambridge and the first of her two Jacks. 'That's right; she was. Of course, I didn't know Peggy then.'

She certainly knows her now. And she came to know Jack Archer all too well. The dashing wartime private became a peacetime publican and drank The Bull's profits. 'Poor old Peggy,' says June. 'She doesn't have much fun.' Her

> **'… I knew exactly how Peggy felt and what she was going through.'**

second Jack, the avuncular Brummie businessman, known to most of the village as Mr Woolley, gave her love and money but their happiness was short-lived. 'When Vanessa [Whitburn] called me into the editor's office and asked me how I felt about a storyline about Alzheimer's, I was all for it,' the actress goes on. 'The more publicity it gets the better.'

Her real-life husband Roger had dementia for ten years before dying from a stroke in 2001. 'He never became as bad as Jack, but I knew exactly how Peggy felt and what she was going through,' June reflects. 'I was asked to talk to the scriptwriters and they gave me a round of applause at the end. That was very touching. The writing has been so good all the way through.' It must have been difficult to read, though. 'Well, I used to get the tears out of the way at home so I could focus in the studio.'

She lives in a village in Surrey. 'A real place, not a commuter dormitory,' she points out. 'Everybody knows everybody else's business.' Mmmm… that sounds familiar. 'The church is divided between happy-clappies and fuddy-duddies. I'm one of the latter. I don't like dancing in the aisles.' Sounds familiar again. 'But in other ways I'm more broad-minded than Peggy,' she insists as she sets off for the studio and Igglepiggle waves goodbye from the screen behind her.

Love triangle:
Clive Lawson-Hope
(Leslie Parker)
with Grace and Phil

to a tea-planter's daughter. Perhaps in an attempt to distract herself from these disappointments, she became friendly with eccentric Lady Hyleberrow, who wanted to take her away on a trip to Ethiopia. Doris was horrified at the idea, and she was persuaded not to go. Dan offered her a job looking after the Brookfield poultry and, for her 21st birthday, he and Doris gave her a beautiful jet-black horse whom she called Midnight.

There was another upset for Doris when Jack gave up his unequal struggle with his smallholding and took his family away to Cornwall, where he set up in a partnership with his wartime friend, Barney Lee, whom Doris mistrusted and Dan thought was a bit of a spiv. Dan bought the smallholding for £1,300. But Doris's doubts were justified when Jack brought the family home again after Barney had started chasing Peggy. Jack decided that he'd had enough of farming, and applied to become licensee of The Bull.

1953

Spies and Lovers

The big talking point of the year concerned the mystery surrounding the identity of thriller writer Mike Daly, who lived at Blossom Hill Cottage. Reggie Trentham, the owner of Grey Gables, tried to expose him as a fraud by confronting him with his supposed fiancée, Valerie Grayson. The astonishing truth was that Mike was a wartime secret agent, who'd ended up in Dachau prison camp, and that Valerie too was an agent, only posing as Mike's fiancée as part of an elaborate cover story arranged by the intelligence services to conceal his real identity. This was good news for Reggie, who'd taken quite a shine to Valerie, the glamorous spy. Within a few months they were married.

Missed Chances

Both Phil's resolution and Grace's loyalty were severely challenged when, in February, Clive Lawson-Hope asked Grace to be his wife. She played for time, perhaps hoping that it might spur Phil into marrying her before it was too late. Phil, though, refused to be budged, telling her that she should do as she saw fit, and carried on saving the profits from his pig business.

In the end Grace's indecision was too much for Clive, who told her that he'd changed his mind. By the eve of Coronation day, Phil and Grace were back together roasting potatoes at the celebration bonfire. Soon after, however, she shocked him by announcing that she'd arranged to go to Ireland for a year on a horse management course. This was enough to make Phil do some serious thinking. Mrs P offered to lend him money to boost his pig numbers, but he was still dithering when Grace took the train from Hollerton Junction. It looked like being a very long year for Phil. He even failed to notice when Reggie's cousin Anne Trentham tried flirting with him at Christmas.

GRACE	Thanks for last night anyway, Phil. It was wonderful fun.
PHIL	Does you good to do daft things sometimes.
GRACE	What's daft about roast potatoes?
PHIL	(LAUGHS) Nothing. But eating them at that time in the morning is just plain daft. Still, it had its compensations. You were enjoying yourself.
GRACE	Oh, I was, Phil. It was almost like … old times.
PHIL	Just what I felt… it was good to see you so happy.
GRACE	Was it?
PHIL	(GENTLY) I know the secret of success now.
GRACE	Yes?
PHIL	Carry a couple of potatoes around and when Grace is a bit down, light a bonfire and roast 'em.
GRACE	You might do a lot worse … You didn't mind me coming to see you before I went to the stables, did you? I felt I – I'd like to – just to say thank you.

Peggy and Jack (Thelma Rogers and Denis Folwell) at The Bull

Just good friends.
Walter and Mrs P

Dan with farm worker
Simon Cooper
(Eddie Robinson)

1954

Family and Friends

Dan and Doris must have kept their fingers firmly crossed when, early in the year, Jack took over the license of The Bull. All went well at first, but Jack seemed unable to commit himself to any venture for long. He split his time between the bar and casual farm work, and then – always fond of a tipple himself – began serving drinks after hours. The brewery found out and made him transfer the license to Peggy, who lost no time in smartening the place up and putting in a few comfy chairs for the customers.

Like Jack, feckless Walter Gabriel was never the most successful of farmers, but in the spring he suffered a serious blow when many of his sheep were mauled by stray dogs. Mrs P took pity on him and intervened on his behalf when the Squire threatened to evict him. By June, Walter had recovered enough to hold a Coronation party in his barn, with Mrs P's new television set as its proud centrepiece.

The Incomer

Tom Forrest, Doris's brother and gamekeeper for the estate, was hurt in a fight with poachers. Suspicion fell on a mysterious, bearded young man who'd recently parked his caravan on Heydon Berrow. When the stranger was also suspected of stealing one of Christine's horses, he proved his innocence by rescuing it from the clutches of local gypsies. The mystery of his identity was solved when Anne Trentham recognised him as John Tregorran, her former university lecturer, who'd won a large sum on the football pools and opted for the simple life. In spite of his dubious welcome from the locals, he accepted Walter's invitation to move his caravan down into the village, and looked set to stay for quite a while.

Patience Rewarded

With Grace away, Phil wrote her letters, worked hard at his pig business and managed to avoid any romantic entanglements until she finally sent him a telegram to say she was coming home. With Reggie's help, he arranged a lavish welcome home party at Grey Gables. This backfired when Phil – delayed by a farrowing pig – arrived late and promptly accused her of flirting with Paul Johnson, a keen horseman and friend of Christine's. Soon after, however, another quarrel over a flat tyre finally prompted Phil to propose, and Grace accepted. It's likely that Dan and Doris were tempted to frogmarch them both straight to the church, but the happy couple picked Easter Monday of the following year for their wedding day. Grace was content; after the bumpy ride of the last four years, another few months didn't seem so long to wait.

Family and Friends ☙

Although it was common knowledge that Squire Lawson-Hope had been in financial difficulties for some time, it came as a shock to his tenants when he announced that he was putting the estate up for sale. Dan had recently sold Jack's old smallholding to Carol Grey, a smart lady from the Home Counties and, after some nail-biting sessions with the bank manager, he managed to raise enough money to meet the Squire's asking price and buy Brookfield. So in July he and Doris ended their days as tenants and became proud owners of their hundred-acre farm. George Fairbrother bought the bulk of the estate and so became the new Squire of Ambridge.

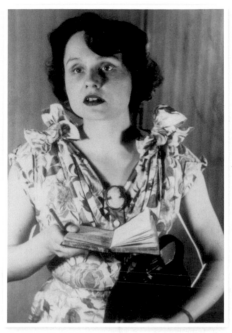

Forever young: Grace Fairbrother (Ysanne Churchman)

After his disappointment over Grace, Clive Lawson-Hope set his sights on Christine. Although, for different reasons, both Phil and Clive's father disapproved of the match, Clive had inherited his own farm in Kenya, and at the end of March he proposed to her. When she turned him down, he gave up on the Ambridge girls and set off to try his luck in East Africa.

Jack, meanwhile, was finding it hard playing second fiddle to Peggy at The Bull. His mood swings and drinking became a big worry for the family, and eventually led to a four-month spell as a voluntary patient at the County Hospital for Nervous and Mental Disorders.

New Arrivals ☙

1955

When Surrey-born newcomer Carol Grey took over the smallholding, she borrowed a pick and shovel and set about converting it into a market garden, working dawn to dusk and confounding the sceptics who thought she'd never make a go of it. She introduced herself to fellow incomer John Tregorran by accidentally knocking him off his motorbike. John (never one to hold a grudge against a pretty girl) responded later in the year by asking her to marry him. Carol assumed he was joking and didn't reply. However, by the end of what had been a busy, if mixed, year for proposals, Ambridge still had one wedding to look forward to.

Celebration and Tragedy ☙

Just one story was to dominate life in Ambridge this year: the dramatic conclusion to Phil and Grace's courtship.

CAROL	(GASPS) Look! She's going back into the stable.
REGGIE	What! No, Grace! Don't do it!
CAROL	She's going in after Midnight! Grace!
PHIL	Grace! Grace! Come back! The roof's collapsing!
	For God's sake, Grace, come back!
REGGIE	Look at that roof!
	(RUMBLE OF ROOF COLLAPSING)
	It's caving.
CAROL	Horrible!
JOHN	Phil! Phil you fool!
PHIL	Let me go! Grace is in there! Let me go, blast you, John!
JOHN	It's suicide! If you – (SMACK: JOHN REACTS)
PHIL	(GOING OFF FAST) Grace! Grace!
REGGIE	Phil, you madman!
CAROL	Don't let him!
	(RUNNING FOOTSTEPS ON GRAVEL. CRACKLE OF FIRE LOUDER. HOOVES APPROACHING AT THE GALLOP)
JOHN	(YELLING) Phil! Phil!
PHIL	(OFF) Look out! Midnight's gone crazy!
	(HORSE TO PEAK AND OFF, GALLOPING ON GRAVEL)
JOHN	Where are you!?
PHIL	(COUGHING, COMING NEARER) Near the tack … can't see… Grace! Grace! Oh my god! Grace! Where is she?

Given the happy couple's past form, some disagreement over the wedding plans was almost inevitable. Grace was not at all flattered by Phil's suggestion that they should bring the date forward and thus save £90 income tax. Phil got the message and St Stephen's church remained firmly booked for 11 April, Easter Monday. On the day, Jack – who'd come out of mental hospital in a much better state of mind – was best man, and Christine a bridesmaid. The bride wore a tulle dress with satin gloves, and (delayed by a faulty limousine) kept a tormented Phil waiting long enough for the organist to play the Organ Voluntary twice over. After the service, Reggie Trentham and friends chased after the car blowing hunting horns, and Phil drove over a ploughed field to escape them. The couple returned from their honeymoon to live at Coombe Farmhouse, let to them for the nominal sum of £1 a week by Fairbrother, who also offered Phil a directorship of his farming business. Man and wife at last, Phil and Grace's only regret was to wonder why they'd waited so long. But their new-found domestic happiness was soon to be overtaken by a terrible tragedy.

On the evening of 22 September, after Grace had overcome her initial doubts and agreed to start a family, a delighted Phil had booked a table at Grey Gables. Also invited to share the celebration were John Tregorran and Carol Grey, who were now going out together, although Carol was holding on fiercely to her independence. Over pre-dinner drinks in the bar, Grace went out to look for a lost earring and was shocked to discover that a fire had begun in the stables. She went to summon help and, as Phil and other guests helped her to rescue the horses, Christine's mare Midnight panicked and bolted back into the burning building. Grace bravely went in after her, was trapped by a falling beam and seriously injured. With John and Reggie's help, Phil managed to drag her clear. On the way to hospital she regained consciousness for just long enough to whisper to Phil that she loved him; a few moments later she died in his arms.

1956

Heartbreak at Brookfield

After the tragic loss of their daughter-in-law, Dan and Doris barely had the chance to draw breath when they were hit by another disaster. It began in January when their farm worker Simon Cooper noticed that two of their pigs were lame. Dan was devastated when the vet diagnosed suspected foot-and-mouth disease. Ministry restrictions were imposed immediately, the farm was quarantined and a policeman stationed at the gate. Dan could only wait and pray while his stock was tested, but at the end of February the disease was confirmed.

Dan lost his entire stock of forty-eight dairy shorthorns, forty ewes, thirty lambs and fifty-three pigs; a lifetime's work slaughtered in a few hours and buried in pits on the farm. Fortunately it proved to be an isolated outbreak caused by some uncooked liver that had been fed to the pigs, and hadn't spread beyond Brookfield. No doubt this was a huge relief for their farming neighbours, but cold comfort for Dan, who began seriously to consider selling up Brookfield and retiring. The farming blood ran deep in his veins, however, and by the time summer arrived he'd used some of his compensation money to buy eighty ewes and a pair of rams. In the autumn he began to rebuild his dairy herd, so ensuring that there would be Archers at Brookfield for at least a while longer. Simon Cooper retired and Dan took on a new farm worker called Ned Larkin.

Grief and Happiness

Doris remained very concerned for Phil, who bottled up his grief and stayed on at Coombe Farm with only his dog Timus for company. Although he kept on working, she could see that his heart wasn't in it.

In an attempt to bring him out of himself, George Fairbrother gave him a cine camera as an early Christmas present. So it was that Phil was in St Stephen's Church on 15 December to film the big family event of the year: Christine's marriage to Paul Johnson. With their shared passion for all things equestrian, the couple had been growing closer, but the match had nevertheless come as something of a surprise to Dan and Doris. Paul had proposed in June, and Christine had amazed her parents by coming home with a beautiful ruby engagement ring. Although she was blissfully happy, Paul's parents fancied themselves a cut above the Archers and made things awkward by trying to delay the wedding arrangements. When the day came, however, all went smoothly. The bride was radiant in a dress of white lace with billowing paper taffeta petticoats, Doris resplendent in violet silk and – not to be outdone – Mrs Johnson suitably chic in a full-length mink coat. Paul's sister Sally, now Christine's partner at the stables, was a bridesmaid, and the newly-weds were escorted to the reception by riding pupils on ponies. Phil kept himself busy throughout with his movie camera.

Dan Archer at work

Phil out with the muckspreader

Christine (Lesley Saweard)

1957

Tom's Trials ◠

Early in the year the whole community was shocked by a dramatic turn of events that overtook Doris's brother, Tom Forrest. After many years of seemingly contented bachelorhood, Tom had recently begun paying some attention to the new barmaid at The Bull, Pru Harris. Although Pru was more admired for her prize-winning chutney than her fashion sense, Tom soon had a rival in Ned Larkin's brother, Bob, a decidedly dodgy character with a taste for gin and peppermint. Although Bob persuaded Pru to go out with him once or twice, he soon began to upset her with his unwelcome advances, obliging Tom to politely warn him off. Later, Tom confessed to Doris that he was tempted to bash Bob's face in. This offhand remark soon came back to haunt him when, in the early hours of 21 February, he and Phil staked out the Fairbrother estate in the hope of catching poachers. Tom struggled with a man in the darkness, a gun went off, and Phil arrived on the scene to find Tom standing over the body of Bob Larkin, shot through the head by his own four-ten. Tom was taken into custody and charged with murder.

Although nobody who knew him – apart from Bob's brother Ned – believed that the death was anything other than a tragic accident, unfortunately for Tom other witnesses had heard him threaten Bob with violence. The police decided to pursue the case and he was held on remand for several weeks, before being released on bail pending trial, the charge now reduced to one of manslaughter. Although he hated the confinement, Tom bore his time in prison stoically. Pru was one of his many visitors and was in court when he stood trial at Borchester Assizes on 4 July. For two days, the whole community held its breath, but justice and common sense prevailed and the jury quickly dismissed the charge. Tom returned home a free man to a hero's welcome – hastily organised by Phil and Walter – and the strains of the Borchester silver band.

Tom Forrest on patrol
(Bob Arnold)

Wedding of the Year ◠

The day after his Uncle Tom's triumphant acquittal, Phil took his cine camera to the village show (opened this year by Humphrey Lyttleton) where his lens was attracted to a pretty blonde girl in a yellow dress. No one seemed to know who she was, but soon after he saw her again, demonstrating a kitchen gadget in a local department store. Wasting no time he chatted her up, found out that her name was Jill Patterson, and asked her out to dinner. It

Jill Archer
(Patricia Greene)

was love at first sight for Phil, but Jill was an orphan used to making her own way in the world and wasn't in such a hurry to give up her independence. Jill's urban background and travelling sales job made Doris wonder if she'd make a good wife for Phil, and Jill seemed to share some of these doubts herself; when Phil first proposed she told him that she'd never marry a farmer.

Undeterred, he kept up the pressure and she finally admitted that she loved him and said yes. He presented her with a diamond engagement ring and they were married on 16 November at St Luke's church, Crudley. She took three months off work to try out the farming life, and was seldom to be far from Phil's side for the next fifty-two years.

Around the Village

25 March – Lady Day – was a sad milestone for Walter, as he was finally forced to abandon his faltering agricultural career and give up his farm. With the proceeds of his farm sale he bought a minibus and set up as village carrier. Mrs P bought him a spotlight as a bus-warming present. But the fates seemed to be set against his new enterprise; later in the year his bus was hijacked by Teddy boys who slashed the seats with their flick-knives. Phil and John Tregorran gave him a nice surprise by paying for the repairs. Walter was back in business.

The other notable event was the arrival in Ambridge of Dan's sister-in-law, Laura, after the death of her husband Frank in New Zealand. Down-to-earth, outspoken and with money to spare, she stayed at Brookfield, then rented a cottage in the village, saying that she planned to be in England for a while.

The Newly-Weds

Although it was quite a steep learning curve for her, Jill soon began to adapt to her role as a farmer's wife, and it wasn't long at all before she announced her pregnancy to an overjoyed Phil. Dan and Doris shared their delight, doubly so when they discovered that she was expecting twins. After the two babies – a girl and a boy – were successfully delivered on 8 August, Phil opened a bottle of champagne in Hollerton High Street and shared it with Walter Gabriel, who was passing at the time. Phil and Jill eschewed the traditional family names and the twins were christened Shula and Kenton.

Although quick to offer her congratulations, Christine found herself envying her brother's happiness, as hers remained a childless marriage. At the end of the year she went for medical tests and was found to be fit and healthy. She and Paul would just have to keep trying.

TOM	Let go o' the gun, you fool, or I'll give you a right pastin'.
BOB	No!
	(WRESTLING CONTINUES. TWIGGY UNDERGROWTH RUSTLING AND SNAPPING)
TOM	(STRAINING) By golly! I know you now, you rascal! 'Tis Bob Larkin!
PHIL	(APPROACHING) Uncle Tom! Uncle Tom!
TOM	Over here!
PHIL	Hold the blighter!
BOB	My wrist –
TOM	Leave hold then! Go on – let go! (GREAT STRAINING EFFORT)
BOB	I'll – (GASP OF SURPRISE)
	(SOUND OF BODIES CRASHING THROUGH BUSH MIXED WITH SINGLE FOUR-TEN SHOT)
PHIL	(NEARER) Uncle Tom! Uncle Tom! Are you all right!
TOM	(PANTS)
PHIL	(NEARER, MORE ANXIOUS) Uncle Tom!
TOM	(ALREADY FEARING THE WORST) Here!... Quick!!!!! Bring your torch. Hurry!
	(SOUND OF PHIL RUNNING IN)
PHIL	(COMING ON) What's happened? You're covered in blo–...
TOM	I'm all right. Shine it on him down there. It's Bob Larkin.
PHIL	(TURNING SLIGHTLY OFF) Bob Lar – .... (AGHAST) Oh my God!

1958

Famous folk who opened the village fete:

HUMPHREY LYTTLETON, 1957

Profile

JILL ARCHER

PATRICIA 'PADDY' GREENE FAILED to impress her tutor in microphone technique at the Central School of Drama. 'You sound like a fairy in hockey boots,' she was told. 'You'll never broadcast.' As it happens, Paddy didn't particularly want a career in radio. She wanted to be a classical stage actress. Instead she became the vocal embodiment of Britain's best known farmer's wife – after the demise of Doris, anyway. 'Jill Archer has stolen my voice,' Paddy proclaims with a clarity that could still reach the back row of the upper circle if called upon.

Admittedly we are in a rather clamorous café opposite the BBC's Mailbox studios. Paddy is about to record what, sadly, turns out to be the last scene with Norman Painting as the steadfast Phil. Their marriage had been the rock around which the sometimes murky waters of radio drama frothed or flowed. Other couples have floated apart while casting around for other fish in the sea. But Phil and Jill? Never. 'Playing a warm, homely voice for fifty-three years can be difficult at times,' the actress confesses. 'Saint Jill I call her. The only awful thing I remember her doing was

running over a deer, and that was an accident. She didn't dare tell Phil for a while.' Nor Brian, perhaps. Wasn't that deer a stock of valuable venison steaks? 'I don't think Brian had been cast at the time.'

As an *Archers* character, Jill goes back – way back to 1957. Difficult as it may be for younger listeners to imagine, she was meant to be what Paddy calls 'a bit of fluff' for Phil. 'It was two years after the death of Grace and he was allowed to look at another woman,' she recalls. He could have more than one look, indeed, because he filmed her with his cine camera, having spotted her across a crowded tea tent at the church fête. Shortly afterwards, he spotted her again, demonstrating a device called the 'Household Drudge' in Mitchells of Borchester. They married just four months later.

Paddy would have preferred them to wait a while. Despite her misgivings about broadcasting, she was rather enjoying playing a sexy blonde. 'I could do sex,' she insists. 'In fact, I got the role by doing a Fenella Fielding.' Note to younger listeners: FF had a husky voice and a breathy delivery that would lead to her being dubbed 'the first lady of the *double entendre*.' Paddy's version of it certainly worked on *Archers* producer Tony Shryane. He was prepared to wait six weeks while the actress fulfilled her early ambitions by travelling around Europe in classical productions with the Oxford Playhouse. For her it made a pleasant change from treading the boards twice nightly in repertory tours of South Wales and remote parts of northern England.

The lure of seven guineas an episode (several hundred pounds at today's prices) for a regular part in *The Archers* was too tempting to turn down, however. 'I remember my first husband saying: "I'll do the posh stuff. You can earn the bread and butter."' Paddy takes another sip of her coffee before recalling the sometimes

'I could do sex …
I got the role
by doing a
Fenella Fielding.'

conflicting parts written for young Jill by the *Archers'* script writers of the day, Edward J Mason and Geoffrey Webb. 'Ted liked sophisticated women who drank gin and tonic and painted their nails while Geoffrey preferred nice country ladies with apple cheeks. In the end I had to go to Tony and ask what I was supposed to do about my rather Jekyll and Hyde character.'

Shryane's somewhat enigmatic response was to advise her to 'play against the lines throughout.' What on earth did that mean? 'Haven't a clue.' Editor Godfrey Baseley soon solved her dilemma, however, by briskly announcing: 'Congratulations. You're getting married. You can cut the sex now.' At the time she was still getting letters from listeners, apparently unable to separate real life from fiction, accusing her of usurping the role of the martyred Grace. Only later did Paddy evolve into radio's equivalent of the Domestic Goddess. One thing that character and actress have in common is a love of cooking. At her home in a village in the Thames Valley, Paddy makes her Christmas puddings even earlier than Jill. 'I spend ten hours steaming the beggars,' she confides. 'You couldn't do that on radio.'

Come to think of it, she wouldn't have done anything on the radio had she taken notice of her microphone technique tutor.

PHIL	How are you?
JILL	I'm fine… simply fine. Have you seen them yet?
PHIL	No… wanted to see you first.
JILL	They're simply wonderful, Phil… honestly…
PHIL	But naturally. And you really do feel all right?
JILL	I told you all along there was nothing to worry about. Well – I was right – there wasn't. (PAUSE) Not disappointed it isn't two boys… 'stead of a boy and girl?
PHIL	Disappointed? Don't be ridiculous… I'm absolutely tickled pink.
JILL	Talking of pink it's a good job I took a chance and had one blue and one pink of everything… 'stead of two blue outfits…
PHIL	Clever girl…
JILL	But they might have brought them in here, for you to see…
PHIL	I'm being allowed to peek at 'em through a window or something. That's the normal routine apparently.
JILL	Well all I want to do is to get back home… then you can see as much as you want of them…
PHIL	Don't be in too much of a hurry, young woman… you have a nice rest.
JILL	Yes… from what I've heard I shall be busy enough when I do get home…!

Wedding of the Year

After his acquittal, Tom seemed to be fonder than ever of Pru, and she of him. Doris was sure they'd make the ideal couple, and wished Tom would get a move on and pop the question. In February Tom finally summoned the courage to do so and Pru accepted. But she had to wait a little longer and it wasn't until 26 September – after Tom's young pheasants were safely reared and put out to cover – that she eventually walked with him down the aisle of St Stephen's. Sadly, however, they were only allowed to enjoy a few weeks of wedded bliss before Pru was diagnosed with tuberculosis and sent to a sanatorium. It was to be almost three months before she was able to return home to her new husband.

Farming Life

It was to be a year of mixed fortunes for Dan at Brookfield. A fire in his Dutch barn destroyed half his oats, and in July six of his lambs were killed by lightning. Laura offered him a loan to help him out, but typically he refused, not wanting to be in debt to anyone if he could help it. Doris then surprised him by having all her remaining teeth removed. In the autumn he took on a new apprentice, James Dean lookalike Jimmy Grange, a hot-blooded youth who played guitar in a skiffle band and soon set the hearts of the village girls fluttering. Towards the end of the year Dan decided to completely reorganise the farm and consulted a land commissioner who advised him to tear down and replace many of his old buildings. Architect Wilfred Sprogett told him this would cost £2,500, a third of which would be paid for by a grant. Dan decided to borrow the rest and go ahead.

1959

Family Ties

There was a chance for Laura – always anxious to be seen as one of the family – to play fairy godmother to Jack and Peggy when the brewery offered to sell them The Bull. The price was too much for them, but Laura offered to help them out with an interest-free loan of £4,000. After some discussion they

How did Phil and Jill Archer dream up Shula and Kenton when those twins, born in August, 1958, were due to be christened? They threw lettered bricks in the air until they came down in a configuration that would give them original names, recalls Patricia 'Paddy' Greene (Jill). 'We actually said, "Nobody's ever been called Shula before." Then listeners started writing in, saying things like "My name's Shula, and I have a friend who just happens to be called Kenton."'

Proud parents. Phil and Jill show off the twins to doting grandparents Doris and Dan

gratefully accepted and, for the first time in her married life, Peggy had the security of owning her home and business. Jack, however, showed few signs of mending his ways. Although full of schemes to turn the place into a gold mine, he kept on his part-time job at the estate, as well as his fondness for a drink and a flutter on the horses. So once again Peggy was left to pull the pints and prove to Laura that she'd made a wise investment.

Wedding of the Year ✑

The arrival of a stonemason was to bring a dramatic change to Mrs P's life, and a big disappointment to Walter. The stonemason (also called Perkins, first name Arthur) stayed at The Bull, where Mrs P served him supper. Unlike her bibulous son-in-law Jack, Arthur was a strict teetotaller, and – much to the chagrin of a jealous Walter, who'd been suffering from migraines – she took

Village heartthrob and skiffle star Jimmy Grange (Alan Rothwell)

Forgive and forget. Ned Larkin (Bill Payne) shares a drink with Tom Forrest, who was acquitted of murdering Ned's brother Bob. Jack and Peggy behind the bar

a liking to him. She asked him round for meals, he dug her garden in return, and then asked her to marry him. Once she'd recovered from the surprise, she took him for a ride in her pony and trap and said yes. They were soon married and left Ambridge to live in London. Walter eventually got over his disappointment and began a small pig-fattening enterprise with Ned Larkin.

Mixed Fortunes

After Grace's death, George Fairbrother's health had begun to fail and he'd struggled to improve the estate and build up a profitable business, even with the help of such a capable manager as Phil. After a worrying fight to prevent a new bypass being built over his land he announced that he'd decided to sell up and leave the village. There was much gossip and speculation about Phil's new employer, Charles Grenville, when he moved into the Manor House. Recently returned from running a large ranch in Africa, Grenville was an old friend of

the Lawson-Hopes, which Phil might have found reassuring.
Grenville kept him on as manager for a six-month trial, but the
first few weeks of the new regime were anything but easy for
him. Grenville turned out to be a demanding employer who had
his own ideas about farming and was quick to criticise Phil over
many of his decisions – even about the pigs, which were Phil's
own area of expertise. The fact that Grenville seemed far more
considerate towards his other employee, Carol Grey, only served
to fuel Phil's resentment.

But as time went on, relations with his new boss got easier,
and Phil was greatly cheered by the news that Jill was pregnant
again, barely six months after the birth of the twins. He was
less happy when Helen Fairbrother returned to visit, bringing
with her plans for a stained-glass window to be placed in the
church as a memorial to Grace. Although still loyal to his own
memories of Grace, Phil was cross that Helen hadn't thought
to consult him first, and he had his new wife to consider; he
worried that Jill might find the whole thing upsetting. Jill
however turned out to be very understanding and the window
was installed with both their blessings. On 18 September, a
thunderstorm heralded the birth of their third child, a son,
delivered at home after a rather anxious labour. It must have
come as some relief to Dan and Doris when his parents crossed
the more exotic names off their list and called him David.
They were still getting used to more sleepless nights when Dan
had a serious fall at Brookfield and broke his leg. He was in
hospital for several weeks, then fell on his crutches and caught
pneumonia. Grenville showed his true generosity by giving Phil
all the time off he needed to help out his father at Brookfield;
but it was to be a long road to recovery for Dan.

Life imitating art? Norman Painting played the organ, like his alter ego
Phil Archer. Indeed he was at the keyboard for the first wedding of
Trevor Harrison, otherwise known as Eddie Grundy

❦

'After the killing of Grace [Archer] made headlines around the world,
everyone at the BBC, from the Director General downwards, realised
that this was a programme not to be patronised as a little series on
farming, made in Birmingham. The public knows what it wants.'

Norman Painting (Phil Archer) a week before he died.

*A parting of the ways for
Walter and Mrs P*

*Estate owner
Charles Grenville
(Michael Shaw) takes
stock of his new domain*

Chapter Two 1960s

Jill Archer was reminiscing, around the time of Phil's death, about the era when farms like Brookfield were awash with workers. 'All the staff and their families were available for lambing and haymaking,' she fondly recalled, looking back to her early experience of becoming a farmer's wife in the late 1950s. Or as Dr Roy Brigden from Reading University's Museum of Rural England puts it: 'Even tenant farmers could field their own football teams in the '50s.'

By the end of the 1960s many farms would have struggled to field a five-a-side team. Trends that began in the previous decade gathered pace. Buoyed up by guaranteed prices for milk and grain, farmers were prepared to invest in new machinery to meet government demands for increased efficiency.

More mechanisation would inevitably lead to the requirement for fewer workers as the 1960s wore on. Four decades later, Bert Fry was an endangered species in Borsetshire when he retired as Brookfield's last general farm worker in December 2006.

On the Land...

- As workforces were going down, acreage was going up and farms were getting bigger. *The Archers* anticipated the co-operative approach to expansion in 1961 when Dan and Phil amalgamated with neighbouring farmers Jeff Allard and Fred Barratt to form Ambridge Dairy Farmers.
- New strains of wheat were introduced along with more artificial fertilisers to boost output.
- Sugar beet was becoming a profitable crop and, in 1963, Dan Archer signed a contract to supply it to a factory in Kidderminster.
- The use of artificial insemination became far more widespread and the farming of pigs and poultry far more intensive. In Ambridge the trend was reflected by Phil setting up a pig unit at Hollowtree.
- Chicken ceased to be the luxury that it had been in the 1950s. Consumption per head doubled between 1960 and 1970 as supermarkets began to tighten their grip on the retail food market.

... And in the Land Beyond the Farm Gate

- The decade was only two years old when the Cuban missile crisis brought the world closer than at any time to nuclear extinction. Fear was widespread in the countryside as well as the cities.
- Having survived the threat of nuclear winter, freezing temperatures descended on the UK, making the first two months of 1963 the coldest since 1740. Power lines came down and villages were cut off by huge snowdrifts. The land remained iced over until March.
- The same year saw the birth of 'Beatlemania'. The group's appearance on *Sunday Night at the London Palladium* caused hysteria and drew a TV audience of over 15 million.
- Home Secretary Roy Jenkins forced through the Abortion Act in October 1967, three months after Jennifer Archer of The Bull, Ambridge, had given birth 'out of wedlock'. Jenkins also formulated a law that would eventually make life easier for her son Adam: homosexual relationships for consenting couples over 21 were legalised for the first time.
- The Summer of Love gave way to student political activism as anger mounted over the Vietnam War. Mick Jagger briefly joined protestors marching towards the American Embassy in 1968.
- Seeing Led Zeppelin in Bath planted the seed of an idea in the head of farmer Michael Eavis to stage an annual festival on his land in Glastonbury. It proved rather more enduring than the festival staged at Grange Farm, Ambridge, by one Joe Grundy five years later.

1960s

Playing Away

The close of the 1950s left Chris envying Phil and Jill's domestic happiness while still hoping vainly for her first child. With her marriage now beginning its fifth year, the new decade got off to an inauspicious start when Paul went down with chickenpox. This turned out to be just a taste of more difficult times to come; soon after he recovered he ran into serious financial difficulties. He'd taken over the family business after the death of his father, but now his mother (never Chris's biggest fan) announced that she wanted to withdraw her share of the capital. Chris nobly offered to sell a horse to help buy her out, but Paul wouldn't let her make such a sacrifice. His own solution to the crisis was to sell out to a company called Octopus Ltd, only to discover – when he went to sign the deal – that it was owned by none other than Phil's new boss, Charles Grenville. Paul was kept on as general manager, but never looked like settling easily into this more humble role.

Doris and Dan in the Brookfield garden (Gwen Berryman, Monte Crick)

Chris began to notice her husband showing distinct signs of restlessness – more particularly after he and Phil came back from a short break in Paris. He talked of getting a travelling sales job, and moving to the Home Counties. This sudden wanderlust wasn't all to do with job satisfaction, however, as Chris was soon to discover. While on holiday with Phil he'd bumped into Marianne Peters, a pretty 20-year-old who'd had a big crush on him as a young teenager, and the two had spent time together in the heady atmosphere of Paris. After his return, Christine's suspicions were aroused when she found a letter addressed to Marianne in Paul's study, and then Phil came across the two of them together in a pub in Borchester. This was enough to provoke Paul's guilty conscience and he confessed to Chris about Marianne, claiming that he'd only been trying to help her out by finding her a job in Borchester. This act didn't fool Chris for a moment, and Paul agreed to end the relationship. Marianne wasn't seen again in Borsetshire.

CHRIS	(SHAKILY) Really Paul... couldn't you be a <u>little</u> more discreet? For my sake if not your own?
PAUL	Oh dear... off we go again. I thought all this nonsense was over and done with.
CHRIS	So did I. It <u>was</u> Marianne Peters I s'pose.
PAUL	(BORED) Yes... it <u>was</u> Marianne Peters.
CHRIS	Don't tell me... let me guess... (SARCASTICALLY) You're getting her another job with another friend of yours ... so you just <u>had</u> to see her again.
PAUL	Now just listen Chris. To start at the beginning as you know I met Marianne quite by accident when I was in Paris with Phil.
CHRIS	(PAUSE) Yes I know although I still don't understand why you didn't tell me, when you got back... or was it the kind of meeting you couldn't tell your wife about?
PAUL	It was a very strange situation altogether Chris... and by now I'd hoped this thing would be forgotten...past history. But let me make it clear from the word 'go' that nothing's happened between Marianne and me...!

Surprise Romance of the Year

John Tregorran and Carol Grey had remained close friends over the years and were generally assumed to be pretty much of an item. Perhaps it was only Carol's fierce independence that was holding her back from making a long-term commitment. In June the couple drew even closer when – by a bizarre coincidence – a painting in John's antiques shop proved the key to unlocking the mystery of Carol's real parents. These turned out to be unmarried artists who had split up when she was two, leaving her to be adopted by her mother's cousin. But if John had hoped that this piece of shrewd detective work might improve his chances with Carol, he was about to be bitterly disappointed. In the autumn Phil and Charles Grenville went to Holland on business, and Carol went with them. On their return, Charles and Carol astonished the whole village by announcing their engagement. It looked as if John had missed his chance and lost her for ever.

Paul Johnson (Leslie Dunn, centre) demonstrates the latest in farming technology to Ned Larkin and Jimmy Grange

Brookfield

As Dan recovered from his injuries he began to suspect that his modest modernisation plans wouldn't be enough to turn the farm business around. When Walter's old farm (now called Wynfords) came up for sale, he saw a chance to expand his acreage, and offered Jack the chance to farm it in partnership with Brookfield. Jack was keen, but Peggy had had quite enough of the farming life and firmly vetoed the whole idea. Instead the farm was bought as an investment by Phil, who leased the land back to Dan. Later in the year, Dan decided to cut costs by joining a milk co-operative with his farming neighbours Fred Barratt and Jess Allard. Their three herds would be run as one business, and a new milking parlour built at Brookfield. As the 1960s began Dan was forced to accept that the writing was on the wall for small farms – for the future, big was almost certainly going to be beautiful.

Carol Grey (Ann Cullen) and Charles Grenville

1961

Sweet Sixteen

While Peggy had been kept busy running The Bull and trying to keep Jack on the straight and narrow, Jennifer had blossomed into a bright and very attractive 16-year-old. She'd already worried her parents by hanging out with local lad Gary Kenton – quite innocently, as it turned out. But the heat was turned up a little after she came back from a Christmas skiing trip in Switzerland. Peggy found a letter to her from a boy called Max, which suggested that Jennifer had been faking it and pretending to be 18. Peggy went into panic mode, fearing a steamy liaison with some shifty foreign ski instructor. Max, however, turned out to be Max Bailey, a perfectly harmless engineering student from Wolverhampton. When he came to visit Jennifer at The Bull, Peggy quite liked him, but Jack drew the line at letting him stay the night. Max took Jennifer out a few times, and in November she went to stay with him and his family. Jack and Peggy had to accept that their eldest daughter was most definitely not a child any more.

Doris collecting eggs watched by Mrs P

Rough Justice ✑

Although Ambridge was scarcely a no-go zone, some villagers at least shared the current concerns about the spread of juvenile delinquency. Charles

Bull regular Ned Larkin enjoys a pint

Grenville had gone so far as to write an article in the *Borchester Echo* calling for the return of capital punishment for young hooligans. This issue may still have been fresh in his mind when, in March, three leather-jacketed youths on motorbikes set fire to a hay-filled barn on the estate. They soon realised that they'd picked the wrong place, however, as they were set upon by Grenville, Sally Johnson and Walter Gabriel. In the ensuing struggle, Walter was knocked unconscious, Charles broke one of the youths' arms with a judo blow and another lad was badly bitten by Walter's dog, Butch. The youths were arrested and at the trial the defense suggested that Grenville's evidence might have been prejudiced by his dislike of teenage hooligans. The judge was having none of it, however. The eldest boys were given two years in prison and the youngest a year in Borstal: exemplary sentences perhaps, but generally seen as a fitting victory for the law-abiding citizens of Ambridge.

Family and Friends ✑

The big social event of the year was undoubtedly Carol's wedding to Charles Grenville which took place on 18 September. Carol wore a dress of heavy

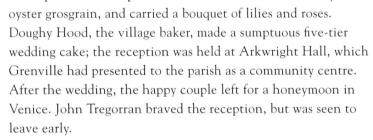

oyster grosgrain, and carried a bouquet of lilies and roses. Doughy Hood, the village baker, made a sumptuous five-tier wedding cake; the reception was held at Arkwright Hall, which Grenville had presented to the parish as a community centre. After the wedding, the happy couple left for a honeymoon in Venice. John Tregorran braved the reception, but was seen to leave early.

Newly-weds Charles and Carol Grenville toast their future happiness

Also among the guests was Walter Gabriel, whose fortunes had been mixed in recent years. Since losing Mrs P, he'd also lost his school bus contract after an accident. He'd then fallen out with his new ladyfriend, sprightly widow Agatha Turvey, over the smell of his pigs. This year Lady Luck smiled on him for a change and he had a small win on the football pools. He wasn't able to hold onto it for long, however; his son Nelson, who'd just left the Air Force, got wind of his good fortune and persuaded soft-hearted Walter to part with £3,000 to help him fund a small engineering business.

1962

Forsaken Love ✑

Over the months following Carol's marriage, John Tregorran still pined for her, becoming moody and short-tempered. Just to make things even harder for him, Carol came across a bundle of his old love letters to her, which were promptly stolen. The thieves then tried to blackmail them both for the princely sum of £200. Carol – who, after all, had nothing to hide – came clean to Grenville, and after a police stake-out the two oddly inept criminals were caught. They turned out be local men, both workers on Grenville's estate. After this, John seemed to try harder to get over Carol and move on. In March he offered his assistant, Dawn Kingsley, a partnership in his antique business. She was a rather meek, dowdy young woman but a shrewd bidder at the auction rooms, and good with the customers. John let it be known, however, that this was to be a business partnership, and no more. It can't have helped him much to know that Carol had taken readily to her new role as Lady of the Manor, and seemed blissfully happy. In December she gave birth to a son, Richard Charles.

Walter at the wheel of his minibus

Paul's Brilliant Career ✑

After seeing off Marianne Peters, Chris – although still longing for a child – might have hoped that Paul would settle down and behave. His old restlessness soon returned, however, and he still wasn't happy working at Grenville's agricultural machinery business. Then, out of the blue, he astonished her by announcing an abrupt career change: he'd decided to give up his job and train as a helicopter pilot. Even more ominously for Chris, this would involve them leaving Ambridge and the riding stables she'd worked so hard to build up. However upsetting this was for her, she stayed loyal to Paul and before long she found herself stuck in a suburban house on the edge of Newmarket. Paul's sister Sally, now married to betting shop owner Toby Stobeman, was left in charge of the stables. Chris missed her horses terribly, especially Midnight, but when she did manage to ride she had a serious fall and Doris went to look after her. It may have been some consolation to her to know that for the time being, at least, there seemed to be no other mysterious young women in Paul's life.

Back at the stables, Reggie and Valerie Trentham decided to sell up Grey Gables, and Sally found herself with a new neighbour: a self-made Birmingham businessman by the name of Jack Woolley.

Famous folk who opened the village fete:

RICHARD TODD, 1962

Ambridge Farmers ✑

Dan's determination to modernise and expand was tested when one member of the dairy co-op – now formally known as Ambridge Dairy Farmers Ltd – ran into difficulties. His neighbour and business partner Jess Allard's two wayward sons were misbehaving and threatening to derail the whole enterprise. Eventually

Dan and Doris with a prize-winning bull, led by Ned Larkin, with Walter Gabriel at his side

1963

Allard decided to sell up. Rather than let the farm go to an outsider, Dan and Fred Barrat sensed an opportunity and approached Phil – who was still working as Grenville's manager – to see if he'd consider taking it on. Phil decided to take the plunge. He resigned from his job and he, Jill and the three children moved into Allard's, known ever after as Hollowtree Farm. Phil lost no time in buying a few of Grenville's pigs and setting up a pig unit.

One Wedding and a Funeral

John Tregorran's long, dark night of the soul finally seemed to be over when he fell in love with Ambridge's pretty young district nurse, Janet Sheldon. It was a shared interest in art that had brought them together; she was a keen amateur potter, and John had taken a couple of her pots to sell in his shop. Not long after, he took her on a touring holiday of the West Country, where he proposed to her. She accepted and they were married in June. If he had any lingering regrets over Carol, he kept them firmly to himself. Janet was married at the Manor House, and Carol witnessed the ceremony. So ended John's days as Ambridge's most eligible – if star-crossed – bachelor. Or so all his friends assumed; fate, however, had other plans. On the afternoon of Hallowe'en, Janet had been over for tea with Carol at the Manor House

and Grenville offered to drive her home. Soon after Carol
had a phone call to say that the car had crashed. Janet
was killed outright, and Grenville seriously injured. After
barely four months' happiness shared with his new bride,
John was alone again.

Paul's Brilliant Career (Part 2)

Far away in deepest Suffolk, Chris was still lonely and
miserable, but putting a brave face on it. She stuck grimly
by Paul who was now qualified as a helicopter pilot and
working for a crop-spraying firm. True to form, however,
Paul soon fell out with his boss, and discovered that his

*Jack Woolley (Philip
Garston-Jones)
at Grey Gables*

new life wasn't quite as glamorous or as lucrative as he'd hoped. Chris must have had
mixed feelings when he eventually resigned. Although his career had reached another
dead end, it meant that they left Newmarket and moved back to Ambridge. Phil agreed
to let them live in the old farmhouse at Wynfords, in return for some renovation work.
Chris's long exile was over, and she was soon reunited with her beloved Midnight.

New Broom

Rough diamond Jack Woolley lost no time in establishing himself as the new
owner of Grey Gables Country Club, declaring his intention to give the place a
complete makeover and develop it into an exclusive holiday retreat for world-
weary business executives. His ambitious plans may have upset some people – one
of his first moves was to buy twenty acres from Grenville for a golf course – but
his down-to-earth geniality soon won him the respect of most villagers. They also
learnt that Jack had a shrewd business mind, and wasn't content with being a
mere hotelier. Among other interests, he opened a rival antiques shop right next
door to John Tregorran's, which – with his own peculiar brand of imaginative
flair – he named the New Curiosity Shop. Every inch the self-made man, he was
willing to give the less fortunate a leg-up if he thought they deserved it, as he
demonstrated when young fellow Brummie Sid Perks appeared in the village. In
spite of Sid's troubled youth (he'd done time in an approved school for breaking
and entering), Woolley saw in him a younger version of himself, and took him
under his wing. Sid became Jack's chauffeur and general assistant, and so had a
chance to prove that he'd put his past behind him.

Terry Molloy (Mike Tucker) played the saxophone in the Cavern Club while studying music and drama in Liverpool.
'I was there from 1965 to 1968, and The Beatles had long gone,' he recalls. 'Northern Soul was all the rage. I played in
the T-Bunkum Band – a mixture of T-Bone Walker and Bunk Johnson. There was still quite a buzz in Liverpool at that
time. All the bands used to end up at the Blue Angel Club and jam till three in the morning.'

1964

Moving On ⌒

After the car accident that killed Janet Tregorran, John struggled to hold his life together and keep his business going. In the end, it was all too much for him, and he left for a long holiday in Spain. Grenville was in hospital for several months, and the village was shocked when they heard that one of his legs had been amputated. Carol dealt with the crisis stoically, and kept herself busy running the home and caring for 1-year-old Richard. The estate was left in the capable hands of Andrew Sinclair, who'd taken over Phil's job as estate manager. Paul Johnson gratefully accepted an offer of a job in Grenville's agricultural machinery firm. Grenville eventually returned from hospital with an artificial leg, but (unsurprisingly, perhaps) he found it hard to settle back into his old routine. Then, later in the year, he abruptly sold off some of his business interests and surprised everyone by setting off to America on what he said was a fact-finding trip. Carol stayed behind with Richard and spent Christmas waiting to hear when her husband planned to return.

Young Tony Archer (Philip Owen) eavesdrops as Sid Perks (Alan Devereux) chats up village belle Joan Hood (Esme Wilson)

Jack and Peggy's Fairy Godmother ⌒

Down at The Bull, Jack's drinking had been no worse than usual, Peggy was keeping the business afloat, and all three children were growing up fast. Anthony William Daniel would soon be a teenager, Lilian was taking her O levels and 19-year-old Jennifer was on a teacher-training course in Walsall. Jennifer's boyfriend Max was now history, and Jack bought her a moped so that she could get home more often. In the previous year Ambridge had won the Best Kept Village competition, and the extra visitors prompted Jack and Peggy to consider adding a new dining room – if they could somehow raise the money. While they were still worrying about this, Laura once again waved her magic wand. There was to be no interest-free loan this time; instead, she presented them with a cheque for the handsome sum of £25,000. The family wondered about the motives behind Laura's generosity (she claimed she was doing it partly to avoid death duties) and worried that all these riches would go to Jack's head. Peggy, however, kept his feet firmly on the ground and the money was put towards the new dining room and other sensible renovations, including a small flat for Laura. Paul tried to persuade Jack to help him buy out Grenville's machinery firm, with no success.

Christine and Lilian (Leslie Saweard, Elizabeth Marlowe)

Grey Gables ⌒

Jack Woolley's faith in his new chauffeur Sid Perks seemed to be justified, as the young lad worked hard, kept out of trouble and made friends in the village. But his chequered past caught up with him one last time when he took his new girlfriend Polly Mead, the Bull barmaid, to the Hollerton Fair. There they bumped into some of the Birmingham bad boys from his old gang, who weren't best pleased to be cold-shouldered by newly reformed Sid. Soon after, his motorbike was stolen and trashed. Sid worried that he'd be in trouble if his new boss found out, but the village PC, Albert Bates, handled the matter discreetly and Jack Woolley was none the wiser. Woolley, besides, had other preoccupations: he had recently got to know Valerie Trentham, now a widow, after she had returned to the village with her daughter Hazel. They became close enough friends for him to ask Valerie to look after his guest house while he went away for a long cruise.

Widow and Mothers ✍

The New Year found Carol still waiting to hear when Grenville planned to come home from America. When the call came, however, he again surprised everyone – not least Carol – by announcing that his future lay in the New World, and he wanted the family to emigrate. Carol hated the idea of leaving Ambridge, but before she had the chance to try and talk him out of it, Grenville succumbed to a sudden brain haemorrhage and died. Carol was left to endure her grief and carry on her life as a widow, living at the Manor House with young Richard. Luckily she had many friends and neighbours she could count on for support; among her regular visitors was John Tregorran, who returned from his long holiday in Spain and quickly picked up on their old friendship. The estate was put up for sale and was bought by Ralph Bellamy, the son of neighbouring landowner Admiral Bellamy, in partnership with Jack Woolley. Grenville's businesses were inherited by Carol, and so she became Paul's employer and partner in the machinery firm. Paul took a liking to young Richard, treating him to presents and generally playing the role of a surrogate uncle. This touched a raw nerve for Chris, who still longed for a child of her own, although as the years went by this seemed ever more unlikely. After some anguished heart-to-hearts, Paul eventually realised just how much it meant to her, and they settled on the only compromise available: in September they adopted a baby boy, Peter.

Laura's Magic ✍

After being so generous to Jack and Peggy, Laura had moved into the new flat at The Bull, which now boasted a strawberry-pink carpet in the ladies' toilets as well as the brand new dining room. In spite of her modest accommodation, Laura was still a woman of considerable means, and took on a handsome young chauffeur by the name of Roger Portillo. And she hadn't yet given up her role as fairy godmother to the Archer family; now it was Dan and Phil's turn to

1965

(FADE IN TRAFFIC NOISES IN BACKGROUND)

(SID AND POLLY ARE WALKING)

POLLY	(DREAMILY) Lovely film, Sid.
SID	Eh? Oh yes… smashing.
POLLY	'Course… that Julie Andrews is worth going miles to see any time.
SID	Yes.
POLLY	(PAUSE) What's the matter with you tonight, Sid?
SID	Eh? Matter? Oh nothing chick… nothing.
POLLY	You've had something on your mind ever since we met.
SID	Ar… maybe… just – well… you know… things.
POLLY	Still worrying about me?
SID	Well I haven't got anything else to worry about.
POLLY	We're still engaged y'know.
SID	Ar… just about.
POLLY	(STUNG) And what's that supposed to mean?
SID	Well… when a couple get engaged the idea is that it's the first step towards getting married. In our case I don't see much hope of that happening for years and years.
POLLY	No mad rush is there? T'isn't a shotgun wedding.
SID	I almost wish it was.
POLLY	Sid Perks… do you mind.
SID	Well at least we'd have to make a move then.
POLLY	(COLDLY) I'm afraid you've picked the wrong girl if that's the way your mind works…
SID	(SIGH) Maybe we've both picked the wrong partner.
POLLY	I'm just not rushing, that's all…

Profile

JENNIFER ALDRIDGE

NGELA PIPER HAS TAKEN delivery of her sea bass and pronounced it 'good'. Well, that's a relief. She is, after all, the woman at the helm of the most-used Aga in Ambridge (since Jill Archer moved out of Brookfield, anyway). What's more, Angela is the author of three books on food and cookery written in the style of Jennifer Aldridge, whose character she has inhabited for 47 years. For now, though, she's sampling someone else's cooking in an incredibly noisy Birmingham restaurant. Grey Gables it is not.

Luckily, a professional actress can always turn up the volume when required and her extremely familiar voice comes through loud and clear. All the same, this place must seem a million miles from home in the peace and quiet of her beloved East Anglia. She and her husband, former BBC news reader Peter Bolgar, recently sold their Georgian mill house, set in four and a half acres of rural Essex. Downsizing? 'Yes, but we also wanted to move closer to the Suffolk border.'

You can bet your life the Aga will have moved there too. Angela shares with Jennifer a love of family and of cooking. 'I just feel that the kitchen is the heart of the home,' she says, 'and I love nothing more than when my [three] children and grandchildren are back home and we congregate on a Sunday morning for coffee and croissants. There might be a Labrador or two wandering round and a cat sitting one of the children's knees.'

Sounds a bit like Home Farm in some ways but not in others, just as Angela admits to being like Jennifer in some ways but not in others. 'I suppose a bit of your personality is bound to seep into the character, and vice versa, when you've been together for forty-seven years,' she ponders. In the early days, there was an almost uncanny parallel between fiction and real life. Back in 1967, Jennifer shocked the nation by becoming pregnant 'out of wedlock', as people said in those days. Society's corsets were loosening only on university campuses and in certain parts of 'Swinging London'.

Jennifer herself was feeling 'all peculiar' during the early stages of pregnancy, as Angela recalls. 'And I was beginning to experience similar symptoms. I remember thinking to myself that I was taking this storyline far too seriously. That was until I discovered that I, too, was pregnant with our first child after six years of marriage.'

Angela gave birth in August, Jennifer a month or so before. The child was christened Adam and he would grow up to feature in *The Archers*' first gay kiss. Society's corsets had loosened considerably in the intervening thirty-seven years. His father was eventually unmasked as Paddy Redmond. 'A cowman!' Angela exclaims in mock shock, sounding for a moment like Lady Bracknell. She is, needless to say, parodying Jennifer Aldridge, the wife of Brian, who would be rather sniffy about a liaison with a farm labourer – or indeed about her daughter marrying a farrier. But back in 1967, she was Jennifer Archer, daughter of an alcoholic publican and an East Ender.

'Jennifer was always the brightest of their children,' Angela points out. 'God knows that doesn't say a lot, but she did go to college, which would have become a university by now. She also became a teacher and won a prize for her writing before marrying the richest man in the village.'

'... she's a bit of an earth mother when it comes to her family.'

Her character is complex, she believes. Snobbish? 'Oh, yes. She does like to keep herself aloof from the Carters and the Tuckers.' But caring? 'Absolutely. In fact, she's a bit of an earth mother when it comes to her family.' And when it came to accepting Brian's son Ruairi into the family – another shock to the nation – her motives were equally complex and multi-layered, Angela feels. 'She saw an innocent little boy whose mother had died. Another part of her made a financial calculation and realised that she didn't want to lose a man who may have treated her shoddily but had provided her with the good life. Yet another part saw a way of reining Brian in, making sure that he didn't stray again and didn't disregard her gay son. And guilt played a part as well.' Guilt? On Jennifer's part? 'Yes, because she'd never given Brian a son of his own.'

That makes him sound rather like Henry VIII, except that Brian only had one child 'out of wedlock'. As far as we know.

Profile
TONY ARCHER

COLIN SKIPP, BETTER KNOWN as Tony Archer, was once photographed with a page three model. On the beach at Borth in Dyfed as it happens. Colin was clad in a jacket and a sporty-looking cap. The model was wearing a pair of skimpy knickers and a somewhat superfluous sun hat. Low cloud and light drizzle prevailed – just as Tony had predicted when grumbling about his on-air wife Pat's suggestion that they spend a holiday in her native Wales. The photograph turned out to be a publicity stunt dreamt up by the Welsh Tourist Board in cahoots with the pictures desk at the *Daily Star*.

'My mother-in-law didn't speak to me for a week after it appeared,' Colin confides. His wife, the actress Lisa Davies, simply observed: 'You look like Eric Morecambe.'

There's certainly a resemblance, judging by the photocopy which he unearths at the couple's home in West London. Must be the mischievous expression behind the sizeable spectacles he was wearing back in 1985. Eric Morecambe had died the previous

year, aged 58. Colin would have been 46. And Tony? He was 34 going on 70. 'Yes, he is a bit of an Eeyore,' the genial Colin concedes. 'We don't have much in common. Apart from anything else, I'd fall over a weed before I picked it up. Half an hour's gardening and I need a rub down with a wet sponge.'

Certainly there's little resemblance between the garden beyond the kitchen window – an estate agent would call it 'manageable' – and the organic acres of Bridge Farm. But then Colin became Tony because of his voice rather than his ability to hoe a leek patch. 'I remember having to wait hours for my audition in 1967,' he goes on. 'When I asked [*Archers* producer] Tony Shryane about the delay, he said: "We're trying to find some lad called Colin Skipp who was in that radio play the other night." I was 28 at the time and I'd played the head boy at a particularly posh public school.'

Ah, the versatility of actors. In reality, Colin was brought up in a mean street that ran along the side of Holloway Prison in North London. The toilet was up the yard and the bath hung on the back of the kitchen door. 'My father was like a cross between Alf Garnett and Albert Steptoe,' he explains. 'He was a former lavatory attendant and road sweeper. But when he was invalided out of the war, he got a job as a general dogsbody at the Gainsborough Studios on City Road. And when [the director] Sidney Gilliat wanted half a dozen kids to play in a scene with John Mills and Stuart Granger, he said "I've got two of those little 'baggars' at home."'

For Colin it was the beginning of an acting career that would take him everywhere from summer seasons in Frinton to playing Cliff in *Look Back in Anger* on the television. He won a scholarship to the Royal Academy of Dramatic Art (RADA), where he met the young Charles Collingwood, an old boy of Sherbourne School, like his alter ego Brian Aldridge. 'As far as I was concerned, he was the sort of silver-spoon-in-the-mouth ex-public schoolboy that I didn't like,' Colin recalls. 'We get on really well now – it would be hard not to get on with Charles – but at that time I had a chip on my shoulder, like Tony. I have to try to rekindle that old resentment whenever Tony comes up against Brian.'

> '... I had a chip on my shoulder, like Tony.'

Playing against his fictional father, Jack Archer, provided Colin with a rather more specific challenge one evening in the 1960s. Jack had developed a drink problem, not unknown among publicans. In one scene he was supposed to be helped upstairs from the bar of The Bull with the support of young Tony. The late Denis Folwell, who played Jack, mistakenly arrived for recording on the wrong day. 'I thought I'd finished for the evening and went off for a few drinks with an old friend who'd turned up in Birmingham unexpectedly,' Colin remembers. 'I must have been well into the fourth pint when a messenger dashed into the pub and asked if I'd do Denis a favour and record the scene there and then. Denis was stone cold sober, pretending to be drunk. I was concentrating very hard on trying to appear sober.'

Ah, the versatility of actors.

be helped. At the end of the summer Fred Barrat, the third member of Ambridge Dairy Farmers Ltd, announced his decision to sell up his share of the business and retire. This was a real blow for Phil and Dan, who wondered how they'd ever raise the money to buy him out. Cue for Aunt Laura to save the day yet again by buying Barrat's land and leasing it back to Phil and Dan. Barrat agreed to sell them the rest of his investment in manageable installments. So it was largely thanks to Laura that the Archer family became the sole owners of what was growing into a sizeable farming business. Dan took on a new farm worker, a young man from Northern Ireland by the name of Paddy Redmond. Lilian, meanwhile, was very taken by Laura's hot new chauffeur, and they started going out together. Roger, however, was not quite what he seemed. Later in the year he confessed to Lilian that his real name was Roger Travers-Macy, and he'd changed his identity after falling out with his parents, who were wealthy and rather grand.

1966

Two Proposals

Valerie Trentham was now well established at Grey Gables, running the riding stables with some help from Lilian. Jack Woolley began to court her in earnest (perhaps seduced by tales of her glamorous past) and by the end of the year they were engaged. Sid Perks had less luck with Polly Mead. When he proposed she happily accepted, but soon after they quarrelled and she broke off the engagement.

The Ambridge Arsonist

The spring began with a series of mysterious fires around the district. The police suspected they were started deliberately, and the villagers organised patrols to

The keeper and the barmaid: Tom and Pru Forrest (Mary Dalley)

try and catch the culprit. The plot thickened when the arsonist struck again, this time at Brookfield, while Dan and Doris were out partying at the Manor House. Although the house wasn't badly damaged, the barn and several outbuildings were destroyed and Doris was devastated. Several villagers came under suspicion, including their former neighbor Fred Barrat, and even Tom and Pru's adopted son Johnny, a rather solitary boy who liked making camp fires. Then, a month or so later, a man was caught trying to burn down a shed at The Bull. It turned out to be Polly's father, Frank Mead, a strict teetotaller, religious zealot and general oddball. The courts accepted his plea of diminished responsibility and he ended his days in the local psychiatric hospital. Poor Polly turned to Sid for comfort, and soon their engagement was back on. The couple were married in September, with Jennifer and Lilian as bridesmaids. Jack Woolley – now married to Valerie – appointed Sid manager of the leisure centre at Arkwright Hall, and found himself a new chauffeur by the name of Higgs.

Happy Endings

Since Grenville's sudden death, John and Carol had been growing
steadily closer. John, meanwhile, was busy consolidating his
business interests; he bought a share in a Borchester bookshop in
partnership with Roger Travers-Macy, who later bought him out.
That autumn, nearly twelve years after his first proposal, he once
again asked Carol to marry him. This time she said yes, and early
in the following year they were married quietly at St Stephen's.
Carol sold the Manor House to Jack Woolley, and the newly-weds
moved into Bellamy's former house, Manor Court. It had been a
very long wait, but John's loyalty and patience were finally rewarded.

*Rebellious young writer
Jennifer Archer searches
for her muse
(Angela Piper)*

Trouble at The Bull

With the Sixties in full swing, Jennifer had entered enthusiastically
into the spirit of the times and was enjoying a fast life as a student
in Walsall. After a particularly wild party she had been evicted from
her flat, much to her parents' disapproval. She redeemed herself a
little by getting a couple of her short stories published, and began
planning a novel. Jack Woolley was sufficiently impressed to ask
her to write a brochure for Grey Gables; and both Jack and Peggy
were proud when, in July, she passed her exams and qualified as a
teacher. Lilian, not to be outdone, rented some stables from Laura
and opened her own riding school. Jennifer managed to find a job
locally, and in September she began teaching at Hollerton Primary.
That wasn't to say she'd left her wild days behind her, however.
There was a row when Peggy discovered that she'd been secretly
going out with Nelson Gabriel, Ambridge's own wheeler-dealer and
general wide boy. This was especially galling for poor Peggy, as Jack
had recently been running up big gambling debts at a Borchester
casino owned jointly by Nelson and Toby Stobeman. But Jack's
misbehaviour was nothing compared to the bombshell that was about to hit the
whole family. Not long before Christmas, Jennifer made a terrible confession to
Lilian: she was pregnant.

*David Latimer, vicar of
Ambridge (Arnold Peters)*

Outcast Jennifer

It had been a miserable Christmas for Jennifer, struggling through the usual family
festivity while all the time nursing her guilty secret. Although Lilian was supportive,
Jennifer wouldn't tell her who the father was. She could guess only too well how her
parents would react when they found out, and surely it was only as matter of time before
her sharp-eyed mother noticed that something was amiss. But when she did confess, it
wasn't to Peggy, but to her Auntie Jill (who was herself now pregnant again). Jill was

1967

Jennifer

(FADE IN MAIL-VAN APPROACHING AT 45-50 MPH)

BROWN   (TO HIMSELF) Here he comes. Torch… (TORCH CLICKS ON AND OFF) … Now then, wait for it… (MAIL-VAN SUDDENLY BRAKES. THERE IS A SCREECH OF BRAKES. THEN SILENCE. ONE PAIR OF FOOTSTEPS RUNS TO VAN. VAN DOOR OPENS)

VOICE   What the –

BROWN   (OFF) Oh no you don't! (CRACK OF COSH)

VOICE   (GROANS AS HE SWOONS) AaaaaaH!

NELSON   Ach – you fool, Brown, I said use judo not a tyre wrench. Oh get on – tape his mouth and into the ditch with him. Quick. (EFFORT AS THEY MOVE HIM A FEW YARDS AND DUMP HIM) Then the wire… I have already freed it from one side.

BROWN   Then it won't take a second to free the other…but boss, this driver would have put up a fight. I had to act quick.

NELSON   We'll discuss that later. I'll take the wire and the strainer back with me in the mail-van. Inside that stack they'll be as safe as the cash itself… Hurry Charles… but not with unseemly haste… It's all going perfectly… exactly as planned. (FADE OUT)

understanding, but when she asked about the father, Jennifer still wouldn't tell. Jill's advice was to come clean to her parents right away, but Jennifer lost her nerve again and went instead to Brookfield. If she'd been expecting any kind of sympathy from her grandmother, she was in for a rude awakening. Doris was horrified at the shame she'd brought upon the family, and told her she must marry the father right away – whoever he was. Jennifer left in tears. Soon after she grasped the nettle and broke the news to her parents. Her worst fears were confirmed by Jack, whose first reaction was to threaten to throw her out of the house. The news came as less of shock to Peggy, who'd begun to guess, but she was nevertheless very upset when Jennifer insisted that she wanted to keep the baby, and still refused to say who the father was.

Jennifer was quite prepared to call Jack's bluff and leave but Lilian and her mother persuaded her to stay on and at least give Jack a chance to calm down. It was Dan who stepped in to remind them all that whatever the circumstances the baby would be one of the family, and surely Jennifer needed their support, not condemnation. Doris relented, Jack cooled off a little and Jennifer stayed at The Bull, braving the muted gossip and knowing looks from the public bar. In April came the worrying news that Jill's baby daughter, Elizabeth, had been born with a narrowed heart valve, which needed corrective surgery. Little Elizabeth recovered well and before long had a new cousin when, on 22 June, Jennifer gave birth to a healthy baby boy. When the word got around that the baby – named Adam – had red hair, people soon made the connection with Brookfield's recently departed farm worker, Ulsterman Paddy 'Red' Redmond. When Laura bluntly asked Jennifer if he was the father, she was unable to deny it. Fed up with being the village pariah, she bravely took her baby son and escaped to Bristol, where she stayed with a college friend before finding a flat of her own. One of her few visitors was Lilian's boyfriend, Roger Travers-Macy.

Police 5

It turned out to be a good year for the village gossips. As if Jennifer's unfortunate condition wasn't enough, early in May Ambridge was buzzing with the news that Nelson (high on the list of the baby's potential fathers) was missing, presumed dead, after a mysterious plane crash. Walter scarcely had a chance to grieve when a mail-van robbery in Borchester led the police to

*Phil, Jill and family
celebrate Elizabeth's
christening*

raid a local farm, where they found Nelson's fingerprints on an empty whisky bottle, supposedly used by the robbers. This prompted another round of lively speculation, none of it very cheering for poor Walter.

The words 'Doris Archer is a prude' were scrawled across Waterloo Bridge back in 1967, the year when London really began to swing. Whoever wielded the spray can was poking fun at the scandalised reaction of the matriarch of Brookfield to news that her granddaughter, Jennifer, was pregnant 'out of wedlock'. But Doris would eventually relent. When little Adam made his entrance, she proclaimed tearfully: 'A baby is a baby and that is all that matters.'

During Jennifer's pregnancy by cowman Paddy Redmond, the strangest series of letters received by actress Angela Piper were from an elderly brother and sister living in the East End of London. 'The first letter assured me that I'd be welcome to stay with them should my irate parents throw me out of The Bull,' Angela recalls. 'The second informed me that they'd decorated the spare bedroom. Yet another one arrived some time later saying: "My brother has been waiting to meet you on Paddington Station." It was terribly sad. I didn't know what to do with them, so I handed all three letters to [producer] Tony Shryane. I never heard any more from them after that.'

49

1969

Charles Brown had narrowly escaped discovery by the Ambridge PC, Colin Drury, while they were preparing to ambush the van. The evidence against him wasn't enough to convince the court, however, and he was acquitted – much to the relief of his loyal father Walter, who'd been convinced all along that his son had been framed.

Problems for Peggy

It was to be a year of mixed fortunes for Jack, Peggy and their family. After last year's health warning, Jack had more or less kept off the booze for a few months, but he was now drinking heavily again. It must have been some small relief to Peggy that at least his drinking and gambling sprees kept him from interfering with the business; when he did show an interest, his whimsical schemes tended only to add to her difficulties. Towards the end of the summer he sobered up enough to decide that they should do more to attract the younger customers. He told Peggy that he'd been inspired by Paul Johnson, Ambridge's other great entrepreneur (who'd narrowly escaped bankruptcy by selling the garage to Ralph Bellamy, and was now planning to make his fortune with an obscure engineering gizmo he'd invented). Jack was convinced that the failure of Paul's coffee bar had left a gap in the market. He waved aside Peggy's doubts and she was forced to grit her teeth and watch as the restaurant was transformed into a 'playbar' complete with jukebox and the latest espresso coffee machine. The opening night on Hallowe'en was a modest success, but later in the year some kids ran riot and Peggy was threatened with a prosecution for breach of the peace. Whatever her problems with Jack, at least she had the consolation of knowing that it had been a much better year for the younger generation. Jennifer was now happily settled in Borchester with Roger and the baby, and in the summer Anthony William Daniel – or Tony, as he now preferred to be called – completed his course at the farm institute and was offered a job on the estate by Bellamy. But the happiest event of the year for the whole family took place on 26 May, when Lilian married her handsome Canadian boyfriend, Lester 'Nick' Nicholson.

Peggy and Carol share the church flower rota with Bull barmaid Norah McAuley (Julia Mark)

Changing Times at Brookfield

Dan Archer was now in his early seventies, and – although he would be the first to deny it – beginning to feel his age. At the end of the previous year he'd been injured rescuing a cow from the slurry pit, and then he struggled though a wet spring to get the wheat drilled. He ended up in hospital with a severe attack of bronchitis. But it would take more than that to keep him away from Brookfield. He was soon back at work, deaf to Doris's pleas that he should think about retiring. To add to his difficulties, Phil was by now becoming very frustrated by what he saw as his father's obstinacy and outdated farming methods. His disagreements with his father over the day-to-day running of the farms became more frequent, much to Doris's exasperation. Eventually, as the summer ended, Dan admitted a partial defeat and announced that he was going into semi-retirement. Phil, Chris and Jack would each get a ten per cent share of Ambridge Farmers; Phil, Jill and the four children would come to live in the Brookfield farmhouse, while Dan and Doris moved into Glebe Cottage (which had been left to Doris by the old Squire's widow, Lettie Lawson-Hope). This was something of a victory for Doris; it was what she'd been urging Dan to do for the last ten years or more. Now she'd finally succeeded, she could hope that the new decade would fulfill her dream of a more leisurely life, where she and Dan would be able to spend a little more quality time together.

Dan and Doris look forward to a happy retirement

Chapter Three 1970s

It's difficult to imagine two more different operations than Home Farm and Grange Farm when they came to the attention of *Archers* listeners in the 1970s. One was run by Brian Aldridge; not so much a farmer as a rancher – 'the JR of Ambridge', no less with 1,500 acres to play with, bought from the Bellamy estate. Three decades on and Brian has reluctantly been forced to hand over more of a share to his stepchildren, with Adam, allegedly, controlling day-to-day management. Grange Farm, on the other hand, was run by tenant farmers Joe and Eddie Grundy who miraculously managed to keep the bailiff from the door until the turn of the century.

Brian swaggered into Ambridge in 1975. His presence meant that the programme could reflect one of the national tendencies that had begun in the 1960s, gathered pace in the 1970s and became widespread in the 1980s – the growth in the big business farmer with an eye for high-yield intensive farming. Brian was part of the future. The Grundys, on the other hand, belonged to the past. Their scams came to nothing and, for the most part, they got by on a wing and a prayer – a turkey's wing at Christmas when, largely thanks to Clarrie's valiant efforts as unpaid plucker, they earned enough to savour some seasonal pleasures.

On the Land...

- Beyond Grange Farm the intensive battery farming of poultry was an all-the-year-round affair that had begun in the 1960s and spread rapidly.
- Pig farming became more intensive as well and there was uproar in the village when Brian proposed setting up an industrial-scale unit.
- An increasingly prairie-like landscape evolved in rural England as hedgerows were ripped out to accommodate bigger machinery for larger fields.
- Britain joined the European Common Market in 1973 and many regional varieties of fruit and vegetable began to disappear.
- *The Archers* reflected unease over the increasing use of chemicals on the land in 1973 when David and Elizabeth were taken ill after eating grain heavily laced with pesticides.
- In the same year the programme also reflected the growing number of apprentice schemes on farms. Enter Neil Carter to Brookfield.
- *The Archers* proved not so good at reflecting the lengthy drought of 1976. Farmers tuning in while surveying their parched acres were surprised to hear that the corn-dryer had broken down at Brookfield.

... And in the Land Beyond the Farm Gate

- Decimal currency was introduced in February 1971.
- Britain was plunged into power cuts and a three-day week the following year as industrial action by the miners slashed supplies to power stations.
- Industrial unrest continued throughout the 1970s, culminating in the so-called 'Winter of Discontent' in 1978–1979.
- Petrol prices soared in 1973 after a political crisis in the Middle East. Inflation reached 26.9 per cent in August 1975.
- Women's Liberation became a political force, and Ambridge acquired its first feminist in the form of Pat Archer.
- Colour television spread as radio audiences continued to decline. Morecambe and Wise Christmas specials attracted TV audiences of over 27 million, comfortably exceeding the 22 million who tuned in to the old Light Programme for Grace Archer's death in 1955.
- The birth of punk in 1976 transformed pop music and fashion. The Sex Pistols' savagely anti-royal 'God Save The Queen' topped every chart except the one used by the BBC in 1977. A wave of patriotism and street parties, however, marked the Silver Jubilee of Elizabeth II.
- Unemployment rose even more sharply after Margaret Thatcher won the election in May 1979.

1970

Sisters and Wives

After Lilian's marriage to 'Nick' Nicholson, the only slight worry clouding their happiness was Nick's continued ill health. He'd been invalided out of the Canadian Air Force with a chronic ear condition which was still giving him trouble. Early in the spring he took Lilian to Canada – partly for her to meet his family, and partly for him to receive some specialist treatment over there. The couple had only been away a fortnight when, on 18 March, Peggy had a phone call from a distraught Lilian to say that Nick was dead. In an ironic twist of fate, his illness was only indirectly to blame; he'd been sleepwalking at the hospital where he was having treatment and had fallen down a flight of stairs, dying instantly. So Lilian's idyllic marriage to the man she loved was tragically curtailed. The family rallied round to support her when she returned, but she showed herself to be more resilient than they had imagined. Within a week she was back at the stables, throwing herself into her work with a determination that Peggy must have been proud of. And it wasn't just the family who was concerned for the young widow. Ralph Bellamy was now Ambridge's most eligible bachelor by a mile and, although the village gossips had already paired him off with his distinctly upper-crust neighbour Lady Isobel Lander, he kept up his friendship with Lilian. She was suitably flattered when, in September, he asked her to play hostess to some of his county-set friends at a dinner party. Although this failed to lead to any greater intimacy, he remained attentive, and just before Christmas the family was intrigued to hear that he'd asked her out for New Year's Eve.

Jennifer, by contrast, seemed quietly content in her marriage. There was a brief panic early in the year over a bizarrely botched attempt by kidnappers to abduct Adam, but little else to disturb her and Roger's life among the arty set in Borchester. Jennifer was soon pregnant again and their daughter, Deborah, was born on Christmas Eve.

LILIAN	(OVER PHONE. VERY SHOCKED) Hello Mum...
PEGGY	Oh hello dear... (AND SHE BREAKS DOWN. NOT OUTWARDLY, BUT INWARDLY TREMBLING WITH EMOTION) .. Oh I'm so sorry to hear...
LILIAN	(STUNNED) Yes it's terrible isn't it?
PEGGY	(SNIFFS, BLOWS, RECOVERS) What are you going to do, dear?
LILIAN	(DAZED, SOUNDING ALMOST DRUGGED) Well... There's an awful lot of things to do, there's got to be an inquest...
PEGGY	Sorry love, the line's not very good – did you say, inquest?
LILIAN	Yes. We think he was sleepwalking.
PEGGY	Oh!... Oh I see... (PAUSE)
LILIAN	We did tell them at the hospital... but they said it'd be all right... even in a private room... (LOST) They said they'd keep a close watch over him... Not close enough, was it?
PEGGY	Oh, it's awful Lilian.. dreadful... I just don't know what to say.. You seem so far away.. I feel so .. helpless...
LILIAN	(FLAT AND WITHOUT EMOTION) Oh don't upset yourself Mum.. I'll be all right.. (PAUSE) .. Lots to do.. lots to be arranged.. I'll keep in touch .. And then, after the... when it's all over.. I'll.. Well I suppose I'll just come home.
PEGGY	Oh yes, please God!... Come home safely to us, Lilian...

All Change at Brookfield

While still looking forward to Dan's semi-retirement, Doris found the preparations for the move to Glebe Cottage more of a wrench than she'd thought. They were leaving behind them fifty years of mostly happy memories, and – as Phil and Jill wanted to re-furnish – many of their surplus possessions had to be sold. Although in the end the move was a relief to Doris, it can't have come as a great surprise to her that Dan found it difficult to step back from the farm, and by the end of the summer was beginning to regret his decision. Jack wasn't too happy either. Although he owned a nominal ten per cent of Ambridge Farmers, seeing his young brother installed at Brookfield brought out his simmering resentment at being left out of the running of the family business. In the end Dan agreed to let him back onto the farm payroll, but without any say in the management. He came on the strict understanding that he was to work part-time under Brookfield's existing farm worker, Greg Salt, and would have to do as he was told.

Walter's Wooing

Among the guests at Jennifer and Roger's wedding was Mrs P, who had since returned to Ambridge after the death of her ailing husband Arthur. Walter lost no time in renewing his courtship of her and in the summer he proposed, only to be disappointed; he now faced stiff competition in the form of Bull cellarman Henry Cob. The two men were soon involved in a fierce rivalry for Mrs P's affections. On her birthday Henry gave her an exotic mynah bird, soundly trumping Walter's sad gift of a budgie.

Eligible bachelor Ralph Bellamy (Jack Holloway)

A Choice for Lilian

If Lilian had any doubts about Ralph's true feelings for her, they were put to rest on New Year's Eve, when he confessed that he wanted them to share a future together. Still confused about her own emotions she pleaded for time, and he agreed not to rush things. Soon after she found herself fighting off the unwelcome attentions of Nelson Gabriel, always ready to try his luck with a single Archer girl. This unsavoury encounter may have prompted her to accept Ralph's offer for her to ride his beautiful thoroughbred Red Knight in the Borchester point-to-point. After she won her race he took her out for a romantic meal and presented her with a wonderful engagement ring. Although touched and flattered, again she hesitated – perhaps unsure if it was her affection for Ralph that enticed her, or the prospect of becoming Lady of the Manor – but a week later she said yes. They were married in style on 3 September, Ralph footing most of the bill. Jennifer was matron of honour, and the reception was held at Grey Gables. The only slight sadness for Lilian was her father's absence from the ceremony. In February, Jack had become so unwell that he'd given up working at Brookfield. In July he collapsed and was rushed to hospital, where he was told that his liver was seriously damaged. He was sent to a rehab clinic in Scotland where he spent the rest of the year, too weak even to attend his daughter's wedding. Tony stepped in to take his place and give Lilian away. Ralph had bought Lilian the Dower House as a wedding present, and it was to there that the happy couple returned after their honeymoon in Venice.

Old hand Walter teaches Tony Archer (Colin Skipp) some basic tractor maintenance

Lilian's wedding to Ralph Bellamy

Lilian slipped easily into her role as Ambridge's First Lady – with her own housekeeper, Mrs Blossom, to take care of the more tedious chores – and invited Dan and Doris to the Dower House for Christmas. As far as the estate was concerned, the match brought rather mixed blessings for Ralph. Tony Archer, his hot-headed and outspoken young employee, was now his brother-in-law; and if that wasn't complication enough, the 1,000 acres that came with the Dower House had its own cuckoo in the nest – a thoroughly feckless and self-righteous tenant farmer by the name of Joe Grundy.

Cold Winds of Change

The Ambridge Protection Society – now chaired by Dan – found a new cause when Jack Woolley proposed turning a hundred acres of land adjoining Grey Gables into a country park designed to attract visitors from nearby towns. Opposition was spearheaded by Robin Freeman, a botanist and ex-POW who worked at the Arkwright Hall Field Centre. He talked up rumours of the village being invaded by thousands of city dwellers, but his campaign came to nothing when Woolley's plans were given the go-ahead. In a more benign development, Hugo Barnaby – an arts and antiques expert and cousin of John Tregorran, recently returned from the USA – bought Nightingale Farm from his niece, Lady Isobel Lander, turned it into a rural arts centre, and installed Laura as his assistant.

1972

A Life-Change for Peggy

After missing Lilian's wedding, Jack had been too ill to leave the Scottish sanatorium for Christmas, although he did manage to call Peggy on their wedding anniversary, and arranged for a mohair scarf to be sent for her Christmas present. When the New Year's rush at The Bull was over, Peggy was told that he was well enough to have a visitor, and went up to see him – the first time they'd met since he'd been sent away, six months ago. It wasn't to be the happy reunion she'd hoped for, however. Soon after she arrived Jack took a sudden turn for the worse; she was still with him when he died, just a few days later. Whatever her private emotions, Peggy showed all her usual strength of character in the way that she dealt with her bereavement. In accordance with Jack's wishes there was no funeral. Peggy instead organised a memorial service at the end of January. She politely declined Lilian and Ralph's offer to take her in at the Dower House, and stayed on at The Bull with the help of her temporary manager, Dick Corbey. Not for long, however. In April, Corbey stole some of the stock and disappeared with the police on his tail. This was all too much for Peggy, and when Jack Woolley urged her to take on a job as his assistant at Grey Gables she accepted. Sid and Polly were delighted when she offered them the chance to manage The Bull (incidentally upsetting Roger and Jennifer, who'd rather fancied running the place themselves). Sid and Polly sold the shop to Jack Woolley. Sid's criminal record barred him from being a licensee, but Polly took over the role and at the end of the summer they began their new life as landlords of the village pub. There were some typically alarmist rumours about Jack Woolley's plans for the shop and post office, but these were quashed when he installed Stanley and Angela Cooper, a reliable father and daughter team, as new managers. Peggy took up her new job and moved into a flat at Grey Gables, her days as a publican now firmly behind her.

Romeo Tony

Like his mother and sister, it didn't take Tony too long to recover from the undoubted shock of Jack's death and start looking to the future. His 21st birthday came only two weeks after the memorial service, and to mark the occasion Lilian treated him to a quiet but sumptuous dinner party at the Dower House. It was also some consolation for him to discover that Jack had left him £2,000 of Laura's gift in trust. More importantly – for his future career, at least – Dan and Phil agreed that he could inherit Jack's ten per cent share in Ambridge Farmers. It was soon back to business as usual for Tony as he cruised the lanes in his brand new MG Midget, hoping to impress any local girls who weren't already wise to him (as was the case with Phil and Jill's French au pair, Michele, and Lilian's assistant at the stables, Roberta). When Hugo Barnaby took on an attractive young teacher, Jane Petrie, to run his summer arts and crafts fair, it wasn't long before Tony's MG was buzzing around to Arkwright Hall – the new venue for the arts centre – like a bee to a honeypot. Jane was something of a drama queen, and bored besides, and was quite happy to lead Tony on for a few weeks over the summer. Tony was putty in her hands, and his work running Ralph's dairy enterprise suffered as a result. There was a big row after some neglected cows strayed and were struck by lightning, and an even bigger one when Ralph blamed him (unfairly, perhaps) for an isolated outbreak of brucellosis. As a result of this, Ralph finally lost his patience and Tony was sacked. He disappeared off to France, and when he came back went straight down to

Laura Archer (Berry McDowall)

DORIS	(CHUCKLING) And to tell you the truth, it's about time I had another little grandson – so what about it eh?
LILIAN	Gran Archer... you're quite wicked – inciting me to promiscuous motherhood like that... No. And now I'm declaring the subject closed. Another cup of tea?
DORIS	Yes please dear...
LILIAN	Pass your cup then.
DORIS	By the way... wasn't Tony going out with that girl of yours at the stables – what was her name – Roberta?
LILIAN	Tony - er – yes, I believe he was but things have cooled off, lately, I hear.
DORIS	That's a pity – she seemed a nice girl, from what your mother said. (INNOCENTLY) Did something go wrong? Tony seemed quite settled, I thought...
LILIAN	Oh, he was, while the fun lasted... (LAUGHING) The trouble was, Roberta had more serious ideas – which scared Tony off very smartly.
DORIS	Nice to hear a modern girl having so much sense... marriage is a wonderful institution you know... (LAUGHING) Even though your grandfather tells me that the first fifty years are the worst...
LILIAN	Well, Ralph and I still have another forty nine to go... but if they're only half as good as this first one, I won't be disappointed... FADE OUT

Brookfield and asked Dan and Phil to take him on. They agreed, but – as with his father before him – on the strict understanding that he pulled his weight. Tony ate humble pie and agreed to do so.

1973

Further Adventures of Tony &

After being sacked by his brother-in-law, Tony seemed to buckle down and work conscientiously at Brookfield. There was some friction with Phil, however (who

still saw him as young and irresponsible), and when an opportunity to move on presented itself Tony grabbed it with both hands. Haydn Evans, a widower from Wales, had recently bought a small farm at the side of Lakey Hill, and – after his son ran off with a local girl – Haydn agreed to take on Tony as a partner to help run his dairy herd. At Michaelmas, Tony left Brookfield and moved up to Willow Farm, delighted at this first taste of real independence. He didn't let this new responsibility interfere with his love life, however, and was soon involved with Mary Weston, his pretty 22-year-old farm secretary.

Tony and Sid Perks swap a joke in The Bull

Trying Times at Brookfield &

The previous year hadn't been entirely trouble free for Jill and Phil and their family. Five-year-old Elizabeth had needed another major operation to correct her heart defect and – although this was a complete success – Jill had begun to buckle under the strain of being a wife and mother. As a result she'd spent some time away in London visiting a school friend, while Chris helped out at Brookfield. The New Year got off to a more promising start with Jill back at home fully recovered and Phil organising a folk choral group for the Ambridge Festival (held to mark the 1,000th anniversary of St Stephen's Church) as well taking charge of the Scout troop. There was a nasty scare, however, when both David and Elizabeth were taken ill after eating grain dressed with pesticide, Elizabeth needing her stomach pumped as a result. Luckily neither of them suffered any lasting harm. The twins took their GCE exams, and Kenton was given a telescope for doing well in his science subjects. Shula shared in his success and was a bit miffed when her parents baulked at rewarding her with one of Lilian's best horses. Phil and Jill had ambitions for her to be a vet, but horse-mad Shula was desperate to follow her idol Ann Moore and become a prizewinning event rider. She compromised by agreeing to stay on and take her A levels while keeping up her riding. If the stresses of fatherhood weren't enough, Phil also had his hands full running the farm. After

Jack and Hazel Woolley (Hilary Armstrong)

Tony left Ambridge Farmers, Phil took on a new apprentice, Neil Carter, who lodged at April Cottage with newly-weds Martha and Joby Woodford. Neil had no farming experience and the next few months proved to be a steep learning curve for him, and a headache for Phil, obliged to put up with Neil's frequent mistakes.

Jack Woolley's Brush with Death

Early in the year Jack began to suffer mild heart problems. His adopted daughter Hazel – now 16, and studying for her GCE exams – came to stay, and persuaded him that it would be better for his health if he went to live at Grey Gables. Jack duly took her advice and sold the Manor House – soon to be renamed Ambridge Hall – to Laura. The move didn't do much for his health, however. In May he was attacked and badly injured by burglars at Grey Gables. Peggy found him unconscious in the lounge bar, and he was in hospital for several weeks, during which time she took charge of running the business. And this wasn't to be the only upset for Jack; he'd only been back for a short while when his wife Valerie told him she was suing for divorce. Their relationship had in fact been in a state of terminal decline for several years. After they were married, Valerie had quickly succumbed to boredom, which she'd relieved by having an affair with Ralph Bellamy (before his marriage to Lilian), and only two years later she and Jack had separated. He was still fond of her, however; her divorce ultimatum came as an unwelcome shock and prompted a severe heart attack. Although he recovered well, he was told to rest by his doctor, and once again Peggy stepped in to help look after his business affairs. Amid all his troubles Jack found a good deal of solace in her company and her invaluable assistance.

A Separation, Three Proposals and a Wedding

1974

For Jennifer, the New Year brought more worries to add to the uncertainty that was beginning to overtake her marriage to Roger. Tensions over his domineering mother – always a bone of contention – had grown worse, and he'd been less than supportive when she'd taken on a part-time job helping Peggy at Grey Gables. They had ended up spending Christmas apart, and Roger had then decided to sell up the bookshop, along with the flat that was their home, and take a job as a travelling rep for a book-dealers. This, he informed her, would take him away for long periods at a time. Although he insisted that he still loved her, and they'd still be man and wife, this wasn't a great consolation for Jennifer, who was soon forced to accept that they were living separate lives. In the summer she took her two young children and went back to Ambridge to live with Christine (whose own husband Paul was now away re-inventing himself as a horsebox dealer in Germany). It was hardly in Jennifer's nature to pine for long, however, and village gossips were soon intrigued to see her out and about in the company of Grey Gables' assistant keeper, Gordon Armstrong. Tony, meanwhile, was still busily pursuing his own love life, with mixed results. In January he decided that Mary

BRIAN ALDRIDGE & SHULA HEBDEN-LLOYD

CHARLES COLLINGWOOD PEERS OUT from the kitchen window across the rolling fields of rural Hampshire, eyes narrowing like a sailor scanning the horizon. 'That's the sea in the distance,' he beams with the air of a man only too conscious of his nautical heritage. As he reveals early on in his autobiography, *Brian and Me: Life on – and off* – The Archers, he is descended from Admiral Collingwood who was second in command at Trafalgar.

Judy Bennett comes from a seafaring family as well. Her father was a captain in the merchant navy and he evidently bequeathed her an abiding love of the briny. Until fairly recently, she used to go body-surfing off the south coast in late October when few would venture in without a rubber suit. 'I'm very warm-blooded,' she revealed in 1998 when interviewed about the brief evolution of her long-term character into a merry widow. Shula Hebden, as she then was, enjoyed flings with the village vet and doctor.

As *Archers* listeners know, Shula went on to marry the vet. Judy, on the other hand, is the off-air wife of Brian – or rather Charles. She may not go swimming in the sea in October these days, but she does enjoy two minutes under a cold shower every morning. 'I find it very invigorating,' she confides.

The couple met in a train corridor in 1971. She was wearing a purple mini-dress and high-heeled boots at the time. 'The train induced a sort of wiggle in her,' Charles recalls in his book, 'and I remember thinking, "Ooh, how lovely."'

Ooh, how very Brian that sounds. But, as the title of his autobiography suggests, they are two different people. 'The voice and the education are the same,' Charles accepts. 'Like Brian, I went to Sherbourne School. But I'm neither ruthless nor wildly unfaithful. And I don't drive a four by four.' So whose is the Range Rover on the drive? 'It's Judy's. I had an XKR Jag until recently, but I've just bought a Mercedes convertible.'

Reliable wheels are essential in these parts for two jobbing actors. Their well-appointed mid-Victorian cottage is part of what is little more than a hamlet. Charles has pulled on his green wellies this morning and trudged over the fields for half an hour to collect the morning papers. It's part of his daily ritual. 'I love it,' he insists. And Judy? 'Well, she's the one who wanted to move to the country. I was all for moving from our old house in Muswell Hill into the middle of London, close to the theatres and restaurants. After ten days I expected her to be begging to go back to the city. As it's turned out, there's no chance of either of us going back.'

Judy nods. 'I'd had enough of London,' she confirms. 'If I have to go to read an audiobook [a regular source of income for an actress with a talent for a wide range of voices] then there's a train from Petersfield that goes direct to Waterloo.' Charles uses it too. But he tends to travel to Birmingham for *Archers* recordings more often than his wife. After all, Brian has become a more prominent character than Shula in recent times. 'It would be churlish to complain,' she insists with a saintly smile. 'I've had a very good innings.'

The cricketing metaphor seems somehow appropriate for a couple who share a passion for the game. Indeed, Charles is an associate member of the MCC. He was once asked by former prime minister John Major if there was anything about the part of Brian that he wasn't happy with. 'Yes,' I replied. 'I'm the only playing member of the MCC in the entire cast and Brian is just about the only man in the village who's never played cricket for the local team.' As it happens, Nigel Pargetter has never played for Ambridge either and actor Graham Seed is also an MCC member.

> 'Like Brian, I went to Sherbourne School. But I'm neither ruthless nor wildly unfaithful.'

But what's a playing member? Well, here's the evidence on the wall of Charles's study, adjacent to a set of Wisdens dating back to 1965. Among several pictures of a white-flannelled Charles is one dating back to his prep-school days. Another has him at Lord's, playing for the Cross Arrows – a team made up of MCC members and employees. 'I was stumped for 18 and very annoyed with myself for getting out,' he recalls. Here's yet another photo of him turning out for The Stage, a team of made up of actors and playwrights. He went on to become club president but, in his early days, it fell to him to ring around his fellow thespians to check on their availability to play. Having exhausted his list and found himself still a player short, he made the mistake of ringing Harold Pinter before nine in the morning. The response was gruff and abrupt. The second word was 'off' and the first has never been heard in *The Archers*. Then the celebrated playwright put the phone down without a pause. 'Tragically for my career,' Charles recounts, 'those were the only two words Harold Pinter ever said to me.'

Still, he's not done too badly out of *The Archers'* scriptwriters, as he is the first to concede. 'I'm so grateful,' he says warmly. 'The writers now are even better than they were when I started. Without them you're nothing, and I've been given the most amazing storylines.'

Well, indeed. And, by his own admission, he was a radio novice compared to his wife when he arrived at the old Pebble Mill studios back in 1975. Admittedly he'd acted on television and film sets as well as the West End stage, but this was altogether different. He watched – and listened – carefully, particularly to the late Norman Painting as Phil Archer. 'To see him eating a full English breakfast with nothing in his mouth deserved an Oscar,' maintains Charles, who also kept an eye and an ear out for the techniques of Anne Cullen (Carol Tregorran) as well as one Judy Bennett.

Shula was already well established when Brian came into the programme. And Judy was also a skilled child impersonator at a time when children were heard but not seen anywhere near a microphone. 'I must have saved *The Archers* a few quid over the years,' she reflects with a smile. Not only did she play Adam before his voice broke but also the young Elizabeth, Kenton and Shula around the Brookfield breakfast table. 'I remember having to swallow quickly before answering a question in a different voice. Tony Shryane [the producer] was in fits of laughter.'

Laughing at the mic is an occupational hazard for actors, especially when they're playing a particularly poignant scene. It's known in the business as 'corpsing'. Charles became only too well aware of the phenomenon during Brian's affair with Siobhan Hathaway and its aftermath, which stimulated so much debate on websites, in newspapers and on the dinner party circuit in the early Noughties. The scenes were steamier than any of Brian's previous dalliances – in more ways than one. His fling with Caroline Bone in the 1980s, for instance, was largely conducted in restaurants and the kisses heard on air were delivered to the backs of hands. This time the kissing was for real. Caroline Lennon, who played Siobhan, was considerably younger than her swain and, according to Charles, warmer and gigglier than the character she played. 'No wonder we'd corpse,' he recalls. 'My glasses would steam up every now and then, or she'd have to push them up my nose.'

Such is the magic of radio, however, that the listening millions remained gripped by the intensity of a drama with consequences that are still unfolding. And such is the nature of radio drama that Caroline Lennon's reward for her part in such a stupendous storyline was to see her character killed off. Charles sympathised

'I must have saved The Archers a few quid over the years...'

but understands. 'It's the way of our profession. The thing that actors sometimes forget is that for the production team the most important thing is the show. Actors are simply the mouthpiece for what has been written.'

Brian would appear to be fairly secure as a pivotal character with the broad acres of Home Farm around him, but Charles is taking nothing for granted. As a skilled raconteur on the after-dinner circuit, he has never been totally dependent on a script. His burgeoning career on various Radio 4 chat shows is evidence enough of that. Verbal jousting with Paul Merton on *Just a Minute* requires a razor-like wit as well as impeccable articulation. 'I have a good rapport with Paul,' he says. 'We always sit next to one another.'

At this point, Judy gets one of her rare words in edgeways. 'I wish it was just a minute,' she observes drily. 'He can talk for half an hour without pause or repetition. Luckily, I'm a good listener.'

*Happy couple Pat
(Patricia Gallimore) and
Tony Archer*

Weston really was the woman of his dreams and duly proposed to her. She didn't exactly jump at the chance to become his fiancée but he eventually talked her round and she accepted. The wedding was set for July but, as the summer approached, Mary first found an excuse to postpone it, and then, while on holiday with her mother, she wrote to him and called it off. Tony was less upset than she might have expected, as by then he'd met Haydn Evans's niece, Pat Lewis, a shrewd and attractive 21-year old who'd been used to looking after a herd of pedigree Welsh Black cattle. When Haydn fortuitously slipped a disc, Pat came down to help run the farm and soon had Tony eating out of her hand. Perhaps a little intimidated by her lively mind, he was slow to act and in the end it was Pat who cooked him a Welsh hotpot and proposed. Tony said yes, thereby setting the tone for a relationship that was to last into the next century and beyond. On 12 December they were married and – after a honeymoon in Tenerife – began their life together at Willow Farm.

Not to be outdone by her children, Peggy was involved in a romantic intrigue of her own. Jack Woolley had become increasingly attached to her and as soon as his divorce from Valerie was settled he proposed. He was disappointed when she decided she wasn't ready to marry again and turned him down. She left her job at Grey Gables and moved into a cottage on the Bellamy Estate. She hadn't been there long, however, when Ralph and Lilian faced a major crisis of their own. Ralph's doctor had told him that he needed a complete rest, and as a result he decided to sell up the estate and move away from Ambridge.

Brookfield

The year got off to a bad start for Phil when some pigs at Hollowtree went down with swine vesicular disease, and the whole herd had to be slaughtered. He re-stocked with a more disease-resistant strain, but at the same time his young apprentice Neil Carter was getting into trouble. After taking a part-time job at a Borchester pub, he'd gone with a girl called Sandy Miller to a party, which was raided by the police. Neil was found in possession of marijuana and arrested. He claimed that the drug had been planted on him, but was found guilty and had to paint Walter Gabriel's porch as part of his community service order. To add to his woes, he failed his farm proficiency test after skipping some of his day-release classes. Phil was not impressed but decided that the lad was keen and deserved another chance.

PAT	… She might be lonely.
TOM	You could say the same about me.
PAT	Are you?
TONY	Sometimes. Everybody is.
PAT	Even when they're married?
TONY	Oh… er… well… Pat?
PAT	Yes Tony?
TONY	I've been going to ask you.
PAT	Go on then.
TONY	… Do you think we ought to cull that cow?
PAT	(BURSTS OUT LAUGHING) Tony! You're lovely!
TONY	What's so funny?
PAT	You are! I thought… (LAUGHS) I thought you were going to ask me to marry you!
TONY	Oh no. I was just thinking about (DOUBLE TAKE) Marry you?
PAT	Yes Tony. Sorry I was mistaken.
TONY	Yeh… er no!
PAT	No? Well go on then!
TONY	Eh?
PAT	If one of us won't say it we'll spend the rest of our lives talking about cows and changing the subject. After all, it's a simple question with a simple answer. And if you can't get around to it, I will. Tony Archer: will you marry me? What about it, eh? (MUSIC UP TO END.)

By contrast, Phil's eldest son, Kenton, had never shown much interest in farming, preferring science and meteorology. This year, after leaving school, he left Brookfield to train as a cadet in the merchant navy. Shula blamed herself for being mean to him and driving him away.

Sid with barmaid Nora

A Keeper's Life ⌀

Nora McAuley, the popular Bull barmaid, took a step into the unknown when she befriended George Barford, a Yorkshire ex-policeman who'd come to work as under-keeper for Tom Forrest. George was a moody loner who turned out to have a drink problem, and early in the year he was found unconscious after a suicide attempt. Although he was still married to his estranged wife – and was stubbornly resistant to any kind of help – Nora risked the outrage of the village gossips by moving in with George to look after him.

Moving On ⌀

1975

The early part of the year was dominated by the break-up and sale of the Bellamy Estate. Although Lilian was loath to leave the security of her home village, she had no choice but to go along with Ralph's plans to leave behind his business worries and visit warmer climes. He decided to keep 1,000 acres – including Bridge Farm – and let the Dower House. The rest of the property and land was sold in two lots, making Ralph a cash millionaire overnight. On 21 January, Lilian bade a sad farewell to Ambridge, having arranged for Christine to take over the stables and the new indoor riding school. She, Ralph, and 1-year-old James spent the year travelling, before eventually deciding to settle in Guernsey. Soon after they left, Carol Tregorran hosted a dinner party to welcome a newcomer to the village: Brian Aldridge, a suave, moneyed, 32-year-old Cambridgeshire farmer who'd bought Ambridge Court Farmhouse – soon to be renamed Home Farm – along with 1,500 acres of the Bellamy Estate (the remainder having been bought by a Mr Barnet). Brian took over the role of Ambridge's most eligible bachelor with some panache. As well as flirting with Carol (while John was away on a trip to America), he was soon practising his distinctive brand of polished charm on Jennifer, who was quite happy to reciprocate. She allowed him to wine and dine her at Borsetshire's finest restaurants, and they spent a pleasant day together at the Royal Show. There was a bit of a wobble when Roger got in touch to tell her abruptly that he'd been seeing another woman, and wanted a divorce; but Brian was on hand to console her, and she was soon helping him host his house-warming party. Like the rest of the family, she kept her fingers crossed and hoped it was only a matter of time before he proposed. At the end of the year, however, she was still waiting.

Joe Grundy (Hayden Jones)

1976

A Small Farmer's Lot

It had been a typically tempestuous few years for widower Joe Grundy and his two sons at Grange Farm. After narrowly surviving one notice of eviction, he'd been hospitalised with farmer's lung, and then had crashed his lorry into the village pump. He'd also threatened to sue for slander after Tom Forrest accused him of deer poaching, and rowed with Dan when his dog was shot for worrying sheep at Brookfield. Rent-day was a perennial crisis, and if there was an easier way to make a living than by milking cows, Joe was determined to find it. His recent attempts at diversification included a short-lived caravan site, followed soon after by a boisterous autocross meeting on his land. This summer he decided (a little late, perhaps) to jump on the Woodstock bandwagon and hold his own pop festival. A large part of the village was immediately up in arms, but the festival went ahead and – for once in his life – Joe had a modest success to celebrate. He followed this up by winning first prize in the Flower and Produce Show raffle: a luxury weekend for two at Grey Gables. He went up to claim it alone and annoyed Jack Woolley by trying to get the other half in cash.

A New Start for Jennifer

After a rather tense Christmas with the family, the New Year got off to a flying start for Jennifer. On New Year's Eve she became an aunt for the second time round when Pat

Jennifer takes her Jacob sheep by the horns

gave birth to a son, named John Daniel. Very soon after that, Brian mercifully put an end to the suspense and asked her to marry him. She didn't need asking twice; her divorce from Roger was finalised in the spring and she and Brian were married at Borchester Registry Office on 29 May. Jennifer swapped Chris's spare room at Wynford's for the luxury of a spacious farmhouse while Brian got used to the idea of becoming stepfather to 9-year-old Adam and 5-year-old Debbie. Jennifer resisted any temptation to become a lady of leisure and kept on her part-time job at Grey Gables, as well as writing her own regular countryside column for the *Borsetshire Echo*. In her spare time she took up spinning and weaving, and for her birthday Brian bought her a dozen Jacob sheep. After all the uncertainties of the last few years, it looked as if she'd finally landed on her feet.

Paul's Brilliant Career (Part 4)

After his venture as a German horsebox salesman had come to nothing, Paul had managed to talk himself into a job in the oil exploration industry. As this was generally happening in places far away from Borsetshire, Chris still saw little of him. This looked set to change in the New Year when he was moved to a desk job in

London, which – he promised – would allow him to work from home three days a week. However much Chris may have wanted to believe him, he soon found reasons why he needed to be in London far more often than he'd hoped. His excuses became ever more transparent and eventually he confessed that he was having an affair with his boss's PA, a woman called Brenda Maynard. After her experience with Marianne Peters, this was all wearily familiar ground for Chris. She spent a few weeks in a hiatus of uncertainty before Paul abruptly announced that he'd ditched Brenda, thrown in his job and was coming back to live with her. A mixed blessing for Chris, perhaps; but at least she still had her job at the stables to support them.

Shula the Rebel

With her 18th birthday fast approaching, Shula was coming to terms with the hard truth that she was never likely to fulfil her burning ambition to become a world-class competition rider. Phil had sensibly insisted that she take a secretarial course as a back-up, but she was in no hurry at all to make use of her shorthand skills. Determined instead to have some fun, she paired up with Kiwi sheep-shearer Michele Brown, and they spent the summer hitchhiking around Europe, where Shula fell for a Spanish boy named Pedro. After she returned she signed on as unemployed for a few weeks while deciding what to do next, her spare time spent pining for Pedro and flirting with Neil, who'd fallen hopelessly in love with her. As the year waned, however, she found a new interest: the *Borchester Echo*'s handsome and audacious new editor, 33-year-old Simon Parker. The two had scarcely met when Simon horrified Phil by publishing a photo of Shula on horseback under the headline 'Hunting on the Dole'. After this dire beginning, Shula might have assumed that Phil's opinion of her new boyfriend could only get better. Sadly this was not to be the case.

Paul's Brilliant Career (Finale)

1977

After finally coming back to live with Chris and Peter (now 12 years old) at Wynfords, Paul showed his good intentions by getting a dull but steady job with an agricultural machinery firm in Borchester. Chris may well have wondered if this was all too good to last; and, true to form, by mid-July Paul's fertile mind was already busy with his next big idea. A few years back Jack Woolley had started a small fish hatchery, which Paul planned to take over and develop into a full-scale trout farm. Jack was understandably wary about going into partnership but agreed to lease him the land. By the end of August, Paul had quit his job, raised a second mortgage on Wynfords and taken delivery of 20,000 seven-inch trout. Chris could only stand by him and silently pray as he talked up the big profits he was sure to net when he sold the fish on later in the year. All went well at first, but in mid-October the almost inevitable disaster struck: a filter was blocked by leaves and all the fish died. If this wasn't tragedy enough, Paul had no insurance, and so lost his whole investment. Jack Woolley offered to waive the rent, but his other creditors were less generous and Paul was forced into bankruptcy. Faced with losing Wynfords, Chris accepted an offer by Dan and Phil to buy the house at the stables and lease it back to her. Paul, however, slipped into a bout of deep depression and early in December he disappeared, leaving a note to say that he was gone for good. Brian eventually managed to trace him to an address in Hamburg, and Chris flew out to see him a few days before Christmas. She returned with the news that he'd found a job out there, and wasn't coming back. She and Peter would have to begin a new life without him.

Lost Innocence

Whatever her father's opinion of Simon Parker (or 'that inky blighter', as Phil had labelled him) Shula was well and truly smitten. Now with a steady job at Borchester estate agents Rodway and Watson, she went out with him at every opportunity, in spite of his habit of turning up late and standing her up on several occasions. She even thought she'd lost him for good when, after a row with Jack, he resigned from the *Echo* and left for Paris. He was back before long, however, and she finally surrendered what remained of her virtue to him in a cornfield on Midsummer's Eve. Fearful for his daughter's happiness, Phil remained determinedly hostile and Simon did little to endear himself to her parents. When he published an article criticising the farming community and calling them 'fat cats', Phil took it as a personal attack. This was all water off a duck's back to Simon the hard-nosed journalist, and Phil could only watch as Shula became ever more beguiled, and hope that she'd somehow find the sense to give the blighter up.

All Change at Willow Farm

The year held big changes in store for Mike Tucker, Ambridge Farmers' dairy manager, and his wife Betty. Mike had shown himself to be a steady and reliable worker, although his role as local rep for the Farm Workers' Union had caused the odd ripple at Brookfield; the previous year he'd helped Phil's stalwart worker Jethro Larkin get compensation after he'd fallen through the calf shed roof. Mike had always had ambitions to be his own boss, however, and early this autumn he saw his chance when Pat and Tony accepted Ralph Bellamy's offer to take on the tenancy of Bridge Farm. This left Haydn Evans looking for a new partner. Mike approached Haydn who agreed to take him on, and so Mike and Betty raised the necessary funds, left Rickyard Cottage and moved up to Willow Farm to run the dairy herd. The only slight complication was a temporary house-share with Pat, Tony and baby John, who were waiting for renovation work at Bridge Farm to be finished. The two couples got on well enough, although Pat soon tired of Mike's large collection of country and western records.

	7. INT. WYNFORD'S FRIDAY, MID-AFTERNOON
	(DOOR OPENS)
CHRIS	I don't think he's back, Dad. The car isn't in the drive.
DAN	He could have put it in the garage, Chris.
CHRIS	Hm. (CHANGE TO INT. HALL) (CALLS) Paul! Are you there?
DAN	And answer came there none.
CHRIS	Looks as if you've come on a wild goose chase.
DAN	I'll wait a bit if I may. We must get this out in the open. He may turn up soon.
CHRIS	Let's go into the living room. (DOOR OPENS ON – CHANGE TO INT. LIVING ROOM)
DAN	You haven't told me what lunch was like.
CHRIS	Lovely. Jennifer pulled out all the stops.
DAN	Good.
CHRIS	And she didn't say a word about Paul. Last time she was … what's the matter?
DAN	I think there's a letter for you. There.
CHRIS	Mm? Ah. It's a note from Paul. Probably to say when he'll be back… (ENVELOPE OPEN)
DAN	Are you all right?
CHRIS	I'll just sit down for a …
DAN	Why? What does he say?
CHRIS	That he won't be coming back. Ever.
DAN	What?
CHRIS	It's quite clear. He says he can't take any more and had to get away so, he's gone for good… (MUSIC – DRAMATIC SIG)

The Keeper and the Widow

Although Chris heard nothing from Paul over Christmas, she clung to the hope that he'd come back to her – and face his creditors – eventually. When Phil wrote a strong letter to him on her behalf, he repented enough to say that he'd be home for his next bankruptcy hearing in May. Chris, meanwhile, found a friend and confidant in her neighbour, George Barford. George had been going through his own difficult times with his live-in partner Nora and his son, Terry. The previous year, Terry had been caught drink-driving in a stolen car, and was given three months' detention; before that, Nora had left him for a short time, and had had a miscarriage. George,

Shula (Judy Bennet)

however, was now firmly established as Tom's under-keeper, a strict teetotaller and an accomplished cornet player. He'd recently begun to suspect that Nora was seeing someone else, and so it came as no surprise to him when she left him for a man who worked at the Borchester canning factory. There was a much worse blow in store for Chris, however: on 10 May, Paul was killed in a car crash in Germany, and Chris suddenly found herself a widow. He was buried over there, and Dan went with Chris to the funeral. Once she'd got over the initial shock, George's friendship was a great support to her. Where Paul had been impulsive and neglectful, George was steady and considerate. As soon as his divorce from his first wife was settled he asked her to marry him and she was happy to accept. The family (apart from Jill) had some doubts about George's past, but Chris put them firmly in their place, and George soon won them round. The vicar, Richard Adamson – after some deliberation – overruled his own PCC and agreed to marry them in St Stephen's. The wedding duly took place in March of the following year.

George Barford (Graham Roberts)

Hard Lessons

Shula's love life was still a worry for her parents. In spite of Phil's simmering disapproval, she showed no signs of dumping Simon Parker; quite the opposite, in fact. The more he messed her around, the more she clung to the relationship,

Angela Piper was driving along the A14 to Birmingham some years ago to record her part as Jennifer Aldridge when her car was hit from behind by a Dutch lorry. The car was a complete write-off. Angela, mercifully, survived with nothing worse than whiplash injuries. A motorcycling vicar, in the mould of Alan Franks, stopped to help. 'He was on his way to a Church conference in Leicester,' the actress recalls. Did he offer a lift on his pillion? 'No, a nice motorist from Bury St Edmonds managed to get me to the old Pebble Mill studios before the end of recording.' Divine intervention, perhaps. Some days later a letter arrived from the vicar to tell her that the entire conference had prayed for her.

Profile

MIKE TUCKER

TERRY MOLLOY EASES HIS way into a crowded pub near the Birmingham Rep, his old stamping ground, and asks for a Bacardi and coke. Not quite the kind of drink that *Archers* listeners would associate with Mike Tucker. But then he leaves Mike in the studio when recording is over, much as Mike might leave his milk float parked up at the end of his round.

Actor and character don't even sound very similar. Terry's voice is posher, as you might expect from the son of an RAF wing commander who spent his childhood at various boarding schools. And his appearance? Well, there is a passing resemblance to Eric Clapton, also well into in his 60s. One of Terry's more unlikely recent roles came at the end of an episode of *Harry Hill's TV Burp* in 2009, when he mimed the words to Clapton's song 'Layla' while dressed in a hospital gown.

'I'd appeared in *Casualty* on the Saturday night,' Terry explains. 'And on the Monday morning my agent took a call from Harry Hill's office saying: "We think your man looks just like Clapton and we'd like him to play out the end of the show." Harry would then have the line: "Isn't it amazing the people you see on *Casualty* these days?"' He pauses, takes another sip of Bacardi, shakes his head and smiles. 'It was bizarre. But at least my street cred went up with my children by 200 per cent.'

One of those children is Philip Molloy, who works as an audio-visual technician at a Birmingham grammar school when he's not playing Will Grundy in *The Archers*. 'Phil and I haven't done many episodes together because our paths haven't crossed that often,' Terry points out. Like any actors, they work to the script and the script has Mike in partnership with Ed – the Grundy regarded by his older brother with about as much affection as a van-load of poachers. Not much brotherly love there. 'Still, it makes for great drama,' his real-life dad suggests.

His own career in drama has largely been spent in this city. Indeed he lived here for twenty-nine years, working at the Rep and the Midlands Arts Centre while being conveniently close at hand to record radio plays at BBC's Midlands' studios and slip into Mike mode when required. Terry has played him since 1973, so they've been together now for nigh-on 40 years. 'I've got to like him because he's part of me,' the actor muses. 'I admire his resolute honesty and steadfastness. Admittedly, he tolerates fools with no gladness whatsoever and only opens his mouth to change feet. But he loves his kids to bits.'

His grandchildren, too, and Mike has been understandably concerned about the effects on Phoebe of the reappearance in Ambridge of her birth mother, Kate Madikane (née Aldridge). 'He was never very fond of Kate, or the Aldridges in general,' says Terry. 'They wouldn't be on the Tuckers' Christmas-card list if it wasn't for the Phoebe connection, and vice versa. Don't forget that Brian once tried it on with Betty.'

Ah, yes, Betty Tucker of blessed memory. Her unexpected death gave Terry the chance to plumb the depths of misery once again. 'Any actor likes to have the envelope pushed,' he says, 'and that was a phenomenal storyline to play. Very intense and very dramatic.' And very different from his home life with the younger, louder and brasher Vicky. 'Yes, it was great fun to play a storyline with a comic edge,' he agrees. 'And until Vicky came along, Mike was in danger of slipping into senile dotage.'

His real-life wife, Victoria, is the retired chief executive of a large charity. The couple now live near Norwich in a village that bears more than a passing resemblance to Ambridge, according to Terry. And do the residents know that he's Mike Tucker? 'Yes, but they've got over it and moved on. That suits me. It means I can walk down the street or to the shop without being bothered.' Even his longest-running television role guaranteed his much cherished anonymity. He was Davros in *Doctor Who* for much of the 1980s. But playing the creator of the Doctor's deadliest enemies, the Daleks, meant that he had to don a hideous mask before the cameras started rolling. 'The older I get,' he grins, 'the more like that mask I look.'

Better not tell Eric Clapton that.

> **'Any actor likes to have the envelope pushed.'**

Profile
PAT ARCHER

THERE ARE TWO PILES of books on the coffee table in Patricia Gallimore's elegant apartment in a Midlands spa town. One is topped by a biography of Barrack Obama, the other is *Barbara Cartland's Etiquette Handbook*. 'That's one of the audiobooks that I record when I'm not doing *The Archers*,' she stresses. And by 'that' she means the Cartland, not the Obama. 'I've even done Mills and Boon,' she admits. Heavy breathing and all? 'Yes, all of that stuff,' she adds in a voice that is instantly recognisable as Pat Archer.

Pat and Pat have been together now for thirty-six years and they have quite a bit in common, apart from the voice and the Christian name. Neither would count Mills and Boon among their bedtime reading and both profess themselves to be feminists. 'I'm up for that,' says Patricia, as we shall call her from now on to avoid confusion. So does she take *The Guardian*? 'No, but I read it when my husband [Charles, a solicitor] brings it home. I buy *The Times* because I like the crossword.'

On air, Pat's feminist principles are being sorely tested by Helen's decision to be impregnated by an unknown sperm donor and Patricia can well understand her qualms. 'I'm all for women having freedom of choice,' she muses, 'but I don't know how I'd have reacted if it were my daughter. There are a lot of issues for a young woman who isn't gay.' Isn't Helen, though, rather disillusioned with men? 'Understandably so, but she's only just over 30. And I happen to think that a good partner is important. I also think that any mother would ultimately, like Pat, support her daughter even if she didn't necessarily support the idea of doing it.' She pauses for a moment before adding with some relish: 'This storyline is a bag of rats in some ways, but it's fascinating.'

Her most demanding storyline in three and a half decades as an *Archers* actress was, not surprisingly, the breakdown visited on Pat after the tractor accident that killed off her eldest son. 'It was quite harrowing,' she confirms. 'If you had children, which I did, you couldn't help but think about them. No parent could imagine anything worse than losing a child.'

Happily, her own grown-up offspring are thriving in London, and Patricia became a grandmother not too long ago through her son, who happens to be called Tom. 'My Tom came first,' she insists as though trying to get one over on the fictional Pat. So here are two Pats with sons called Tom. Both Pats regard themselves as feminists and read *The Guardian*. The actress will be telling us next that she's into all things organic.

Well, yes. She even wrote a book in 1999 called *Patricia Gallimore's Organic Year*. 'Unfortunately,' she recalls, 'it soon became out of date because a lot of the farm shops that I'd featured were closed down by a major outbreak of foot-and-mouth.' Two major survivors that she came to know well were Prince Charles's Highgrove and

> **'No parent could imagine anything worse than losing a child.'**

Garden Organic, the national research centre at Ryton, Warwickshire. 'An adviser from Ryton helped me design the little walled garden that we have at the back of this place,' she confides. 'We grow organic herbs there.' No veg? 'No room. But we grew lots when we had a big garden at our old house.' Organically? 'Oh, yes.'

Patricia readily concedes that her interest in matters organic directly evolved from her role in *The Archers*. She and Colin Skipp, who plays husband Tony, became Soil Association celebrities, invited to events all over the country. 'We were the after-dinner turn at a college in Cirencester, sharing the platform with Willie Lockretz, an eminent professor in nutrition science at Tufts University in Boston. He has since become a keen online *Archers* listener. He emails us now and again to tell us how fond he is of the Grundys.'

Patricia leans back in her armchair and smiles. The daughter of a naval captain, she was born in Bath and finished up in the Midlands when her father retired from the navy and worked for ICI. 'I've never worked on a farm,' she says. Well, that's one thing that differentiates her from Pat. 'I've never made yoghurt either. Not that keen on it, to be honest. But if I occasionally have it with some fruit for breakfast, it has to be organic.'

Inevitably.

Dan and Doris with family and friends in The Bull

pretending she was OK about his flirtations with other girls and biting her tongue when he made caustic remarks about marriage. Phil and Jill could only hope that when the end inevitably came, he'd let her down gently. A vain hope, of course. During a May Day picnic on Lakey Hill, Simon casually told her that he'd got a job with a London paper. Soon after he was out of her life, never to return. A hard lesson for Shula, who retreated to her room to nurse her wounds, and so it was a while before she paid much attention to Phil's new student worker, Nick Wearing. Tall, blond and ex-public school, Nick first lodged with Martha Woodford, before moving in with Neil and Michele at Nightingale Farm. His first conquest was Jennifer's au pair, Eva, who fell for him on a badger-watching expedition. When Shula began to renew her interest in life, she and Nick started going out together. Shula found his youthful zest for life therapeutic, although – to begin with, at least – he still found himself competing with the ghost of Simon Parker.

Colin Skipp (Tony Archer) met his wife, the actress Lisa Davies, when they were doing a summer season in Guernsey. They married in 1970 and their daughter, Nova Skipp, is now a successful singer and actress on the West End stage. 'She used to be known as Tony Archer's daughter,' says Colin. 'Now I'm known in the business as Nova Skipp's father.'

Two Jays ⌘

In the previous year Brian and Jennifer had celebrated the birth of their daughter, Kate, who had arrived on 30 September. In the spring Jennifer employed a German au pair, Eva Lenz, and by the summer was looking for ways to fill her spare time creatively. She hit upon the idea of running a craft studio from a converted barn at Home Farm and persuaded Jill to join her in the venture, which they called the Two Jays. Business was slow at the start, and they held a big launch party to try and attract customers. Things weren't helped when Walter took away his carved wooden animals – which had been selling well – and set up his own 'Wally G' craft shop. They ran into more trouble when they discovered they didn't have the necessary planning permission to use the barn and by October Jill had had enough, and pulled out. She was left with £150 in debts, which Phil agreed to pay off for her.

Hard Times at Grange Farm ⌘

To say that Joe Grundy's two sons, Alf and Eddie, had been a disappointment to him would be giving them too much credit. Neither of them had shown any inclination to follow their father into the farming life, and both had recently been involved in a shady scrap metal business near Gloucester. In the spring Joe went down with 'flu and was found abandoned and delirious by his neighbour from Ambridge Farm, Mary Pound. His dairy herd was infected with brucellosis, and, in a final twist of the knife, his favourite hob ferret, Turk, was killed in a trap. Joe touched rock bottom, and sought refuge in his fiery home-made scrumpy. His dire predicament finally aroused a spark of conscience in his younger son Eddie, who returned to help his father pick up the pieces. Joe was compensated for his slaughtered cows, and he and Eddie started a small turkey-rearing business. So Grange Farm escaped bankruptcy, and the Grundys struggled on to fight another day.

Wanderers ⌘

As winter turned to spring, Shula's pain slowly began to heal and she and Nick spent more time together. By early summer she was wondering about visiting Michele, who was back in New Zealand. When Nick suggested they hit the hippy trail and travel together overland she jumped at it, although it was something of an uphill struggle to persuade her parents that this was a good

1979

As Brian Aldridge the actor Charles Collingwood has been married to Jennifer (Angela Piper) as long as he has been with his real-life wife Judy Bennett (Shula). Nearly thirty-five years is plenty of time to get used to seeing your hubby in cosy – and sometimes not so cosy – domesticity with another woman. 'It's only a job,' Judy shrugs. And did she feel the same when he was pursuing other women? 'Oh, yes. We're actors.' All the same, she had some fun after Brian's passionate embraces with Siobhan were broadcast to a breathless nation. 'Every now and then I'd receive a one-word text message,' Charles recalls. 'It read simply "Bastard".'

Eddie and Joe

idea. Phil ended up by caving in and giving her an advance on her 21st birthday present. She took leave from her job at Rodway and Watson, and in July she and Nick set off from Hollerton Junction to Calcutta. The trip didn't quite go as planned, however; in September her parents were slightly perturbed to hear that Nick had gone on alone to Australia, and Shula was looking for a job in Bangkok. In the event Shula was home by November, sun-tanned but penniless after her money and passport were stolen from her hotel. She spent the tail end of the year doing odd jobs and hanging out with her new friend: a well-bred and sophisticated former Bull barmaid, now working at Grey Gables, called Caroline Bone.

Back to the Fold

Now that Eddie was back under the Grange Farm roof, Joe's life became a little easier. With a handy compensation cheque in the bank, he took a break from the burden of twice-daily milking, and didn't rush to replace his dairy herd. In the spring came the news that Eddie was engaged to his girlfriend, fun-loving divorcee Dolly Treadgold. As a long-time widower, Joe welcomed the prospect of having a woman back in the Grange Farm kitchen. He made a token attempt to add a few feminine touches to the house, only to be disappointed when the young couple rowed and called the whole thing off. A few weeks later, however, they made up and it was all back on. Joe cheerfully decked out the turkey shed and ordered food for the reception, but the day before the wedding, Eddie bottled out and called it off again, unnerved by Dolly's wandering eye. As if all this wasn't aggravation enough for Joe, Alistair Sinclair gave him a deadline to shape up the farm or face eviction.

Farming Fortunes

Phil and Jill had now been married for twenty-one years. Over that time Phil had become a respectable pillar of the local community, and a JP on the Borchester Magistrates' bench. Jill had now returned to being a full-time wife and mother after the collapse of the 'Two Jays', although she still found time to help organise village events and deliver meals-on-wheels for the WRVS. When not worrying about his various children, Phil was busy as ever trying to build up and streamline Ambridge Farmers. Dan was now 83 and firmly semi-retired, although still helping out on a casual basis, mostly with the ewes. David – after failing his maths A level – had given up the idea of going to university and started a course at agricultural college, intending to come back and work full-time at Brookfield. This was reassuring for Phil, who shared with Dan his hopes that David would one day take over the farm; and it must have added to his confidence when he bought another thirty acres from nearby Meadow Farm, paying £1,725 an acre. To fund the purchase he arranged to sell Hollowtree to Brian, but this fell through when Brian's plan for an industrial-scale pig unit met with fierce opposition. Phil ended up raising a mortgage from the Agricultural Mortgage Association to buy the land. From Dan's original 100-acre

Phil and Jill talk shop at Brookfield

holding, Brookfield had now grown into a thriving business of 465 acres, with a dairy herd of 110 milking cows, plus 60 breeding sows at Hollowtree, and a flock of around 200 ewes. His workforce included his new cowman, Graham Collard, with Jethro Larkin as a full-time worker, together with Neil – who now mostly looked after the pigs – as well as part-timer Fred Wakefield. Never one to rest on his laurels, Phil knew only too well that farming was an ever-changing and competitive business, and as one decade ended he was already planning how best to face the challenges of the next.

PROCESS

Twice a year the writers and production team gather for a long-term planning meeting. It's from all-day gatherings like this that major storylines emerge, such as Ruth's never-quite consummated dalliance with cowman Sam and the insemination of Helen. Some ideas are so outlandish that they're thrown out immediately. Others are fleshed out at a further meeting on the first Monday of every month.

'Four writers then have from the Tuesday evening to the following Wednesday to write their synopses for a month's storylines,' editor Vanessa Witburn explains. 'I go through them with my senior producer Julie Beckett and we ring them on Thursday with our notes. Each of those four writers then has eleven days to write six episodes each – seventy-five minutes of drama. We do the script-editing in two days flat. Judy and I meet on the Friday morning to read each other's scripts and check that we're in tune. Then we call the writers on Friday afternoon and they have the weekend to do the re-writes. We're in studio with those scripts two weeks later.'

But they're hardly idle during the intervening fortnight. They're working on more than one set of scripts at any one time as well as editing what has been recorded the previous month. The actors spend just six days in studio recording a month's worth of scripts.

Profile

KATHY HOLLAND

BEDROOM SCENES ON THE radio leave everything to the imagination. 'It's all about suggestion,' says Hedli Niklaus, lifting an eyebrow suggestively. In her long career with *The Archers*, she has experienced at least two such scenes – first as Kathy Holland, the schoolteacher who fell for Sid Perks, and then as Kathy Perks, landlady of The Bull, enjoying a dalliance with PC Dave Barry. 'I seem to have had a predilection for policemen during my thirty-two years with the programme,' she laughs. 'I once played a German au pair at Home Farm, Eva Lenz, and she ended up marrying the village bobby of the day.'

No, Brian Aldridge did not try to exercise droit de seigneur during the au pair's time under his roof. His eye was still steadfastly focused on Jennifer in those days. 'When I first started listening to the programme, at university in the 1960s, it was Tony who had all the girlfriends,' Hedli recalls. 'My first appearance was as Libby, the milk recorder, distracting him while Pat was away having a baby.' And did anything come of it? 'No, Libby was just flirtatious enough to annoy Peggy.'

Hedli remembers when couples supposed to be in bed together on the radio sat side by side on chairs. So she was rather taken aback to arrive at the old Pebble Mill studios in Birmingham one day to find a double bed installed. Alan Devereux, who played Sid until the character died unexpectedly, declined to get in it. Instead he sat on the side, feet on the floor, like a character in a 1950s TV sitcom. A shrewd move as it turned out. 'The phone was supposed to ring during the scene,' Hedli remembers.

'And because the bed was so much lower than the mic, I couldn't get out quickly enough to answer it. They had to record the whole thing again.'

She's laughing once more and it comes as no surprise to learn that, although she admires Kathy as a character, she'd like her to have a few more humorous lines. But then, as she readily concedes, Kathy's life has hardly been a bed of roses. Even her relationship with Ambridge's Mr Fun, Kenton Archer, has ended in tears. She has also been a rape victim and endured the indignities of the subsequent court case. Good, meaty storylines, for sure, and she has been grateful for them. 'But the most exciting for me was the two-hander that I played with Alan when Kathy found out about Sid's affair with Jolene,' Hedli insists. 'It's quite a challenge to engage an audience with just two voices for twelvE and a half minutes. Every time you did a scene with Alan, you never quite knew where it was going, and I like that. He was fun to work with.'

Her real-life husband, Leon Tanner, sometimes performs with the Royal Shakespeare Company. They live in Warwickshire and we're talking nearby, in the unlikely setting of an industrial estate off the A46. The shelves in this unit are crammed with boxes of Bull jigsaws, 'dum-di-dum' shoulder bags and fridge magnets featuring Lakey Hill.

'Every time you did a scene with Alan, you never quite knew where it was going.'

There's more, much more, because this is the nerve centre of Archers' Addicts, which celebrates its 21st birthday as the programme marks its 60th. Hedli has developed the 5,000-strong fan club into what she calls 'a small business with a limited turnover'. She evidently relishes meeting the listeners, be it at a garden fete or on the high seas during one of AA's summer cruises.

Paradoxically, perhaps, she also enjoys the anonymity that comes with being in a long-running radio series. 'My voice has been recognised once in M&S, twice in Tesco and once in the cafeteria at the National [Theatre],' she says happily. There was another occasion, ten years ago, in the rather more salubrious surroundings of St James's Palace. Prince Charles was hosting *The Archers'* 50th-anniversary party and Hedli had the task of discreetly ushering Camilla Parker-Bowles, as she then was, into the throng. 'The first thing she said to me was: "I'm so glad your divorce has come through."' By that she meant her divorce from Sid. In real life, Hedli has remained married to Leon since 1973. They met in Torquay. 'I was playing the maid in a play called *Poole's Paradise* and Leon played the bishop,' she recalls. 'When we got married, the headline in the local paper was: "Actress weds Bishop".'

Rather less mundane was the truth: 'Actress weds Actor'.

Chapter Four 1980s

Tony and Pat Archer went organic, Neil Carter went into battery farming and Mike Tucker went bankrupt. Yes, the 1980s proved to be an eventful decade for the farming folk of Ambridge as *The Archers* continued to reflect the ongoing changes in the countryside while anticipating trends that would become more widespread in the 1990s. Tony and Pat's organic venture, for instance, was planned as early as 1984 when eschewing the use of fertilisers was still considered an activity for oddballs.

Brian Aldridge also anticipated the growth of the environmental movement when he constructed a farm pond in 1988. In Brian's case, needless to say, it was the public relations value rather than any principled stance that guided his hand. His head, meanwhile, took a nasty blow the following year when he was attacked by a mad cow, anticipating the BSE crisis which would devastate beef farming in the 1990s.

Memories of war-time food shortages were fading fast. The problem now was one of over-production. Politicians throughout the European Community faced awkward questions about grain mountains and milk lakes. Agriculture, it seemed, was not bound by the unsubsidised rules of the market which had become the new political mantra in the UK. It was time for action.

On the Land...

- Milk quotas were introduced in 1984, restricting dairy production. Joe Grundy blamed those 'beggars in Brussels' for curbing the cash flow for honest farmers like himself. But at least Grange Farm stayed in business – for the time being at least.
- Mike Tucker's bankruptcy came in 1986, reflecting the squeeze on milk production and agricultural returns in general. Credit had become more easily available as the financial markets became more competitive, but repaying mounting debts was not so easy for former farm workers who had moved into management.
- The loss of Mike's Ambridge Farm meant that Neil Carter had to look elsewhere to house his 1,000 battery hens, an enterprise that began in the early 1980s and came to grief in 1990.
- Set-aside was introduced in 1988 to curb over-production. Farmers were paid for the first time to set aside a proportion of their land to let nature take its course with minimal husbandry.
- Farmers were being encouraged to diversify. Brian went into deer farming in 1987 and began shooting weekends in partnership with Grey Gables.

... And in the Land Beyond the Farm Gate:

- Unemployment soared in the early years of Thatcherism as the collapse of traditional industries continued. The Specials' 'Ghost Town' caught the Zeitgeist in the summer of 1981 as unrest spread through the big cities.
- In the suburbs and villages, meanwhile, street parties greeted the wedding of Prince Charles and Lady Diana.
- Even more flag-waving the following year greeted victory in the Falklands War.
- The retail and service sectors of the economy began to boom and supermarkets strengthened their growing grip on the food market.
- Out went the pin-striped City gent and in came a new breed of financial trader with 'wedges' of cash even bigger than their brick-like mobile phones.
- 'Yuppies' emerged – young upwardly mobile professionals. Older couples, like the Snells, followed them out of urban areas into the countryside.
- Villages like Ambridge became home to many more commuters, like Richard Thwaite.
- Edwina Currie was forced to resign in 1988 after claiming that most eggs in the UK carried salmonella.
- Two years later, Neil Carter was forced to destroy his salmonella-ridden battery hens and Mrs Currie's mentor, Margaret Thatcher, was forced out of office. The two events were not related.

1980

Mid-Life Crises ✑

The old decade closed with Peggy's two daughters both married to wealthy husbands: Jennifer quite happily with Brian in Ambridge, Lilian rather less so with Ralph in Guernsey. On a recent visit, Jennifer had found her sister disenchanted, thoroughly bored with the affluent yachting set, and – not unlike her father before her – having the odd G&T too many. Deliverance was at hand, however. Towards the end of the previous year Ralph's health had begun to fail, and early in the New Year he had a fatal heart attack. At the age of 32, Lilian was a widow once again. There was to be no pretence of mourning this time around; as she confided in Jennifer, her main feeling was one of relief. She was now a single, wealthy woman, the sole owner of the Berrow Estate, whose tenants included her brother Tony

*Back down to earth.
Jennifer and Brian*

and his wife Pat at Bridge Farm. When she visited Ambridge she scandalised the village (and upset Peggy) by passing the time with Eddie Grundy at the Cat and Fiddle, Ambridge's notorious spit-and-sawdust dive. She also spent time at Nelson Gabriel's newly opened wine bar, and invested a small sum in his antiques shop. It may have come as something of a relief to Peggy when she decided to return to pick up her life in Guernsey.

Jennifer, meanwhile, narrowly avoided being caught up in a scandal of her own. Daughter Kate was now approaching her 3rd birthday and could safely be left in the capable hands of au pair Eva Lenz, and so – when not busy with her handicrafts and her flock of Jacob sheep – she found herself with a little more free time on her hands. John Tregorran was also at something of a loose end, with his wife Carol very preoccupied running the market garden. He encouraged Jennifer to join him for a series of lectures on local history at Borchester Tech, and they shared the odd extracurricular drink at the pub around the corner. When John suggested they collaborate on a survey of the history of Ambridge, she embraced the idea enthusiastically, recruiting the help of Laura and Colonel Danby, Laura's lodger at Ambridge Hall. She and John spent a good deal of time together as they poked around the local fields and ditches and it wasn't long before people began to notice, not least Brian and Carol. At first Jennifer tried to laugh off her husband's increasingly barbed remarks, insisting that she and John shared a common interest, and nothing more. She was forced to revise this opinion rather smartly, however, when John made a pass at her in a bluebell wood. She let him down gently but firmly, and very soon after he left on a working trip to America.

New Romance for Shula ✑

After her adventures in the Far East, Shula's life settled back into dull routine at Easter, when she went back to work at Rodway and Watson. She found some light relief in her growing friendship with Caroline, but in her bleaker moments despaired of ever finding the man of her dreams in Borchester. Enter a dishy young solicitor – and former Borchester under-14 Judo champion – by the name of Mark Hebden. Mark was everything Simon Parker was not: punctual, well-behaved, considerate, and polite to her parents. Jill and Phil held their breath and crossed their fingers, but Shula wasn't to be rushed into anything. In spite of Mark's many virtues, he could sometimes appear – well, just a little bit dull. While doing his best to make Mark feel welcome at Brookfield, Phil continued his steady consolidation of Ambridge Farmers. In the summer, David returned from agricultural college and helped him expand their ewe flock to 300. To cope with the extra ewes they extended an area of sheep handling pens at Marneys, a group of farm buildings on the outskirts of Brookfield. David also started going out with Jackie Woodstock, the bubbly and vivacious daughter of a local quarry owner. Mark, meanwhile, carried on being kind and attentive to Shula, helping with the Brookfield haymaking and taking her up in a hot-air balloon over Lakey Hill. He was also there to comfort her when, on 26 October, her grandmother Doris died quietly at home in her chair. Shula grieved along with Dan and the rest of the family, and was touched to learn that Doris had arranged for her to inherit Glebe Cottage. Doris hadn't been long in her grave when Mark showed a more testosterone-driven side to his character by publicly criticising the local magistrates, calling them 'amateurs' for convicting a pair of hapless hunt saboteurs. As luck would have it, Justice of the Peace Phil Archer had been on the bench at the time, and must have felt a dull sense of déjà-vu as he once again found himself pilloried in the local press by one of Shula's boyfriends. Shula's relationship with Mark hit a low patch, but had bounced back by New Year's Eve, when he asked her to marry him. She said yes.

MARK	(DEEP BREATH) I wanted to ask you something.
SHULA	(CHEERFUL) Fire ahead.
MARK	What do you think about me?
SHULA	What do I? Well, I think you're very nice. I like you. I like you very much.
MARK	Do you love me?
SHULA	Do you love me?
MARK	I asked you first.
SHULA	I – might. But only if you love me.
MARK	Oh that's all right, I do. Very much.
SHULA	(SMILE) Now can I have a kiss?
MARK	Well – there was something else.
SHULA	Oh?
MARK	Would you like to marry me?
SHULA	Marry you? You mean – get married?
MARK	Yes.
SHULA	(PAUSE) Was that a proposal?
MARK	Yes.
SHULA	That's the first one I've ever had.
MARK	(SLIGHTLY IMPATIENT) Shula –
SHULA	It's a bit of a surprise – I mean I wasn't expecting it – yes, I will.
MARK	(MAKING SURE) You will marry me?
SHULA	Yes, if you want to. Yes, definitely. Shall we go and tell everyone—
MARK	Hang on Shula – you can have that kiss now.

Shula's Change of Heart

1981

After the heady romance of Mark's proposal, the wedding plans took on an ominous momentum of their own; or so, at least, it seemed to Shula. The date was set for 26 September, and Mark presented her with the Hebden family engagement ring: three opals in a Victorian setting. She, Phil and Jill were invited over to meet Mark's parents, Reg and Bunty, a staid couple from the smart suburbs of Borchester, keen on bridge and golfing. Shula struggled with the small talk and found it all quite stressful, to say the least. Although still committed to Mark, she began to feel a little suffocated by her engagement and found some light relief in the company of yet another journalist: the *Borchester Echo*'s roving reporter, Robin Catchpole. Full of charm and yet with a streak of alpha-male arrogance, Robin made no secret of his attraction to her, and she was happy to flirt with him at the Wine Bar. When he told her he loved her, however,

Eddie serenades Clarrie Larkin (Trevor Harrison, Heather Bell)

she backed off and stayed true to her loyal fiancé. The wedding preparations gathered pace; dresses were chosen and the marquee ordered. Having no intention of evicting Dan from Glebe Cottage, she and Mark bought a small terraced cottage in Penny Hasset, which they set about decorating. But as the fateful day drew nearer, Shula's doubts increased. Sensitive as ever to her fluctuating emotions, Mark offered to postpone the wedding, but with only six weeks to go it all became too much for Shula. Saying she still loved him, she called it off. Mark was devastated. Although hugely disappointed, both Phil and Jill were understanding. To help her get over it all, Caroline took her away for a month's holiday in Scotland. Mark sadly stayed on alone at the cottage in Penny Hasset.

The Affair That Never Was

Early in the year, Jennifer held an exhibition in her studio to mark the completion of her landscape survey. Although John was back from America, he'd apparently learnt his lesson and kept a determinedly low profile. There was a good turnout from family and friends, including Tony and Pat, whose third child was due very soon. The last two years at Bridge Farm hadn't been easy for them; their daughter Helen – now approaching her 2nd birthday – had been born with a dislocated hip, and was in a splint for the first three months of her life. This had been a difficult time for Pat, who'd become tired and run down. Tony's innate pessimism seemed borne out when, soon after, he'd contracted tetanus from a rusty nail, and his pigs had gone down with swine vesicular disease. Rather ominously – given his family history – Tony's response to all this stress was to spend more time at The Bull. Their son, Thomas, was born on 25 February. Later in the year, Jack Woolley's Borchester Press published a book of the results of the Ambridge survey. Although John's name appeared on the cover with Jennifer's, their collaboration was strictly professional.

Eddie Gets Hooked

The past year or two had been no worse than usual for Joe and Eddie at Grange Farm. Joe had begun to rebuild his dairy herd after the brucellosis, and had secured Eddie's full-time commitment in return for a regular wage. The previous year Eddie had done some building work for Jethro Larkin at Woodbine Cottage, and had started going out with Jethro's daughter, Clarrie. In spite of her father's strong disapproval, the two became close enough for Joe to begin to hope that he'd soon have the daughter-in-law he'd been waiting for. He'd have to wait a while longer, however. Eddie wasn't about to let his courtship interfere with his ambitions to become a country and western star. His first attempt at a proposal was pre-empted by a once-in-lifetime chance to make a demo tape with Borsetshire's answer to Dolly Parton:

*Eddie and
Clarrie's wedding*

buckskin-clad Jolene Rogers, aka the Lily of Leyton Cross. Clarrie knew a serious
rival when she saw one, but wasn't about to give up without a fight. When Eddie's bid
for stardom collapsed, leaving him disappointed and broke, she struck a deal: she'd
pay off his £500 debt from her savings if he agreed to marry her. She and Eddie finally
exchanged their vows at St Stephen's on 21 November. Clarrie paid for the ring.

Newly-Weds

Clarrie's life as a Grundy got off to a shaky start when she and Eddie returned
from their honeymoon in Torremolinos to find her newly furnished 'bridal
suite' bedroom full of Joe's discarded furniture. This was to set the tone for her
neverending, uphill campaign to bring order to the domestic chaos at Grange
Farm. For Eddie, by contrast, it proved to be a relatively painless adjustment
to married life. He was quite happy to have his meals cooked and his clothes
washed, and by the summer Clarrie was expecting their first child. However, the
farm accounts were as fragile as ever and – in spite of Clarrie's part-time job at
The Bull – their frequent cashflow problems became a bone of contention. Later
in the year, a big row blew up after Clarrie spent a few pounds of her wages on
clothes and nursery decorations for the baby-to-be. This was beyond the pale
for Eddie who pinched a tenner from her savings and went on a bender with

1982

*Eddie toasts the
arrival of baby William*

*Sid comforts his daughter
Lucy (Tracy-Jane White)
after the death of Polly*

his brother Alf in Gloucester. While he was gone Clarrie (now heavily pregnant) fell down the stairs and was rushed to hospital. A repentant Eddie hurried to her bedside but fortunately both Clarrie and her unborn baby were unharmed. Their son, William, was born in February of the following year.

The Long Separation

Although forced to accept Shula's decision to call off their marriage, Mark remained deeply upset. Over the months that followed he'd made an attempt to talk it over with her, but she'd found this too hard to handle and asked him to keep away. Mark then made a concerted attempt to move on, first going out with a girl called Suzanne, and then embarking on a full-on affair with David's ex, Jackie Woodstock. She moved into his cottage, and together they joined the Borchester Buzzards hang-gliding club. Before long they were engaged. Although Shula could hardly complain, she found this unsettling, and hated the idea of Jackie sharing the cottage she and Mark had planned to nest in themselves. Her only distraction was a half-hearted fling with a 40-year-old ex-hippy, Ben Warner, who lived for a time in a tent at the end of Mark's garden. This relationship eventually petered out, shortly before Ben was convicted of a series of minor burglaries.

In May, Mark found himself with a new client when Nelson was arrested by local CID officer, Detective Sergeant Dave Barry, on suspicion of handling stolen goods. The goods in question were part of a batch of antique furniture and knick-knacks that Nelson claimed to have bought in all innocence from a Welsh dealer, Thomas Guthrie. He'd sold on some of the items – including a perfect Jacobean oak gate-legged table, at a bargain price of £400 – to Peggy. Although she was perhaps the least likely villain in Borchester, Peggy had to suffer a searching interrogation by a cynical DS Barry before he would accept that she wasn't part of an illegal antiques ring. Convinced, nevertheless, of Nelson's dodgy dealing, he pursued the case relentlessly before being forced to abandon it through lack of evidence.

Tim Bentinck has been playing David Archer for 28 years. For much of that time he has also been the voice of the Piccadilly Line on the London Underground. 'It was a nice thought, when my kids were at school, that I was telling them to "mind the gap". I've gradually been replaced across the network in recent times,' he adds. 'But I've survived at Russell Square Station.'

Loss and Liberation ⌁

The year started on a tragic note for Pat. In February she was driving to the cash and carry with her friend Polly Perks when the car skidded and collided with a milk tanker. Although Pat wasn't badly hurt, Polly was killed outright, leaving a grieving Sid to comfort his 10-year-old daughter Lucy. In spite of this terrible trauma, Lucy went on to pass her 11-plus exam and in the autumn started at Borchester Grammar, where she soon became friendly with her form teacher, Kathy Holland.

Back at Bridge Farm, Pat and Tony's life had slipped into a fairly joyless routine. Pat had 100 hens and three young children to care for, and when Tony wasn't grumbling to her about the farm he was moaning to the regulars over a pint or three at The Bull. So perhaps it was in a bid to hold on to her sanity that Pat began to show an interest in the burning political and social issues of the day. She bewildered Tony by becoming a spirited supporter of CND and of the women protesters at Greenham Common. She also went to a commemoration service for the victims of Nagasaki with the vicar and his wife, where they lit coloured lanterns and floated paper boats down the Am. And if all this left Tony struggling to keep up, she then changed their daily newspaper to *The Guardian*, which (she said) was the only paper to take women seriously. Perhaps there was a message there somewhere for Tony.

Farming Fortunes ⌁

1983

Now in their sixth year at Willow Farm, life for Mike and Betty Tucker had brought its usual ups and downs. Their son, Roy, was now turning 5, and his sister Brenda was 2. Mike had built up his own successful milk round, although – after a TB outbreak the previous year – he'd been unable to sell his own milk and was forced to buy it in from a local dairy. With the spring came a fresh challenge when his partner, Haydn Evans, decided to sell up the farm and retire. Mike and Betty couldn't afford to buy him out, and for a time prospects looked bleak for Mike's business. But as luck would have it, their neighbours Ken and Mary Pound also decided to retire, so leaving a vacancy at nearby Ambridge Farm (now part of the Berrow Estate). Mike and Betty took over the tenancy of the 165-acre farm, and Mike set about building up his own herd of Ayreshire cattle. Willow Farm was sold and split between Brookfield and Home Farm. Phil's lot included the farmhouse, which he sold on to a semi-retired Derbyshire farmer named Bill Insley for £82,500, along with 15 acres of farmland.

Jethro Larkin meets Bill Insley (Ted Moult), the new owner of Willow Farm

In the late summer Bill moved in and sought Neil's advice about his plans to breed rare pigs. Neil, meanwhile, had rented a henhouse from Mike and started an egg round. He also embarked on a rather bashful courtship of Susan Horrobin, the eldest daughter of Bert and Ivy, who lived in cheerful squalor at No. 6 The Green with their six children and various pets. Neil won Susan's heart

Profile
DAVID ARCHER

THE 12th EARL OF Portland has suggested that we meet at his club. 'No, not the Athanaeum,' says the reassuringly familiar voice of Tim Bentinck over the phone. 'This club's quite informal.' Quite expensive, too, as it turns out. In one of his other roles, as David Archer, the Honourable Timothy would expect at least two pints of Shires for the price of one bottle of German lager. But then we're a long way from Ambridge as well as being a long way from the ground. His club occupies the 32nd floor of Centre Point in the heart of London's West End. It's full of what Tim calls 'arty types and City boys'.

So does membership involve some kind of initiation ceremony?

'No, but it helped in my case that I knew Stephen Fry [a devoted *Archers* fan].' They began a correspondence in the early days of email and cemented their friendship over lunch at the House of Lords, which Tim calls 'my other club'.

Before the hereditary peerage was silenced, he made occasional forays into the debating chamber but never spoke. 'If I did, the headlines would be all about what David Archer said in the House,' he points out as the lights of London gleam beneath us like so many millions of gems spilled over a dark cloth. 'Don't forget that I'm really a jobbing actor.' As Mr Fry put it with a succinctness honed in his Twittering days: 'You've got a title, Tim, but you're not entitled to anything.' So where did the title come from?

'My father took it from his ninth cousin after various branches of the family had died out. And he only did it because he wanted to have a forum to sound off about environmental issues. He was well ahead of his time. Back in 1994, he said, "I urge you, my Lords, to keep your Green hats on.'"

By that time, the 11th Earl of Portland had been running an organic smallholding in Devon for 18 years. 'I spent a year helping him to set it up,' his son recalls. 'I've birthed a lamb, milked a cow and driven a tractor. So when I'm playing David, I can not only picture it but feel it.' He even looks the part. At 57, Tim is six years older than David but he appears fit in a rugged sort of way.

He's married to a milliner. Judy Bentinck designs very posh hats. The couple have two sons at university – one studying philosophy in London, the other pop music in Cheltenham – and they live in a Pooterish Victorian villa in North London which they've been restoring for nearly thirty years. Sounds a bit like painting the Forth Bridge. 'It is,' Tim confirms. 'But I like working with my hands, and it only cost us £32,000 back in 1982.'

That was quite a year for him one way or another. He started playing David and also took the lead in *The Pirates of Penzance* at the Theatre Royal, Drury Lane. 'I'd started off as second understudy,' he confides. But he was in the right place at the right time when first Tim Curry and then Chris Langham found themselves indisposed. That, in turn, led to an offer to play the part of Tom Lacey, the Cavalier hero in a TV Civil War drama called *By the Sword Divided*. 'I had shoulder-length hair and a gold earring when I went up to Birmingham to record *The Archers*.' Not exactly the average listener's idea of David Archer. 'No, but Paddy Greene [his fictional mother Jill] thought it was wonderful.'

> 'I had shoulder-length hair and a gold earing when I went up to Birmingham to record *The Archers*.'

Tim and his fictional wife, Ruth, make an odd couple at the microphone. He's 6ft 3 while the actress Felicity Finch is 5ft 1. 'I tend to stand with feet as far apart as possible while Flick is almost on tiptoe,' Tim confides.

His favourite scene in twenty-eight years of the role was playing the moment when Ruth's dalliance with Sam the cow man finally dawned on David. 'It's the only time I've really felt nervous before a recording,' he says. Did he feel the storyline was credible? 'Oh, yes. People do behave out of character every now and then. Hopefully David and Ruth are the moral centre of the programme. If that gets tested, it's a damn good thing,' he adds before calling for more German lager. This time the waiter brings with it something appropriate for a titled man with no entitlement.

Peanuts.

Profile

JOE GRUNDY

JOE GRUNDY AND JAMES Bond: spot the difference. Not as easy as you might think. The actor Edward Kelsey was once mistaken for Sean Connery by a rather excitable waiter in Menorca. Edward was a guest of June Spencer (Peggy) who has a home on the island. 'The waiter knew that she was an actress and probably assumed that I was someone quite famous,' he surmises.

Looking at the veteran actor across a pub table, the mistaken identity seems not quite as daft as it sounds. Edward was born in the same year as Connery (1930), which makes them both ten years younger than Joe. Both have white beards, dark bushy eyebrows and hairlines that have not so much receded as disappeared over the horizon. Not surprisingly, however, there was much merriment among the *Archers* cast when the story was relayed to the old Pebble Mill studios in Birmingham.

Trevor Harrison, who plays Eddie Grundy and is a good friend off-air, was never likely to let Edward forget. 'I got you a pint because you look like Sean Connery,' he said, when they met up in London one day and he bought the first round. 'We were sitting outside on a summer's day,' Edward recalls, 'and just after Trevor said it, a woman passing by simpered, "Ooh, he does look like him."'

A grin is visible behind the beard which then parts further to allow access for another swig of dark ale with an earthy name. We're in a bar near Guildford Station that bears as much resemblance to The Bull as the actor's life does to Joe's. He has declined the offer of a pint of organic cider on the grounds that he prefers the products of the grape and the hop to the apple.

At home he likes a decent bottle of wine. He lives in Surrey with his Swedish wife Birgit. They met at a dance, and Edward remembers proposing just after they'd visited the 1951 Festival of Britain on London's South Bank. He was doing his national service with the RAF at the time. Still to come was three years' training in the drama section at the Royal Academy of Music. Like quite a few *Archers* actors, he emerged with the Carlton Hobbs Award which guaranteed a six month contract with the BBC drama department during its golden age.

Another thirty years would pass before he took over the role of Joe from his old pal Haydn Jones. In the meantime, he had cut his teeth in theatre as a regular member of the Guildford Rep, playing everyone from Jimmy Porter to Polonius – an angry young man to 'a tedious old fool', as Hamlet called him. 'I've played old men since I was knee high,' he chuckles. The theatre critic of the *Surrey Advertiser* in the 1950s was moved to describe young Edward as 'a master of bizarre accents'. So how did he settle on the right rustic brogue for the grandfather of Grange Farm?

'I stuck as closely as possible to the way Haydn played it. He was Welsh but he used a sort of Hampshire burr.' Just as well, then, that Edward was born

'I've played the role of old men since I was knee-high...'

there and brought up in Petersfield. His mother was a dressmaker, and one of his earliest memories is of swallowing a safety pin when preparing to play a supporting role to the Ovaltine Girl in a carnival tableau, aged 3. Luckily he didn't do himself any long-term damage and he's really putting on that wheeze when Joe succumbs to a convenient attack of farmer's lung. 'Sometimes it's a bit difficult to stop coughing, mind you,' he admits. 'It's a good job we're not doing it live.'

Edward takes as a compliment the suggestion that his character has become the natural heir to Walter Gabriel as the loveable old rogue of Ambridge. 'I remember my first scene in *The Archers* was with Chriss Gittins [Walter], Bob Arnold [Tom Forrest] and George Hart [Jethro Larkin]. It was nervewracking but I was accepted. And, yes, I suppose we Grundys have usually provided some comic relief among the more serious storylines.'

Until, that is, they were finally evicted from Grange Farm and banished to the purgatory of Meadow Rise ten years ago. 'We used to come out of the studio feeling completely exhausted and emotionally drained,' he recalls. 'But the director very kindly provided a bottle of wine afterwards, which helped.'

Rather more than cider might have done.

Profile

BRENDA TUCKER

AMY SCHINDLER IS INVOLVED with three or four very different families – on air, on screen and in real life. As Brenda, she is a Tucker who may one day become an Archer if she ever gets around to marrying Tom. As a burgeoning scriptwriter, she has occasionally orchestrated the mayhem involving the Harpers in BBC One's manic comedy *My Family*. And as the daughter of author, screenwriter and fervent Manchester City fan Colin Schindler, she once played her own grandmother in a TV adaptation of his book *Manchester United Ruined My Life*.

So are you, too, sky blue through and through, Amy? 'I didn't have much choice, even though I grew up in Muswell Hill [Spurs territory]. I once brought home a boyfriend who was a United fan. Dad could just about deal with it because the guy came from Manchester.' Not a London-based glory-hunter then? 'Exactly.' And did the boyfriend last long? 'No. I don't think we could ever have watched a derby match together.'

Amy takes a sip of her skinny cappuccino and stifles a yawn. 'Sorry. Haven't had much sleep,' she explains. 'The boiler's playing up at home.' That's a few miles up the road from where we're sitting now, overlooking a bus shelter in Queen's Park (Rangers territory) on the west side of London.

Her mother's side of the family come from a long way west of here – Santa Barbara, California, to be precise. She died nine months before Amy was called upon to play Brenda's reaction to the death of Betty Tucker. 'I was quite numb doing those scenes at first,' she admits. 'I sounded terribly stilted. So I did something that I don't usually do and went into the scene as me as much as Brenda. I used to cry during the read-throughs, but it helped that the scenes were beautifully written. Everything was so well thought through. I felt that it was really truthful.'

In truth, Amy and Brenda have little in common. One is a country girl in her late 20s, the daughter of a bankrupt tenant farmer-turned-milkman, who is now making her way in the employment of a rather dodgy businessman with the help of a 2.1 in marketing from Felpersham University. The other is a Metropolitan actress in her early 30s who read history at Cambridge and evidently inherited some of her father's writing talents. 'I was at a dinner party the other night and, when one of the guests found out that I'm in *The Archers*, she rang her mum, thrust the phone in my hand and said, "Talk to her in that accent."' Amy duly obliged by adding Brenda's rural twang to her natural voice in the way that a city-dweller might slip into a pair of wellies for a weekend away in the country.

But what does she think of Brenda as a character? 'I'm fond of her in the way you might feel about a slightly goofy cousin,' she explains. 'She's very unlike me insofar

> **'I used to cry during the read-throughs… I felt it was really truthful.'**

as she's quick to react and doesn't really think before she speaks.' A bit like her dad? 'Absolutely. But that directness means that there's no side to her.'

If playing Betty's death was emotionally draining – understandably so in the circumstances – then the scenes with her fictional stepmother Vicky have been a joy to Amy. 'Rachel [Atkins] is a terrific actress and so much fun to work with,' she says. Not quite as well known to the wider world, however, as Angelina Jolie with whom Amy appeared in the 2007 film *A Mighty Heart*. 'Mine was only a small part and I was just in a couple of scenes with her,' she stresses. 'She was very sweet but quite a bit smaller than I'd imagined.' At this point it seems worth asking the question that Brenda might well have blurted out: Did Brad [Pitt] come to visit her?

'I think he was there at one point, but I didn't see him.' Amy, it transpires, was more interested in working with the director Michael Winterbottom because 'he's always open to suggestions from actors.' Which brings us back to her writing career. She has recently produced a pilot script for the BBC which she describes as a historical comedy set in the 17th century. 'You have more control as a writer than an actor,' Amy muses. 'I don't have to be employed to sit in my study and write.'

She just needs to ignore the noises made by that old boiler.

after rescuing her runaway pig, Pinky, which she'd won at the Ambridge Fete. In December he took her away on a short break to London, although Susan insisted that he book them separate rooms.

Tally-Ho

For Shula a dull winter turned into a distinctly loveless – or at least a boyfriend-less – spring. Being single was made all the harder by the knowledge that Mark (after dumping Jackie Woodstock) was now dating his boss's daughter, blonde rah-girl Sarah Locke. In spite of this sobering news, when Mark came alone to the harvest supper (Sarah having a prior engagement) Shula thought she glimpsed a spark of his old affection for her. This gave her the courage to ask him out for a drink, only for him to announce that he and Sarah were now engaged. Perhaps on the rebound from this, she started going out with Borsetshire's original Hooray Henry, Nigel Pargetter, after he fell off his horse while out hunting over Brookfield. The only son of Gerald and Julia Pargetter of Lower Loxley Hall, Nigel was filling in time as a swimming pool salesman, when not swilling claret at the Wine Bar or engaged in drunken pranks with his chum Tim Beecham. Shula found his lively company a welcome distraction from her dismal routine at Rodways. She partnered him when he dressed in a gorilla suit to take her to a fancy dress ball, and again as he led a drunken conga through Grey Gables, holding a stuffed stag's head as a proud mascot. Jill soon became quite fond of him too. Phil politely declined his offer of a special discount on a swimming pool and wondered (a) when he'd ever get a proper job and (b) when Shula would ever find herself another boyfriend as sensible as Mark.

Prodigal Daughter

In the late summer Jack Woolley's ex-wife Valerie died alone in her flat in Brighton. Despite their long estrangement, Jack was badly shaken by the news. When he went down to her funeral he repaired his difficult relationship with his adopted daughter Hazel, who'd been living in London, and invited her back to stay at Grey Gables. Given Hazel's recent track record (she'd only bothered to contact Jack when she needed money), Peggy was immediately suspicious of her motives. In Jack's eyes, however, she could do no wrong. He bought her a new car, overlooked her rudeness to Caroline and even forgave her when she tried to sack his gardener/chauffeur Higgs. After a few weeks, however, she tired of the country life and returned to London, though not before aiming a sly kick at Jack's beloved Staffordshire bull terrier, Captain. Jack was very sad to see her go, Peggy and Caroline less so.

1984

Diversions

As winter turned to spring, Shula continued to seek distraction in the company of Nigel, who was only too happy to oblige. He took her to the hunt ball, afterwards staying over at Brookfield, where he startled Phil and Jill by blundering into their room whispering 'tally-ho!' at dead of night. He afterwards claimed he was looking for the bathroom. But Shula betrayed enough of her secret longing for Mark to make Nigel jealous; when he found out that Mark had joined the local skydiving club, he bravely volunteered to do his own sponsored jump in aid of the church organ fund. In June, Shula found another distraction in Caroline's plans for an NSPCC fashion show at Grey Gables. In a remarkable coup, Caroline used her aristocratic connections to invite a special guest, the Duke of Westminster. But to Jack's everlasting wonder and delight, the Duke brought along a special guest of his own: none other than NSPCC patron, HRH Princess Margaret. Jack wore a white tuxedo with silver braid and named a suite of rooms in her honour. Soon after, Nigel's cheerful exuberance got him into deep trouble when – after a night out with Shula – they mistakenly drove off in someone else's car. They were both arrested and charged with TDA. Shula persuaded Mark to defend her and was let off, while Nigel was lucky to get away with a £200 fine.

Jethro swaps a country tale with Tom Forrest in The Bull

The whole incident only served to bring Mark and Shula closer together, and at one of their meetings he stunned her by confessing that it was all over between him and Sarah Locke. Before she could do much about it, however, he left to begin a year's work placement in Hong Kong. Shula bade him a fond farewell at the airport, but it looked as if she'd missed her chance once again. Full of sad regrets, she broke off with Nigel, who sought some brief consolation in the company of her sister Elizabeth (who'd just been expelled from her boarding-school sixth form) before being packed off to a farm in Kenya by his exasperated parents. For him, as for Shula, the party was most definitely over – for the time being, at least.

Nigel Pargetter (Graham Seed) gets to know the locals in The Bull

Pat's Brief Encounter

The past year had been an uphill struggle for Tony as Pat had become ever more involved in her political consciousness-raising. She'd enrolled on a course in Women's Studies at Borchester Tech, where she made friends with a militant arch-feminist called Rose, who stayed for a time at Bridge Farm after trouble with her boyfriend. More worrying for some – especially Peggy – was the gossip surrounding Pat's association with her course tutor, Roger Coombes. The two were spotted together in a quiet corner of the Feathers in Borchester, and people began to notice that she'd had her hair cut and started using make-up for the first time in years. Alarm bells finally began to ring for Tony when she went off to a feminist conference in Camarthen at which – no surprise – Roger was a lecturer. She returned in a state of some emotional turmoil, and spent the night in the spare room. Tony knew better than to confront her directly, and instead disappeared off to a mysterious conference of his own. When he came back he told

Celebrity Appearance: 1984 – Princess Margaret and The Duke of Westminster opened the NSPCC fundraising fashion show at Grey Gables her that he wanted to give up their reliance on chemicals, and convert the farm into a fully organic business – was she with him, or not? Pat took a few days to think hard and then said yes, she was. She renounced her infatuation with Roger, gave up her women's studies course and soon became a committed champion of the organic movement, never (as far as we know) to look back.

Two Birthdays

In spite of holidaying with Neil in separate rooms, early in the year Susan discovered she was pregnant. In February they married, and their daughter, Emma Louise, was born on 7 August. A month premature, she suffered from jaundice, but was soon well enough to come home to the flat at Nightingale Farm. Later in the year the couple had a windfall when their landlord, Hugo Barnaby, offered them £4,000 to move out so that he could sell the house. Neil and Susan went on the council housing list and moved into No. 1 The Green – just a few doors down from the Horrobin family. This was a little too close for Neil, but he was happy to have a real house of their own. Clarrie, meanwhile, was also pregnant again. In August her brother-in-law was seriously injured in a car accident and Clarrie – now eight months pregnant – went to Great Yarmouth to support her sister Rosie. She was about to come home when she went into labour and was still there when son Edward was born on 28 September.

Mrs Antrobus shares a posy with Peggy

1985

Dog Woman

Early in the year another newcomer moved into the village – nine newcomers, if you include the eight Afghan hounds that Marjorie Antrobus installed in the outbuildings of her new home at Nightingale Farm. Recently returned from Rhodesia after the death of her ex-army husband Teddy, Marjorie had first visited Ambridge when she came to give a talk at the WI entitled – rather ambiguously –'the colourful life of the Afghan'. She then took a liking to the village and bought Nightingale Farm from Hugo Barnaby. Known by the Grundys – and others – as the Dog Woman, she and her beloved pets soon became a familiar sight as they tramped the local footpaths. Her concern for the welfare of animals wasn't limited to dogs, however. Upset by the cramped living conditions of Neil's battery hens, she daringly 'rescued' one from its cage. She took it home to love and care for and named it Jessica.

Two Friends, Two Romances

In spite of Caroline Bone's sophisticated good looks and aristocratic connections, she was still waiting for a Prince Charming to enter her life. Over the past year or two she'd first been courted by enigmatic ex-SAS officer Alan Fraser, until he suddenly disappeared; she'd then fallen for naval pilot Paul Chubb, only for him

A group of Ambridge friends hit the streets of Borchester. Nigel leads Caroline Bone (Sara Coward), Nelson Gabriel (Jack May), Jennifer and Elizabeth

to marry another girl. Perhaps disheartened by her bad luck with single men, she allowed herself to be distracted by the smooth charms of the most definitely non-single Brian Aldridge, and the two of them began a discreet affair. He treated her to lavish meals in out-of-the-way restaurants, and sneaked her off for romantic liaisons in London. The burden of deceit soon became too much for Caroline, however, and she walked out on her job and disappeared. Brian tracked her down and persuaded her to come back, promising not to bother her again. He kept to his word (on the whole) and – for a while at least – Jennifer was none the wiser.

Former *Archers* editor Liz Rigbey on life...

'Christopher Carter and Alice Aldridge were my two babies. And it makes me feel very old now if I switch on and hear their grown-up voices and remember that I conceived them.' (Christopher was born with a hare lip which gradually repaired itself over the ensuing years to the point where he became Ambridge's 'babe magnet'.)

... and death

'Chriss Gittins, who played Walter Gabriel, was very old and ready to die but I sometimes believe that he hung on to life just for me. I visited him at home quite often and we had a good friendship. I made a great fuss of him and, whenever he talked about dying, I'd say, "Don't you dare. Now don't let me down, Chriss." And he didn't. He died the day I left.'

99

Brian's wandering eye

The only person Caroline confided in was her close friend Shula, who found it hard to sympathise, in spite of being caught in a compromised relationship of her own with dashing vet Martin Lambert. Martin was good company and very keen on her, but all the time Shula's heart was in Hong Kong with the absent Mark. She'd been writing him gossipy letters since he left, but received rather bland replies. In July she cracked under the strain of separation and bought a last-minute air ticket to Hong Kong. Mark played the perfect host, but it wasn't the romantic reunion she'd so desperately hoped for and she came home defeated and tearful. Just a few days later, however, she had a telegram from Mark to say he'd be back in Ambridge the next day. She met him at the airport and he then took her for a walk on Lakey Hill and proposed. The couple were married on 21 September. The bridesmaids were Elizabeth and Kate Aldridge (now a rather spoilt 7-year-old), Nigel was best man, and – thanks again to Caroline's connections – the reception was held in the grandeur of Netherbourne Hall. After a honeymoon in Scotland, they went to live in a flat in Borchester's trendy Old Wool Market. Shula's long heartache was over at last.

Back on the Farm

Both Shula's parents were naturally delighted to see her happily joined with the man she loved. The only member of the family absent from the celebrations was Shula's twin Kenton, busy with his life in the far Antipodes. After a minor

David with girlfriend Sophie Barlow (Moir Leslie)

crisis over the bridesmaid's dresses, David's girlfriend Sophie Barlow – a fashion student at the local art school – stepped in and saved the day by finishing them off beautifully, forcing Elizabeth to accept that perhaps she wasn't such a total airhead after all.

Elizabeth was on shaky ground herself by keeping up her relationship with the occupationally challenged Nigel, now reincarnated as an ice-cream salesman.

Aside from the romantic intrigues of his offspring, Phil had plenty else to occupy his mind. In February, his Aunt Laura had a bad fall while out picking snowdrops and contracted pneumonia. Just a few days later she died, leaving Phil as one of her executors. At the comparatively youthful age of 74, Laura had neglected to make a proper will, and Phil had the difficult task of telling her long-time close friend and lodger Freddie Danby that he wouldn't inherit Ambridge Hall. Early the following year, Freddie moved to a bungalow at Manorfield Close, and the house was put up for sale.

Lunchtime at The Bull. David at the bar with Nigel, Tom, Jethro, Elizabeth and Mark Hebden (Richard Derrington)

In the autumn, it was Dan's health that began to cause concern. Now 89, he collapsed at Glebe Cottage and went to live at Brookfield for a few days, returning after being supplied with a panic button in case it happened again. Walter became jealous and pestered Nelson for a panic button of his own.

Single Dad

Now a widower for three years, Sid had become friendly with Lucy's teacher Kathy – who was now renting his cottage in Penny Hasset – and had gone so far as to date her once. Soon after, however, she disappointed him by going out with DS Dave Barry, now living at the Police House. For Sid this can only have added to the stress of being a publican and a single father, and in July he was hospitalised with a perforated ulcer. He was soon back at work, but on a special diet and with orders to ease up on his workload. While he was away Lucy stayed with Kathy for a few days, and when Sid took a fortnight's holiday she drove them to the seaside and stayed the night in Lucy's room. The next day, however, she hurried home to be with Dave.

Profile
CAROLINE STERLING

CAROLINE STERLING HAS VERY little in common with Sara Coward. One is of aristocratic pedigree, apparently descended from the de Bohuns who fought at Agincourt, and related to Lord Netherbourne. The other was brought up on a council estate in South-East London. Her father worked for the Co-Op. Yet Sara has played Caroline for over thirty years and, even when she's not on air, she speaks with a very similar voice – beautifully modulated vowels interspersed with consonants as clipped as the hedges around Netherbourne Hall. So who was your Professor Higgins, my fair lady?

'I never had elocution lessons,' she maintains. 'I was just brought up to speak proper,' she adds, slipping for a moment into the phraseology of the 'Sarf' London that she long ago left behind. A bright grammar school girl, she was tipped to go to Oxford and her parents encouraged her to do so. They were appalled when she insisted that she wanted to act and headed off to Bristol University to study English and Drama in the late 1960s. Then it was back to the Guildhall School in the Barbican from which she emerged, like several future *Archers* actors, with the Carlton Hobbs award for radio drama.

So how on earth did she finish up living in a small town on the borders of Warwickshire and Worcestershire and a dead ringer for Borchester if ever there was one? 'I moved up to Leamington Spa to study acupuncture for three years,' she says between sips of Lapsang Souchong (very Caroline) in her compact but characterful cottage just off the main street. 'The money I earned from *The Archers*, bless them, paid for the course.'

By the time she qualified, she had played the role of Ambridge's 'posh tottie' for over ten years. Ms Bone certainly played the field. 'Yes,' it was a wonderful succession of affairs,' she says, smiling as if at a fond memory. Of course, her character may well have felt like sticking needles into Brian Aldridge once that particular dalliance died the death, but why would an actress want to be an acupuncturist? The answer to that is discussed elsewhere in these pages. For now, suffice it to say that acupuncture was an extension of her interest in matters Chinese. There's a fat tome on the Art of East Asia in the book case, next to a Scrabble board. 'I'm addicted to Scrabble,' she confesses. 'I play on the internet and I've got nine games on the go at the moment.'

Sara lives alone with a lurcher called Sati, the long, twitching nose of which she is currently shooing away from the chocolate biscuits. She was playing Lady Macbeth in Southampton when she was spotted by Vanessa Whitburn, the current editor of *The Archers*, who was then one of several directors. It was 1979. 'Heaven knows what it says about my Lady M, but Vanessa evidently saw something and offered me the part of Caroline. At first I turned it down, partly because I didn't want to be typecast in a series going out every evening, partly because I didn't think the money would be that good and partly because childhood had made me slightly allergic to *The Archers*. My grandmother lived with us for the last two years of her life and she insisted on having it on every lunchtime, evening and Sunday morning. She was rather deaf and it blared out through every room in the house.

> **'My grandmother ... insisted on having it [*The Archers*] on every lunchtime, evening and Sunday morning.'**

'Luckily, Vanessa persisted. She rang me at home and promised me three things – that the money was better than I thought, that I'd have a lot of fun and the part would be a maximum of three months.' Sara pauses before adding: 'They obviously forgot to stop booking me.' So it would seem. Over thirty years on and she's still playing the part, although Caroline has stopped playing the field. 'Marriage is usually the kiss of death,' she muses. Well, it certainly was for Caroline's first husband. The ageing Guy Pemberton had a heart attack after six months of wedded bliss. 'At least that made me an interesting widow,' she suggests, 'until I settled down with the very hale and hearty Oliver.'

The Sterlings now run Grey Gables which she managed for so many years for 'Mr Woolley', as she called her boss until retirement – despite her aristocratic connections and his humble origins in Birmingham. He called her Caroline.

Sadly, Jack Woolley wouldn't know what to call her now.

Profile

NIGEL PARGETTER

GRAHAM SEED HAS SPENT plenty of time up on stage looking out at the audience. Indeed he was in George Bernard Shaw's *Major Barbara* at the Birmingham Rep back in the early 1980s when he was headhunted by *The Archers*. Enter Nigel Pargetter in a gorilla suit – one of several jolly japes that the inheritor of Lower Loxley got up to in his feckless youth. This afternoon, however, he will be in the audience looking up at the stage from a seat in the stalls. 'My daughter Nicola is a theatrical producer and she got me a couple of matinee tickets for the Vaudeville,' he says in those plummy tones as his white BMW inches through the traffic.

It's just before 11 a.m. and the show doesn't start for another three and a half hours. But our snail-like pace suggests that he really ought to set off now if he's ever going to make it from West London to the West End – especially as he has to pick up his 91-year-old mother on the way. Instead we're on our way to his house from the tube station. Mummy will have to wait a little longer.

'She is a bit like Julia,' he concedes, recalling with considerable affection the actress Mary Wimbush who played his fictional mother. By now we have turned off the clogged main road and pulled up outside the rather bijou terraced property that Graham shares with his partner, Denise Silvey, another theatrical producer. 'She's responsible for *The Mousetrap*, which has been running almost as long as *The Archers*,'

Graham points out after sinking into a chair beneath a large picture by the pop artist Joe Tilson in which the word 'Seed' is repeated from the top of the frame to the bottom. 'My former wife was quite happy for me to hang on to that one after our divorce,' he smiles wanly. 'I don't think she wanted to be constantly reminded of my name.'

At this point he answers the phone and says: 'Nigel, do you mind if I call you back.' It's a reminder, if any were needed, that Graham and his fictional character are as different as this compact house is from the sprawling rural splendours of Lower Loxley. Admittedly they both went to public school – Rugby in Nigel's case and Charterhouse in Graham's. If Graham rather than Nigel was involved in the debate over the education of Freddie and Lily Pargetter, he would be against them being despatched to boarding school.

'I boarded from the age of 7 and I couldn't understand why I was being sent away,' he recalls sadly. 'My parents ran a hotel off Baker Street so it wasn't a background of great wealth and privilege. But they worked hard and evidently wanted to give me a good education.'

At least Charterhouse equipped him for two of the great passions of his life: acting and cricket. He successfully auditioned for RADA at 17 and emerged well equipped to earn a living as a professional actor for the next forty years. 'And cricket's a good hobby for an actor if the periods out of work coincide with the summer,' he suggests. Like Charles Collingwood (Brian Aldridge), he is a member of the MCC and, like Charles, he's mildly miffed that his character is not considered good enough to play for the Ambridge team. 'It's probably thought that Nigel would drop too many catches,' he admits.

'I go to the gym and walk a lot. Mind you, I still enjoy wine.'

Graham, on the other hand, is still turning out as wicketkeeper-batsman for a team called the Invalids, made up of thespians and media folk. 'We play at some lovely village grounds,' he enthuses. 'I still enjoy travelling around this country.' Just as well. When we meet, he's enjoying a rare few days at home half way through a tour of theatres that has taken him from Scotland to the south coast of England. This is a man who still relishes being up on stage looking out even more than being in the audience looking up. 'It's what I trained for and now I need to keep fit for,' he says. 'I go to the gym and walk a lot. Mind you, I still enjoy wine.' Making it as well as drinking it?

'Oh, God, no.'

Vineyards are thin on the ground in West London. Cars, buses and taxis are not. It's time to rejoin that clogged main road in the hope of getting his mother to the West End before the curtain rises.

Profile
LIZ RIGBEY

TAKING OVER *THE ARCHERS* editorship in 1986 was 'a bit like climbing aboard the *Mary Celeste*,' says Liz Rigbey. The previous editor William Smethurst had done much to revive the programme's fortunes and bring to it a much needed comic edge. Ambridge was being talked about once more in positive terms. Even *Marxism Today* had declared *The Archers* to be a fashionable mixture of 'young fogeyish nostalgia and radical chic'. Could WS do the same for *Crossroads*? Central Television was evidently prepared to pay him a lot of money to find out.

'He took most of the office staff, virtually all the writers and a good few of the actors,' Liz recalls. What's more, it seems, he bowed out with two major storylines already recorded. Dan Archer was killed off and his grandson David became engaged to Sophie, who was more into fashion than farming.

And Liz? By her own admission, she knew more about farming than drama. She was an agricultural journalist who had been making programmes that were broadcast early on Saturday mornings. 'I was very interested in

drama but had almost no experience beyond a BBC course which had shown me how difficult and different it was. So it wasn't just that I was captain of the *Mary Celeste*: I didn't have a clue how to navigate.'

Nonetheless, she didn't flinch from an early decision to give *The Archers* what she calls 'more dramatic depth and complexity of structure.' Dispensing with Sophie as a potential bride for David was symbolic of the changes to come. She would be replaced with someone altogether more rooted in the soil. The future Ruth Archer was an agricultural student when she came to Brookfield. What's more her voice was as rare in rural Borsetshire as the mating cry of the red kite. 'I love the accent of the North East,' Liz enthuses. She wanted this north-easterner to grow into 'one of the strong, sensitive, sensible, stable farming women I'd met on my travels as a journalist.' Why? 'Because you need a strong union at the centre of the programme.'

'...you need a strong union at the centre of the programme.'

Sophie's brief reappearance helped to destabilise that union for a while. 'But I had no doubts that David and Ruth would last,' Liz insists. 'Without that marriage the programme would just shatter in all directions. It would be the sort of mistake a foolish, short-term editor might make, but not Vanessa [Whitburn, the current editor].'

Apart from Ruth, the Rigbey reign over Ambridge saw the introduction of two characters with comic potential. One was Bert Fry – 'someone who makes the frantic lives of people like me look like one breathless dash,' says the woman who was working 100 hours a week to steer the *Mary Celeste* back on course. The other was Lynda Snell. 'I was determined to bring in Lynda like a lion, so that she'd have a long way to go before she flattened out. Thanks to [the actress] Carole [Boyd], she probably never has.'

Liz's admiration for Carole knew no bounds when she pitted her against Barry Humphries at a live Dame Edna show. 'There was no rehearsal or hobnobbing beforehand and very little hint of what he would say when he plucked her from the audience, apparently at random,' she marvels. 'But Carole brought the house down when she picked up on Dame Edna's mock-serious tone while discussing decorating, and ad-libbed that her favourite colour was Eau de Nil.'

It was a triumph not only for the actress but also the editor who was given a timely boost in 1987 when *The Archers* won a Sony Gold Award for its 'outstanding contribution to broadcasting'. The celebratory lunch at Broadcasting House turned out to be a poisoned chalice, however. Liz and several of the cast went down with hepatitis – the result of poor hygiene in the kitchen which has long since been remedied. The actor Charles Collingwood played Brian's flirtation with Betty Tucker while he was a not-too-delicate shade of yellow. 'I can't imagine how Charles made it into the studio, let alone summoned the energy to sound frisky,' says Liz, who was chairing script meetings while a similar colour and feeling just as debilitated.

Exhaustion forced her to give up the editorship in 1988. Today she writes psychological thrillers under her own name and ghost-writes autobiographies. She lives on the south coast, but she should, perhaps, look inland when she wants to recall the time that she steered the *Mary Celeste* away from the rocks.

1986

An Era Ends ✑

The spring brought a sad but not wholly unexpected event that was to have repercussions for most of the Archer family. On 23 April – St George's Day, and Phil's birthday – Dan was helping Elizabeth right a fallen ewe when he collapsed and died. Although deeply mourned by all who knew him, it was perhaps a fitting end to what – in the words of his brother-in-law Tom Forrest – had been a long life and a good one. As Doris had wished, Glebe Cottage together with its contents was passed on to Shula. She and Mark decided to move in after some renovation work, including the re-thatching of the roof, had been completed. Dan also left Chris and Tony £20,000 each as a recompense for their shares in Ambridge Farmers, so leaving Phil and Jill as sole owners of the family business. This created a problem of its own, however: in November Phil discovered that Dan's will had left him with a bill for Capital Transfer Tax amounting to over £50,000. As he had no ready capital left to pay it off, this provoked a major financial crisis at Brookfield. Phil was faced with the dilemma of either selling land in what was then a weak market or taking on an expensive mortgage. First Mark and then Brian offered to come to his rescue and buy shares in the farm, but he turned them both down, not wanting to compromise his control of the business. David even made him consider selling the Brookfield farmhouse but Jill vetoed the idea, unless as a very last resort. By the end of the year, Phil was forced to bite the bullet and decided to sell the eighty-five acres of land near Willow Farm that he'd bought from Hadyn Evans only three years before. It was put up to be auctioned early in the following year.

Although Elizabeth voiced some resentment at being left out of Dan's will, she was too preoccupied with her busy social life to make much of a fuss. Early in the year she dumped Nigel for a time in favour of his friend Tim Beecham, only to be dumped herself. She turned back to Nigel again – letting him give her driving lessons – before setting up over the summer as a rival ice-cream saleswoman. Throughout all this her academic studies took a back seat, and she ended up failing one of her two A levels. By the end of the year she was trying to sell advertising space for the *Borchester Echo*. David, meanwhile, had been growing ever closer to Sophie Barlow, in spite of some friction over her determinedly old-fashioned attitude towards pre-marital relationships. In July he proposed to her and she

DAN	Now let's have a look at you.
ELIZABETH	Don't bend grandad, I'll do it.
DAN	Poor old girl, how did you get down there eh?
ELIZABETH	(BENDS) Sheep are so stupid. (GRUNTING) She's a terrible weight.
DAN	Not like that! You're holding her wrong.
ELIZABETH	(BENDING, HEAVING) Get up you stupid animal!
DAN	She can't help it! (BENDS DOWN) All you have to do is (PANTS)—
ELIZABETH	Grandad don't! Let me do it please!
DAN	(BENDING) Get hold of them in the right place.
ELIZABETH	Yes all right—
DAN	You don't want to get them upset.
ELIZABETH	I didn't upset her! Honest – did I sheep?
DAN	Just give a chance for her feet to get a grip—
ELIZABETH	Grandad she's too heavy!
DAN	Now....
ELIZABETH	And you're too old!
DAN	Just stand back and be a good girl Elizabeth—
ELIZABETH	Oh for heaven's sake—
DAN	(SIGH) (FALLS)
ELIZABETH	Now look what you've gone and – Grandad? Oh no! Oh my God! Grandad!! (BIG THEME)

David talks farming with his sister Elizabeth

accepted. Although they made no early wedding plans, they bid unsuccessfully for a run-down house at auction. The engagement may have also given added impetus to David's campaign to become a full partner in the farm. Phil wasn't yet ready to give him the responsibility, and said a firm no.

Feeding time at Brookfield. Jethro, Brian and Phil

Bankrupt Mike

The New Year brought a financial Armageddon for the Tuckers at Ambridge Farm. With his small dairy herd and his milk round, Mike had been struggling to make ends meet for some time. In the second week of January the bank began to bounce his cheques; his phone was cut off, and a dozen of his cows repossessed. Mike struggled on for a few days, but the bank finally called in his overdraft and he was forced to declare himself bankrupt. So began a gruelling year for the Tucker family. Six weeks later all their remaining stock and equipment went under the hammer at a farm sale. Although the family was allowed to stay on at the farmhouse until Michaelmas, Mike now had no source of income and was forced to look for work wherever he could find it. He applied unsuccessfully for milking jobs and took on casual work at Home Farm and other farms locally. In the autumn he was offered a few weeks' work as a live-in herdsman in the south of the county, Betty and the children taking temporary refuge at The Bull. By the time he returned, Betty was desperate enough to accept an offer of a cleaning job for the Aldridges in return for cottage accommodation on the farm. With a roof over their heads, and with Mike now back delivering milk for Borchester Dairies, things were slowly beginning to look up again.

Another Romance

In spite of being upstaged by DS Barry, Sid wasn't about to give up on Kathy Holland. This year he continued to woo her, with increasing success. As her landlord, he was never short of excuses to call round to her cottage in Penny Hasset; he also took her to the fair, and for a meal at a Japanese restaurant. Much to the resentment of a jealous Dave Barry, they were soon close enough for Sid's daughter Lucy to worry about the potential fallout when her classmates found out about the relationship. Early in December the couple went out to collect holly and on the way home Sid proposed. Still unsure of her true feelings, she gently turned him down. Undeterred, Sid kept trying and at the third attempt she said yes. Although their engagement didn't go down at all well with Lucy, they were married at Borchester registry office in April of the following year.

Sid and Kathy (Hedli Niklaus) sign the register

1987

Trouble on the Home Front ✑

Early in the year Phil and David were forced to sit by and watch unhappily as eighty-five acres of Brookfield land was auctioned in two lots to pay their tax bill. The first lot of fifty-five acres went to a mysterious buyer for £77,000 – less than Phil had originally paid for it. The other thirty acres failed even to meet its reserve and he was forced to withdraw it from the sale. To add insult to injury he only discovered the identity of the first buyer some weeks later when Brian's bulldozer arrived and began removing a hedge. With some of the tax bill still left to pay, Phil came under pressure to sell

Nigel and Elizabeth kill time together

some of the land for a small housing development, provoking fierce opposition from villagers – including his own son-in-law, Mark, now a local SDP councillor. In the end it was Nelson – representing a local builder – who suggested that they sell instead some old barns for conversion into housing. Planning permission was granted, and so Brookfield's financial troubles were solved.

Both David and Elizabeth's personal lives proved more problematic, however. Elizabeth became involved with handsome 34-year-old wine dealer Robin Fairbrother, who turned out to be the half-brother of Phil's first wife, Grace. Jill found this rather hard to deal with, but there was worse to come when Elizabeth discovered that he was already married. She promptly threw a glass of wine in his face and dumped him. Luckily she was able to find some consolation in the company of Nigel, who had recently returned from the City after an abortive attempt to make it as a financial whizzkid.

David and Sophie's romance also hit a bumpy patch when Sophie defied Elizabeth's low opinion of her mental powers by landing a job with a top London fashion designer. The couple agreed to postpone their wedding plans indefinitely, and their separation gave them both time to reflect. There was a far worse trauma in store for David, however. In June he and Jethro Larkin were out clearing timber when Jethro was killed by a falling branch. Although everyone – including Jethro's daughter Clarrie – accepted that it was no more than a terrible accident (a verdict confirmed at the inquest), this did little to ease David's sense of guilt. When Sophie came back for the funeral, things were difficult between them. Soon after, he went to visit her in London and came back with the news that the relationship was finally over. He threw himself into his farm work, and at the end of the summer a new employee began a year's work experience at Brookfield: 19-year-old Geordie agricultural student, Ruth Pritchard.

'About 20 years ago, I did a scene with Paddy Greene [Jill] and we did it in one take. The director – can't remember which one – said: "You'd think they'd been married for 40 years." We took that as a great compliment.'
Norman Painting (Phil Archer)

NIMBY

When rumours of Phil's housing plans began to spread, among the most vocal protestors were two recent newcomers to the village: computer expert Robert Snell and his wife, Lynda, a former Sunningdale socialite and a keen campaigner for – well, almost any deserving cause. The couple had bought Ambridge Hall after Laura's death and almost immediately clashed with their neighbour Brian Aldridge over the signposting of his footpaths. They were also quick to point out that Phil's original housing scheme would not only blight the landscape but also threaten the nearby rookery. Although the scheme was dropped in favour of the barn conversions, Lynda accused Phil of hypocrisy when he subsequently made a substantial donation towards the village minibus scheme. To begin with, the Snell's crusading attitudes won them few friends but that gradually changed as they settled in and adjusted to the ways of the country. Lynda made an unsuccessful bid to become a member of the Parish Council, and in the autumn Robert's giant conker made a big impression at The Bull conker contest.

Romance for Caroline

One of the first to arrive at the scene of Jethro's tragic accident was local GP Matthew Thorogood. After spending some time in Papua New Guinea, Matthew had bought Willow Farm after Bill Insley died suddenly from a heart attack. Instead of choosing to live there, he took on the lease of Ambridge Farmhouse from the Bellamy Estate, where he set up a surgery in one of the outbuildings. He soon became involved in a romance with Caroline, who eventually moved out of Grey Gables and went to live with him (much to Peggy's disapproval). It wasn't always an easy relationship, however. Caroline was cross when he considered buying the farmhouse without telling her, and although he made amends by booking a romantic break in Florence, he then blew it by inviting Mark and Shula to join them. In spite of all that, Caroline stuck with it, and it wasn't until the summer of the following year that they finally parted.

Nelson serves wine bar customers Caroline and Shula

The Course of True Love

Ruth Pritchard's first few months at Brookfield hadn't been easy. Brought up in the suburbs of Prudhoe, her only previous farming experience had been time spent on a kibbutz in Israel. David's doubts about the wisdom of taking on such a young and unskilled worker had seemed justified when she made a series of early mistakes, including the contamination of a batch of milk with iodine, and killing a neighbour's vegetables with drift from the sprayer. But her dedication and willingness to learn slowly won him round and as the New Year began there were hints that he was beginning to appreciate her for more than just her natural instinct for handling dairy cows. He took her out on Valentine's Day, but when

1988

Jill and Phil look forward to their Christmas pudding

Nelson mourns the death of his father Walter

he tried to push things a little further she told him firmly that she wanted them to remain Just Good Friends. David's response was to throw himself into the arms of the nearest willing girl – the first named Annette, and the next Frances, who lived in Borchester with her two young daughters. His life wasn't about to get any easier, however; in the summer, his brother Kenton called from Australia to say he was coming home. After an absence of almost fifteen years – apart from the odd visit for weddings, and most recently for Dan's funeral – sailor Kenton swaggered back onto the Brookfield stage to be greeted by Phil and Jill as the prodigal son. He immediately annoyed David by calling him 'Dave', and then by persuading Phil to buy him a new performance car on the farm. At first he was vague about his plans, but soon admitted that he was taking voluntary redundancy from the merchant navy, and asked for a job on the farm while he decided his next move. David was less than overjoyed when Phil agreed to take him on and pay him a wage. Kenton's relaxed timekeeping and perfunctory attempts at farm labour only led to more friction between the two brothers. More galling still for David – who'd recently been dumped by single mum Frances – was Kenton's casual flirtation with Ruth, who seemed quite happy to be the object of his attentions. This did, however, serve to remind David just how much he loved her himself. Two weeks before she was due to leave Brookfield, he went to her flat at Nightingale Farm, and opened his heart to her. This time she told him she was very happy to be more than just friends, and by the end of September they were engaged. Phil had also agreed to make David a full partner in the business, at last. On 3 November came the sad news that Phil's Uncle Walter had died quietly from pneumonia at the grand old age of 92.

Just a few weeks after this – on 15 December – Ruth and David were married. It would be a while before they could settle down together, as Ruth had to finish her year's course at Harper Adams Agricultural College. In the meantime, Phil arranged to have a bungalow built for them at Brookfield. The two brothers were now back on good enough terms for Kenton to be David's best man. Although late for the rehearsal, Kenton made it to the church on time.

Jack and Peggy Archer's son was known as Anthony William Daniel until, like Anthony Wedgwood-Benn, he became plain Tony. The two Tonys have nothing in common politically, however. Tony Archer was most put out in the 1980s when his on-air wife Pat cancelled his *Daily Express* in favour of *The Guardian*.

Family Planning

Now entering the third year of their marriage, Shula and Mark were happily ensconced at Glebe Cottage with its newly thatched roof and Mark's carefully managed compost heap at the bottom of the garden. After Andrew Sinclair's retirement, Shula had taken over his job as manager of the Berrow Estate (owned by Lilian), and – although Mark's own job was giving him a few headaches – she persuaded him that it was time for them to start a family. He embraced the idea with slightly less enthusiasm and soon after upset her by accepting a job with a large law firm in Birmingham. His subsequent long hours and daily commute did little to help Shula's attempts to get pregnant; neither did his suggestion that they leave Glebe Cottage and move to be closer to his work. Realising how much she hated this idea, he backed down gracefully, and by the end of the year they were still trying hard for that baby.

David with his new bride,
Ruth (Felicity Finch)

Brian's Nemesis

1989

This summer was to bring an abrupt change of fortunes for Ambridge's most dedicated philanderer, Brian Aldridge – a change that was also to have consequences for Brookfield.

Since the end of his affair with Caroline, Brian had continued to push his marriage vows – and Jennifer's patience – to the limit. His roving eye had settled first on their home help and tenant Betty Tucker. His shameless (if unsuccessful) advances had proved too much for poor Betty, and when the chance had come to rent their old home Willow Farm from Matthew Thorogood, she and Mike had quickly decamped there with their two children. Betty was now working at the village shop. Unabashed, Brian by then had already begun to pursue sultry red-headed horsewoman Mandy Beesborough. Jennifer, however, was rapidly getting wise to his ways and it was partly in an attempt to rescue their marriage that they had decided to have another child. In September of the previous year Jennifer – now 43 – had given birth to daughter Alice.

But this symbolic event did little to bring them together; at the time of the birth Brian was off with Mandy at the races. After another showdown a slightly chastened Brian turned his attention to more acceptable current affairs, standing as a candidate in the local elections. But – as he soon discovered –

As well as playing Mike Tucker, Terry Molloy has appeared in more than 500 plays. In 1981, he won a Pye Radio Award (forerunner of the Sony) for his performance in Ron Hutchinson's play *Risky City*. 'It was only broadcast once,' he reflects, 'and that was on Radio 3.'

Two cakes? Jill helps Phil celebrate his 60th birthday in style

Celebrity Appearance: 1989 – Terry Wogan came to Grey Gables to join in a celebrity golf tournament

politics is a risky business. While canvassing at Grange Farm he was tossed by a BSE infected cow, hitting his head against a brick wall. The resulting injury didn't seem too bad at first, but soon after he needed emergency surgery, first for a blood clot on the brain, and then for a more serious cerebral abscess. He spent some time in hospital and when he came home, in time for Alice's postponed christening, he was still weak and hardly able to work. Worse still was to follow when, while out in a cornfield at harvest time, he collapsed and had a fit. The diagnosis was post-traumatic epilepsy. Brian was put on strong medication and told that he wouldn't be able to drive for two years. Although this inevitably upped the pressure on Jennifer, she at least had the consolation of knowing that – for a while, at least – Brian seemed to lose his zest for chasing other women.

Ruth and David, meanwhile, had a few problems of their own. Ruth had now finished her course at Harper Adams, but the promised bungalow was still awaiting planning permission, and so the couple were living at Brookfield. This led to tensions between Ruth and Jill, who each had very different ideas about the role of a farmer's wife (Jill's definition included keeping the kitchen tidy and cooking proper meals). So when Brian, struggling to cope at Home Farm, offered David the role of his farm manager, with a nice little cottage thrown in, David said yes. This suited Ruth, but Phil wasn't too happy, and neither – after a month or two – was David. Fed up with being used as Brian's chauffeur and general dogsbody, by Christmas he was back working for Brookfield. But Brian let the couple stay on in the cottage for the time being, and Ruth began a year's work placement at Home Farm.

Kenton the Entrepreneur

The year began with an unpleasant health scare for Kenton, the returned traveller. Over Christmas he'd been losing weight and feeling weak and listless, and this led to a series of blood tests to try and establish the cause. A few village gossips were quick to diagnose AIDS, but it turned out to be nothing worse than an overactive thyroid gland. Having by now firmly decided that he wasn't cut out to be a farm worker, Kenton began to look for more adventurous ways to make his fortune. His first attempt – a shaky financial business in partnership with an ex-naval friend – led to him narrowly avoiding prosecution for illegal stock dealing. He soon bounced back, however, and in the summer he saw his big chance when Nelson put his antiques business up for sale. Although the family (David in particular) were initially sceptical, Kenton made full use of his disingenuous charm and eventually persuaded Phil to help him out. Using the remaining profits from the barn conversions, Phil managed to scrape together £50,000 and gave it to Kenton as an advance on his inheritance. This still left him £50,000 short, but his twin sister Shula somehow convinced Mark that it would make a sound investment. Kenton wasn't too happy when Mark demanded £400 a month rent, but bit the bullet and in October he held a party to celebrate the opening of Archer's Antiques. David shook his hand and wished him luck.

Brian and Jennifer
with baby Alice

Ambridge Underclass

Early in the summer Susan Carter was reminded of her less savoury family connections when she discovered that her brother Clive's 17-year-old girlfriend, Sharon Richards, was pregnant. Sharon gave up her hairdressing course and came to live for a while at the Horrobins, before Susan took pity on her and offered them a room at No. 1 The Green. This arrangement didn't last long and soon they were on the move again, this time to the vicarage, when the new vicar Jerry Buckle scandalised half the village by taking them in. It was here that Matthew Thorogood delivered the young couple's baby daughter, Kylie, in October. In spite of Jerry's good intentions, Clive showed few signs of becoming a responsible father and disappeared six weeks later, along with Sharon's portable stereo.

The Childless Couple

It was now close to a year since Mark and Shula had first decided to start a family, and there was still no sign of it happening. As the year began, their failure was causing tensions in their marriage. Mark upset Shula by telling Matthew Thorogood about the problem without letting her know, and suggesting that she made an appointment at his well-woman clinic. Shula's first tests proved normal, but when she was eventually persuaded by Mark to see a gynaecologist, her secret worries over her fertility made her cancel the appointment. There was a big row when Mark found out, and he went off in a huff to stay with friends in Birmingham. But after three weeks they were back together, and Shula braced herself and made another appointment. She then discovered that she'd had endometriosis (a cellular disorder of the uterus). The good news was that she was still fertile; so there was nothing to stop her and Mark having that baby they so desperately wanted.

Profile
LYNDA SNELL

Eddie GRUNDY WAS BEHIND a hedge doing something unspeakable to a small rodent when he heard a rather strident, slightly nasal voice that he would consider affectedly posh. 'Excuse me,' it brayed. 'What do you think you're doing?'

Lynda Snell was perhaps too advanced in years to be considered a yuppie, even in 1986. But she and her beloved Robert were, in other respects, embodiments of that 1980s phenomenon whereby the upwardly mobile began moving out of London and the Home Counties and into the more rustic shires of Middle England. 'They soon started trying to tell people who'd been in the countryside for generations how to run their lives,' recalls Carole Boyd, the actress who has made Lynda's one of the most distinctive voices on radio.

The Snell sniff was her creation. She introduced it from an early stage to express disapproval or hurt feelings or simply the opening of the hay fever season. Here was a woman determined to seize the challenge set by the production team, led by editor-of-the-day Liz Rigbey, to create a larger-than-life figure with comic potential. 'At the time I was a big fan of *Dallas* and *Dynasty*,' Carole recalls. 'They were an absolute hoot because the characters took themselves so seriously. So I decided to do that with Lynda and be rather unpleasant with it.' But didn't the production team object? 'They said it wasn't quite what they had in mind but, on reflection, they thought they'd go with it.'

As the years went on, the softer side of Lynda would occasionally seep through the veneer. 'Deep down she's quite kind and means well,' Carole muses. 'She sees the good side in a character like Vicky, but also feels the need to improve her.'

We're talking in the immaculate front room of the bungalow that she shares with husband Patrick in a quiet, tree-lined road in deepest Surrey commuter land. No, not Sunningdale, but not too far away. Carole was brought up in the somewhat less salubrious surroundings of Wood Green in North London before the family moved south to Balham. Her father was an electrician and her mother, second generation Irish, a nurse. 'What money there was went on school fees,' Carole recalls. She was sent to a convent school where her flair for acting soon came to the fore. 'My most memorable part was playing Badger in *Toad of Toad Hall*, aged 9.'

Eventually she was badgered into going to university in Sheffield rather than following her heart and heading for drama school. That came later. First there was a spell working in the record department at WH Smith's in Fleet Street after failing her part ones. It was the mid-1960s. Newspaper hot-metal presses were thundering away nearby and vast amounts of vinyl were flying over the counter. 'I liked The Beatles, of course, but my real passion has always been for classical music,' she confides, sounding rather like Lynda for a fleeting moment.

Her other passion is for the stage, and one of the highlights of her career was the year she spent in Scarborough working for Alan Ayckbourn's theatre company. But her vocal talents were the

'"Don't tell me," he kept saying. "You're that woman."'

key to her career. They were spotted early and meant that she left the Birmingham School of Speech and Drama with the Carlton Hobbs award, named after one of radio's most distinguished actors. 'It gave me a six-month contract at Broadcasting House and an Equity card,' she says. The intensive training that she received in microphone techniques would prove invaluable. Indeed, her first role in *The Archers* came as early as 1968 when she was brought in to play county-set shepherdess Fiona Watson.

Apart from extensive radio work, Carole is highly regarded as a reader of audiobooks. One bathroom wall at the Surrey bungalow is liberally hung with framed awards testifying to the quality of her work. Here's one for Ian McEwan's *Atonement* and another for George Eliot's *Middlemarch*. Oh yes, and *Postman Pat*. She does the voice-overs for the women's and children's parts in the CBeebies version. 'I went down to Eastbourne to do the recording,' she says, 'and the taxi driver recognised my voice.' From *Postman Pat*? 'No, from *The Archers*. "Don't tell me," he kept saying. "You're that woman."'

Yes, 'that woman'. Eddie Grundy and Brian Aldridge have referred to Lynda with the same disparaging words ever since she arrived from Sunningdale and appointed herself the saviour of small rodents and other Borsetshire wildlife.

Profile
RUTH ARCHER

THE DIMINUTIVE FIGURE OF Felicity Finch emerges into the foyer of Broadcasting House looking anything but the stereotypical farmer's wife. In that respect she has something in common with Ruth Archer. Ruth is more likely to have her hand in a rubber glove rather than an oven glove – thrust up the back end of a Friesian rather than delving into an Aga and emerging with something wholesome for supper. 'Or tea as she would call it,' says the actress who has played her since 1987. 'I'm always having this argument with Tim [Bentinck, her on-air husband]. He won't accept that, where I come from, you have your "dinner" at lunchtime and your evening meal is your "tea". You don't have supper any time.'

It's a good natured dispute that appears to be based on regional rather than class differences, despite Tim's links to the aristocracy. 'We get on very well and he even took Paddy [Greene, his on-air mother] and me to lunch at the House of Lords.' Or dinner, as Ruth would call it. Like her alter ego, Felicity is from the North-East. The daughter of a quantity surveyor and a teacher, she hales from Teesside rather than Tyneside, although she was first recruited to the role on the recommendation of a director at the Newcastle Playhouse. Her accent is less pronounced than Ruth's. That may be because she now lives (alone) in South-East London when she's not travelling to far-flung places for the BBC.

Not just to Birmingham to record for *The Archers* but to Rwanda and Afghanistan, if you please. When we meet, she has recently returned from

Kabul in her dual role at the BBC. She has one foot in the drama department and the other in documentaries. Indeed, she has spent the early part of this afternoon in the *Woman's Hour* studio editing tapes for a package on Afghan boxers. Female ones, as it happens. (Another stereotype gone.) 'They have their sights set on the Olympics,' says the roving reporter through slightly frothy lips. We've moved to a noisy Italian café and she's using her spoon to scoop up the remains of her decaf cappuccino.

'You're the chorus to what's happening elsewhere.'

Felicity, or 'Flick' as she's known to her friends, has been to Afghanistan four times in the past ten years or so. Her first visit to Peshawar was in 1999 to advise on *New Home, New Life*, a radio series devised by the BBC World Service, translated into Pashto and Persian and transmitted over the border from Pakistan. The idea was to use drama to get across public health issues, like awareness of landmines or child immunisation programmes, in a way not dissimilar from *The Archers* in its early years conveying information from the Ministry of Agriculture. 'I was able to go to Kabul for the first time in 2003 after the Taliban had been driven from power,' she recalls. 'It was easier then for a westerner to walk down the street than it is now.'

She evidently has a curiosity about the world and a taste for adventure that makes her a natural. 'I've always loved Radio 4 documentaries,' she says and, like any would-be journalist with ambition, she made the most of being in the right place at the right time. *Archers* editor Vanessa Whitburn introduced her to the head of features at BBC Pebble Mill in the days when the programme was recorded there. That in turn led to a chat with her equivalent on *Woman's Hour*. 'Maybe,' Felicity ponders, 'she wanted to see what Ruth Archer looked like.' Maybe. But the upshot has been a burgeoning journalistic career, producing work not only for *Woman's Hour* but also *You and Yours* and *Saturday Live*. She was even nominated for a Sony Award in 2005 for her documentary *Will He Change His Socks?* about a Down's syndrome boy trying to live life in the mainstream.

Meanwhile, her fictional character has survived breast cancer, almost consummated a relationship with a flirtatious herdsman and given birth on air – a meaty challenge for an actress who has never had a child. She also claims to relish the more humdrum storylines. 'You have to give as much to them as anything else,' she insists. 'You're the chorus to what's happening elsewhere.'

For Felicity that means being a mother of three and a farmer's wife, albeit one more likely to pull a pizza out of the microwave for 'tea' than something wholesome out of an Aga.

Chapter Five 1990s

The Milk Marketing Board was finally abolished in 1993. EU milk quotas had already reduced the volume of what dairy farmers could produce. Now they were going to lose their guaranteed price. It's a wonder that the Grundys managed to survive at Grange Farm until 2000. Then again, Joe was only partially telling the truth when he blamed Brussels bureaucrats for 'cutting us off in mid-stream'. Milk quotas also helped him and Eddie by increasing the price that they received for their calves and cull cows.

Elsewhere in Ambridge and, indeed, the rest of rural England, 'diversification' was the new buzzword. Farmers were being paid to manage the land rather than increase production and nobody cottoned on quicker than Brian Aldridge. Much as he favoured a free market, he wasn't going to turn up his nose at the cheques that arrived through the letterbox as he converted the pond into a fishing lake and added an off-the-road riding track to the Home Farm portfolio. Jill Archer, meanwhile, was opening Brookfield as a Bed and Breakfast guesthouse.

Tony would moan about the comparatively paltry grants available to organic farmers, but Bridge Farm wasn't doing too badly. Pat secured a lucrative contract to supply Underwood's with ice cream and yoghurt and, in 1992, she and Tony opened a farm shop.

On the Land...

- Farmers became increasingly keen to bypass the supermarkets and sell directly to the public. Apart from farm shops in the countryside, farmers' markets began setting out their stalls in towns and cities. The trend continued in the Noughties when Jennifer and Pat combined to sell Home Farm strawberries and Bridge Farm cream in Borchester while dressed in tennis gear at Wimbledon time.

- Environmental issues were rising up the agenda. Farmers who had been encouraged to rip out hedges became eligible for grants to put them back again. Brookfield was one of them, much to Phil's bemusement as he reflected on the irony.

- Trials of genetically modified food faced fierce opposition from environmentalists. Tom Archer – or 'Tommy' as he was known back then – was arrested and tried for trashing a field of GM oilseed rape on his Uncle Brian's farm. The court eventually accepted that he had a 'lawful excuse'.

- The BSE crisis came to a head in 1996 when the government admitted that 'mad cow disease', caused by feeding recycled but diseased sheep carcasses to cattle, could threaten human health. The market for UK beef collapsed and even The Bull in Ambridge stopped serving steak and kidney pie.

... And in the Land Beyond the Farm Gate

- Computer technology advanced rapidly and the worldwide web began to insinuate itself into the national consciousness. The first cyber-café opened in London in 1994. Within a decade the idea had reached The Bull.

- The National Lottery was launched by John Major's government, offering dreams of wealth beyond the imagination of the Grundys. Winning the jackpot? Eddie probably had more chance of unearthing another Saxon hoard with his metal detector.

- The Sunday Trading Act of 1994 allowed shops to open on the Sabbath, although the larger stores were restricted to six hours. Pubs had the option to open longer, too, every day of the week and The Bull took advantage. It's now open all day, from morning coffee to last orders.

- In 1997, New Labour was elected overwhelmingly, Princess Diana died tragically and Dolly the sheep was created scientifically after being cloned in a Scottish laboratory. In Ambridge, meanwhile, sheep continued to reproduce conventionally, leading farmers' families to spend long hours in the lambing sheds.

1990

Hope and Disappointment ✍

In spite of Shula's all-clear diagnosis the previous year, by the summer she was approaching her 32nd birthday, and there was still no sign of a baby. It was some consolation to her to know that at least she and Mark were now as happy as they'd ever been together, but that didn't stop her longing for a child. Then, in October, she missed a period. She and Mark did a home test, which proved positive. It looked as if their dream of starting a family was about to come true at last; but they were in for a bitter disappointment. Just a few days later she began to have a sharp pain in her side, and was rushed to hospital. Mark returned with the devastating news that Shula's pregnancy had been ectopic: the embryo had been growing in a fallopian tube, instead of her womb. Shula was home by bonfire night, feeling emotionally drained and miserable, after having the damaged tube removed. Although she was still technically fertile, the trauma and sadness drove a wedge between her and Mark. In December he was surprised and hurt when she told him she wanted to go on the pill. After a few days' emotional turmoil – and a long walk on Lakey Hill – she relented, and after a difficult Christmas, the New Year saw the beginnings of a reconciliation.

SHULA	I went to see him before Christmas.
MARK	And what did he say?
SHULA	I told him I wanted to go on the pill.
MARK	Why? Surely that's the very last thing—
SHULA	Actually he thought it was a very good idea.
MARK	I don't understand. I thought the best thing we could have done was to try again.
SHULA	No. According to Matthew, some women feel the way I do after they've had an ectopic pregnancy. They then go on the pill for about three months.
MARK	Well if that's what Matthew advises.
SHULA	(HESITATES) The thing is… no it doesn't matter.
MARK	What?
SHULA	Nothing.
MARK	Shula, there's something you're not telling me. I can't help if you…
SHULA	The thing is, it's not just for three months.
MARK	But you just said…
SHULA	I just said what Matthew advises.
MARK	But you don't agree.
SHULA	I've decided I want to do it permanently. I can't face it all again.
MARK	Permanently? What are you saying Shula?
SHULA	Don't you see Mark? I don't want to go through it all again. Ever.
	(MUSIC)

Second Time Lucky ✍

It was no secret that Jack Woolley still carried a torch for Peggy, more than fifteen years after she'd turned down his proposal of marriage. Over the past year or so he'd thought he'd seen his chances slip away as Peggy had begun to enjoy the company of Godfrey Wendover, an ex-naval officer (nicknamed 'Captain Pugwash' by Tony) who'd rented one of the Brookfield barn conversions. He and Peggy had been to the Three Counties Show together, and ran a stall at the village fete dressed as pirates. But an ill-judged joke from Godfrey about Peggy's beloved cat Sammy had finally ended their relationship, and so Jack was now free to resume his gentle courtship of the woman he'd loved for so long. She accepted his invitation to a Valentine's Day dinner, and in the summer they spent a pleasant day together at the Chelsea Flower Show. In October he finally summoned the courage to propose to her again, and this time she accepted. She and Jack brushed aside the practical difficulties and chose New Year's Day of the following year as their wedding day. Nelson was best man, and Tom sang a psalm during the service. Peggy wore cream silk chiffon with a peach hat, and a prussian blue velvet going-away suit. There was even a matching bow tie for Jack's dog, Captain.

New Arrivals

It wasn't a promising start to the year for Tony. Over Christmas and the New Year, his sister Lilian had been around the village on one of her occasional visits from Guernsey, and had begun to drop hints that she was thinking about selling up some of the estate. The first Tony knew for sure, however, was when he received a letter from an agent offering him first refusal on the purchase of Bridge Farm. After much grumbling to Pat and complaints to his sister, he decided that he didn't want to take on a mortgage, and turned her down. In the spring, Lilian put the whole estate up for sale. Tony was also coming under pressure from Pat and Lucy Perks (among others) to let Clive's ex Sharon Richards and baby Kylie move into his caravan. After more grumbling, he eventually conceded, only to regret it soon after when eldest son John – now just 15 – developed a serious crush on Sharon. Although his feelings were sadly unrequited, she went as far as to let him take her out to the wine bar (where Nelson refused to serve him) and – as a special treat – to empty her chemical toilet. It was something of a relief to both his parents when he left in the autumn to study agriculture at Brymore School in Somerset. By then, Tony and Pat (now busy producing yoghurt at Bridge Farm Dairy) had already been introduced to their new landlord, and owner of the Berrow Estate: a dapper and personable 35-year-old Scotsman by the name of Cameron Fraser. His easy Celtic charm soon won him friends around the village. Among his early admirers were Elizabeth (soon to begin a job as a journalist on the *Birmingham Evening News*) and Caroline, still single after her break-up with Matthew Thorogood. She and Cameron soon embarked on an affair. He added some much-needed excitement to her life, taking her to Ascot and whisking her off to Scotland for some grouse shooting. By the autumn, however, she was beginning to see a less glamorous side to his character. He was brusquely unsympathetic over Shula's ectopic pregnancy, only concerned with finding someone to cover at the estate office. They fell out again when he refused to go with her to Jack and Peggy's wedding, preferring to celebrate Hogmanay alone in Scotland. In spite of this, they managed to patch up their relationship, which limped on into the New Year.

Jack and Peggy celebrate their wedding

Cameron Fraser (Delaval Astley) and Caroline

123

1991

Trouble on the Estate

As the year progressed, more villagers began to see the hard-nosed businessman that lurked beneath Cameron Fraser's superficial charm. Shula – in her role as agent for the Estate – found herself at the sharp end as she clashed with him over his often high-handed management decisions. But it was after a farm accident

*Mike Tucker
(Terry Molloy)*

that Cameron really began to show his true colours. In May, Mike Tucker was employed to do some casual work on the Estate. As he was helping to hitch up a trailer, a hydraulic pipe snapped and hit him in the eye. Although at first he hoped it was nothing more than a severe bruise, soon after he was diagnosed with a detached retina, and lost sight in that eye. Facing an investigation from the Health and Safety Executive, Cameron put pressure on Susan, who'd witnessed the accident, to say that she hadn't been watching when it happened. Mike – who'd warned the Estate farm manager that the trailer hitch was faulty – pursued a compensation claim, with the help of Farm Workers' Union rep Neil Carter. Cameron then tried to buy Mike off with a paltry £5,000, less than a fifth of the value of the potential claim. As the case dragged on over the summer, Mike struggled to keep working and for a time Betty took over his milk round. In spite of Tony's misguided attempt to cheer him up with a gift of an eyepatch, by the end of the year he had slipped into a bout of deep depression. In December, haunted by the accident and his recent years of struggle and failure, he set out to torch a barn on Jim Ascott's land, where he'd been hoping to graze some sheep of his own. Luckily he was stopped by Eddie Grundy, but his subsequent rows with Betty culminated in her packing her bags and taking the kids to The Bull, where they stayed until Mike was found sobbing alone on Christmas Day and agreed to treatment for his breakdown. He recovered over time, and the accident was not without a silver lining. Mike was awarded £33,000 in compensation and, when Matthew Thorogood put Willow Farm up for sale, he and Betty used the windfall as a deposit to buy their old home.

Cameron, meanwhile, had avoided any official blame for the accident. Although the HSE decided to prosecute, it was the Estate manager Geoff Williams who was the fall guy. By then Caroline had had enough of Cameron's devious ways and finally broke off the relationship. Waiting in the wings was Elizabeth, now back from her job in Birmingham after a bout of glandular fever. She had fewer scruples about Cameron's managerial style and, determined to impress him, she accepted his invitation to go out hunting. When she fell off her horse, his strong arms were there to rescue her, and before long she was deeply in love.

Reconciliation ⟡

After the emotional roller-coaster ride of the past few months, Mark and Shula's life gradually took on a more settled routine. They spent time together working out at the gym, and riding their new mountain bikes around the lanes. The healing process was helped still further when, in June, Mark left his job with the Birmingham law firm and set up his own practice in Borchester, taking on a new partner, 29-year-old Usha Gupta. She and Mark got on well from the start, which Shula found a little unsettling, but she soon accepted that this was a purely professional relationship. By the end of the year, although still hoping for a baby, she was able to put it to the back of her mind and concentrate instead on the good things that she and Mark already shared.

Daughters and Lovers ⟡

In June, Jennifer's eldest daughter Debbie surprised everyone by coming home early from her second year at Exeter University, where she was studying French and English. She told Jennifer and Brian that she'd managed to get a year's sabbatical, but was vague about the reasons. Eventually she confessed to her mother that she'd had an unhappy love affair. Again she was economical with the details; her family only discovered the truth in the autumn, when her ex-lover came to see her in Ambridge. Rather then the expected fellow-student, he turned out to be a 40-year-old Canadian lecturer, Simon Gerrard. It also emerged that it was Debbie who'd tried to end the relationship after finding him with another woman, but – as far as Simon was concerned – the affair was far from over. While in Ambridge he tried to win her back and persuade her to go with him to Canada. The situation came to a head when Brian found an angry Simon apparently trying to manhandle her, and threw him out. Furious with Brian for his strong-arm tactics, Debbie left too. A few days later, however, she was back, saying that she'd ended the relationship for good. After that, Brian might have hoped for a few months' space to rebuild his relationship with his stepdaughter, but fate had other plans. On Christmas Eve, during a lull in her birthday celebrations, a stranger approached Debbie in The Bull and introduced himself as her father, Roger Travers-Macy. Once she'd got over the bombshell she managed to keep it to herself for a few days before arranging a surprise meeting between Roger and her mother. She quickly realised that – even after all these years – her two parents had outstanding issues of their own to resolve and discreetly left them to it.

Celebrity Appearance: 1991 – John Peel was staying at Grey Gables. Eddie gave John a music cassette that John took away

In *The Archers*, it was Usha who introduced Ruth to the joys of salsa dancing. In real life, it was the other way around. 'I've always had a passion for South American dancing,' says Felicity Finch [Ruth]. 'When we were up in Birmingham for recording, I persuaded Souad [Faress, Usha] to come with me. We had great fun flinging each other around.'

1992

Fraudster Fraser ✑

Elizabeth began the New Year as she'd ended the old – totally besotted with her new love, Cameron Fraser. He in turn seemed to find her youthful vivacity beguiling, but she was puzzled and a little upset by his emotional hang-ups; he seemed unable – or unwilling – to commit himself whole-heartedly to their relationship. Adding to the complications was her new job working for her old flame, Nigel Pargetter. Since the death of his father, Gerald, in 1988, Nigel had grown up fast. He'd inherited the vast and crumbling Lower Loxley Hall, which was in dire need of major refurbishment. Determined to save his ancestral home, he'd begun to open it to the public, and was now planning to turn part of it into a conference centre, with Elizabeth as his marketing manager. She and Nigel danced and had fun together at the hunt ball, prompting a jealous Cameron to take her out to the coast for the day. Here he claimed that he'd once been cruelly jilted by a girl he loved, and this had made him over-cautious with his emotions. She was quite happy to buy this (rather glib) explanation, and the relationship seemed back on course again. Not for long, however. She soon began to feel tired and ill in the mornings, and eventually Debbie shrewdly persuaded her to take a pregnancy test. It was positive; Elizabeth was carrying Cameron's baby.

ELIZABETH	(SOBS) You don't really care at all, do you?
CAMERON	Lizzie—
ELIZABETH	Don't lie to me Cameron! As soon as I told you, I could see—!
CAMERON	I won't pretend I'm overjoyed, but I do care for you, honestly—
ELZABETH	No you don't, you don't care for me or the baby, you just want to get rid of it. You...
CAMERON	Okay go on, call me what you like – but I'm only trying to do what's best for both of us.
ELIZABETH	You mean what's best for you! You think it's just another problem and so long as you pay enough it'll go away!
CAMERON	If that's what you really think then it's no use me arguing with you.
ELIZABETH	You never even asked what I wanted! You never even stopped to think!
CAMERON	Okay, I'm sorry, maybe I should—
ELIZABETH	Oh just forget it! It was stupid of me even to think that you might have wanted— (MORE SOBS)
CAMERON	Lizzie, Lizzie, come on - this won't do any good—
ELIZABETH	No don't touch me! Don't come near me—
CAMERON	If there's anything else I can do—
ELIZABETH	It's too late for that. I don't want your money. I don't want anything else from you, ever!

Shocked and frightened, at first she kept the news to herself, unsure how to break it to Cameron. Jill knew a case of morning sickness when she saw one, however, and made her confess. She was horrified by the news, but Phil took it more calmly, and promised to support his daughter, whatever the outcome – as Dan had spoken up for his pregnant niece Jennifer, twenty-five years before. However, both her parents were worried by her naive assumption that she could simply keep the baby, marry Cameron and live happily ever after. She was in for a cruel disappointment. When she finally told Cameron, he was appalled and immediately offered to pay for an abortion. She left in tears. Afterwards he cooled off a little, offering to support her financially if she kept the child but ruling out any question of marriage. Still she clung on to the relationship, hoping to win him round. It was a very difficult and painful moment for Shula, when she found out about the pregnancy; it seemed a bitter irony that her younger sister could succeed accidentally where she and Mark had failed for so long.

But unknown to Elizabeth, her pregnancy was only one of many problems facing Cameron. As well as his interest in the Berrow Estate, he also ran an investment business in Scotland, and rumours began to spread that he was in financial trouble. At the Estate office, Susan Carter (now the Estate secretary) was fielding calls from angry investors trying to recover their savings. By mid-April, the stress began to tell on Cameron, who leant on Elizabeth for emotional support. At the end of the month she was delighted when he told her that he needed a break, and offered to take her with him. But it wasn't to be the romantic holiday she'd been hoping for. On the way to the airport, they stopped at a pub, and Cameron went to the gents, telling her he'd be back in a minute. That was the last time she ever saw him. Abandoned and distraught, she had to hitchhike back to Ambridge. Any lingering hopes that he might come back to her were dashed when members of the Fraud Squad arrived in the village and began questioning his former employees. The sordid truth was that Cameron had been recklessly gambling away his innocent punters' money on high-risk investments. Among his victims locally were Caroline – who lost £60,000 – and Mrs Antrobus. Cameron had done a comprehensive vanishing act, never to be traced, leaving a shell-shocked Elizabeth still carrying his child. After some resistance from Mark, Shula offered to adopt the baby; but a few days later Elizabeth took matters into her own hands and had an abortion. Shula was bitterly angry and upset, and the subsequent rows led to a serious rift between the two sisters, which by the end of the year showed few signs of healing.

Celebrity Appearance: 1992 – Britt Ekland was playing in pantomime in Birmingham. William won a competition – the prize was tickets for the family and meeting Britt back stage (Eddie had cheated)

Old Flames

The shock return of Roger Travers-Macy caused big emotional ripples not just for Debbie and Jennifer, but also for Brian, who wasn't about to welcome his wife's ex-husband with open arms. Unsurprisingly, perhaps, Debbie found it all hard to deal with and – although saying she'd stay in touch with Roger – kept her distance. It was a very different matter for Jennifer. In spite of Roger's past form the old spark between them quickly re-ignited and they embarked on a torrid affair. Under the smokescreen of researching Brian's new plans for a riding course, Jennifer sneaked off for secret liaisons at every opportunity. She wasn't quite clever enough to fool

For better, for worse: Grundy togetherness

Peggy, however, who began to wonder about her frequent requests to babysit Alice. Debbie also began to suspect. Jennifer was now in too deep to back out easily, and even began to think hard about her marriage when Roger urged her to leave Brian. But in the end her guilt and her loyalty to her family proved the stronger, and she told him it would have to end. Not before time; just a few days later, she was quietly and subtly warned off by Brian, who'd guessed all along. A chastened Jennifer put aside her regrets and returned to the fold, never to stray far again.

Vive La Différence

The past year or so at Grange Farm had brought the usual round of penny-pinching and money-making scams, the most recent being Joe's attempt to become a millionaire by bottling their spring water. A combination of a dead calf, local opposition and lack of investment had put an end to his dreams. In the spring a

Profile
USHA GUPTA

W HEN SHE FIRST PLAYED Usha in *The Archers*, Souad Faress experienced a flashback that wasn't particularly pleasant. 'It reminded me of being ill,' she explains. 'I heard the theme tune and, for a weird moment, I went right back to the days when I used to go down with bronchial pneumonia every winter and drift in and out of consciousness with the radio on by the side of the bed.'

Perhaps it wasn't the best idea to expect a girl who had been brought up in Africa to play goalie in the school hockey team when the school was in Southport and the wind was whipping off the Irish Sea. So did that flashback to childhood illness make her feel ambivalent about taking on the role? 'Not at all,' she insists. 'I'm an actress and I love radio. I happily took over the part from Sudha Buchar who was very busy as a regular with *EastEnders*.'

Souad arrived in Ambridge in the mid-1990s just in time to have acid thrown in her character's face by racist thugs. Strange as it seems now, they were mates of that hot-headed tearaway Roy Tucker. 'I would have liked to see Roy come and work for Usha as a solicitor's clerk,' she muses. That storyline never did take wing. But it was Souad and Jamila Massey (the formidable Auntie Satya) who first suggested that Ambridge's only Hindu should marry the vicar. 'Well, I'm a character very unlikely to have a relationship with somebody from exactly the same background,' Souad points out, 'and I try not to think in boxes. So I said to one of the directors: "Get me the vicar and I'll marry him."' It would put in motion a storyline that brought her relationship with Shula out of the freezer and into the spitting fat of full-scale animosity. But there was one minor problem: Ambridge was between vicars at the time.

Enter the Reverend Alan Franks on a motorbike. Well, to be honest, the motorbike came later and the hitch-up with Usha later still. 'Nothing is too rushed in *The Archers*,' the actress nods approvingly. But didn't the motorbike bring you together when you clambered aboard the vicar's pillion? 'That's right. I was dressed as a chicken at the time.' A chicken? 'Yes, I was running a marathon in fancy dress.'

By now we're beginning to talk as though actress and character are one and the same. In real life Souad has run no more than a quarter of a marathon. 'But I did do a lot of running on the spot in the studio when Usha was in training,' she asserts before adding with a modest smile, 'Actors have to be fit and have stamina.'

And be perpetually youthful, it would seem, although Souad is coyer than most about revealing her age. 'I want to continue playing a wide range of roles across the age spectrum,' she maintains. Incredibly, she once played the mother of Dev, the not-exactly-youthful shop-keeper of Coronation Street. Yet looking at her smooth complexion and un-

'Nothing is too rushed in *The Archers*...'

gnarled hands, it seems an extraordinary piece of casting.

On the table between us is a teapot. So, at a push, you could call this interview afternoon tea with the vicar's wife, albeit in a Birmingham hotel rather than the vicarage at St Stephen's. The woman who plays a Hindu married to a Christian clergyman was born a Muslim. 'I no longer go to the mosque,' she admits, 'but it's a bit like being a Catholic – once a Muslim always a Muslim.'

Her father was Syrian and her mother Anglo-Irish. An exotic heritage to be sure, but rather different from Usha's British Asian background. 'There are still parallels between us,' Souad points out. 'We both left Africa overnight with our parents – Ghana in my case, Uganda in Usha's – and arrived on these shores with the clothes we were standing up in. And we both know what it's like to be "the only one in the village".' She means the only ethnic minority representative, although it might be pushing it to call Southport a village. 'OK, it's a seaside town,' she concedes. 'But there are only three main streets with the sea one side and flat farmland running all the way to Manchester the other.'

Not the best place to play goalie in bleak midwinter hockey matches. Still, at least the annual spell in the sick bed gave her a somewhat feverish introduction to *The Archers*.

Profile

ELIZABETH PARGETTER

ALISON DOWLING IMAGINES HERSELF growing a couple of inches whenever she steps up to the microphone to play Elizabeth Pargetter. 'I see her as quite leggy,' she says rather wistfully, 'while I'm only five foot three. And a half,' she adds. Petite, you might say. 'Yes, but I always wanted to be tall and graceful like the top ballet dancers.'

Ballet was a passion from an early age. 'I was into a tutu almost as soon as I could waddle,' she recalls. By the time she was 11, in 1972, she was good enough to win a place at the Barbara Speake Stage School in Acton, West London. Home was in Clapham, a mere hour and a half away by public transport. Boarding was not an option. Apart from anything else, her mother was struggling to bring up four children while separated from her husband, a blues singer living in Malta.

So different from the home life of the first lady of Lower Loxley, you might say. Today Alison still lives in London with her partner and two sons, aged 11 and 12. 'We have a small house with a big mortgage,' she smiles. 'No garden, never mind an estate. No outbuildings, no lake, no staff.' No ambitions to live in the countryside either?

'I think about it every now and then, but really I'm a townie at heart.' Town is where the work is – London most of the time and Birmingham when required by the *Archers* production team. For the past twenty-six years, she has been driving up the motorway at regular intervals to use her beautifully modulated voice as the farmer's daughter who was expelled from boarding school, embarked on a succession of dalliances with unsuitable boyfriends, flirted with journalism, became the belle of Nelson's wine bar, fell pregnant to the dastardly Cameron Fraser, underwent an abortion, married into 'old' money and gave birth to twins. Oh yes, and then she almost brought about the fall of the house of Archer by demanding her cut of the Brookfield acres.

Alison uses her own impeccable received pronunciation to play Elizabeth. But she can turn her hand to any accent required if called upon. This, remember, was the girl on the Clapham omnibus, travelling to stage school every day absorbing the babble of diverse tongues that are part of daily dialogue in a great cosmopolitan city. When we meet for lunch – coffee in her case – in Shaftesbury Avenue, she has come straight from a Soho studio where she has been recording various voiceovers for *Nanny McPhee 2*.

'It could be anything from a pair of talking wellie boots to re-voicing a part that hasn't quite produced the sound that the director requires,' she explains. Alison has done a lot of this kind of thing from an early age. 'I was the voice of Tommy as a little boy in The Who's rock opera,' she reveals. At the time she was a little girl. Indeed she's proud to say that she worked through most of her

> **'I was the voice of Tommy in The Who's rock opera.'**

childhood, helping to take the financial strain off her hard-up mum. 'I think it helped that I had ringlets and blue eyes,' she muses. 'My first part was as a little Jewish girl in Ken Russell's film about Mahler and, after that, they kept coming.' Everything from *Pollyanna* to *Grange Hill* as a child, *Crossroads* to *Emmerdale Farm* as an adult. By that time, the dedication required to be a top ballet dancer had fallen by the wayside. 'I'd developed too much of a liking for a beer and a curry,' she admits.

These days she appears quite happy with the radio and voiceover work. 'No make-up or costumes are required. There's no hanging around and I can get home to my kids.' One of those kids is just a few months older than Lily and Freddie, those twin bundles of joy whose secondary education – to board or not to board – has been the cause of some heated discussion at Lower Loxley. To Alison it doesn't seem five minutes since she was required to keep a straight face while telling her on-air husband, the actor Graham Seed: 'You'll never guess, Nigel. I think I'm pregnant.' As if he didn't know. 'At the time I was not far off giving birth and fat enough to be carrying twins,' she says, recalling one of the times when she was growing outwards rather than upwards while playing Elizabeth.

disheartened Clarrie read a magazine article about cheap farms in France, and set out to convince Joe and Eddie that they should think about searching for the good life beyond the channel. Joe proved stubborn but Eddie was soon won round and he and Clarrie signed up for a farm viewing trip in France. They scratched around for the ferry fare and set off in May with a second-hand tent, a borrowed lilo and some tins of corned beef. In spite of Clarrie's grand hopes, they soon found out that the life of the small farmer was no easier in France than in Borsetshire. Eddie was rapidly disillusioned by the whole experience, but it was something of a cultural epiphany for Clarrie, who came home a devoted Francophile. Eddie became irrationally jealous when she persuaded the Grey Gables chef Jean-Paul to translate her Roche Voisine tapes. More significantly, she soon became one of the main supporters of the plan to twin Ambridge with the French village of Meyruelle.

1993

Armed Robbery

After Jennifer's near-disastrous affair with Roger, she and Brian soon had other problems closer to home. Their dysfunctional daughter Kate – now 15 – had been involved in a series of minor misdemeanors, which culminated in a police caution after she'd been caught joyriding with her boyfriend in a stolen car. In desperation, her parents had brought in an educational psychologist, but Kate found a more sympathetic counsellor in Lynda Snell. In the spring, however, she was involved in one of the most dramatic events in the recent history of Ambridge – and this time she was in no way to blame. On 22 April, she and sister Debbie had strolled down to the village shop to buy a can of cola. As they waited for Betty to serve Jack Woolley, two hooded youths burst in, one of them with a shotgun, and demanded the money from the till. Kate made a brave – if misguided – attempt to dodge out and sabotage their getaway car, but was manhandled back in by the thieves, and they were all held at gunpoint until the robbery was over. The shock was too much for Jack, who'd been fitted with a pacemaker, and he collapsed, unconscious, as the two men escaped with a meagre couple of hundred pounds and some cigarettes. Jack was rushed to hospital, and although he was lucky enough to make a good recovery, the crime stunned the whole village, and all of its victims were thoroughly traumatised. Kate blamed herself for taking Debbie into the shop, and worried her parents again when she became moody and withdrawn; Betty remained stressed and paranoid and needed emotional support from her husband Mike. But the one village resident who was to suffer the most was Susan Carter. Betty had thought that she recognised one of the thieves as Susan's brother, Clive Horrobin, and a few days after the robbery he was arrested and charged. Under questioning he admitted the crime and shopped his accomplice, Bruno. Susan – who

Neil and Susan Carter (Brian Hewlett and Charlotte Martin)

had been gently trying to distance herself from her dubious family background – was deeply shamed and mortified.

Far worse was to follow, however. In August, Clive escaped from a prison van while on remand, and a few days later he turned up in Susan's kitchen, asking her for money. Frightened and confused, Susan complied and let him go, without telling the police. Over the next few weeks she carried on sending him cash when asked, and in September he came back again asking for more money, and for her to help dye his hair. Although urging him to give himself up, she gave way once again, but this time Clive was forced to flee after being discovered by Neil. By the end of the month, Clive was in touch again, and pressured her into bringing his passport and some clothes to a Birmingham coach station. But his attempt to flee the country failed, and two weeks later he was re-arrested. Believing his sister had somehow betrayed him, he told the police that she'd helped him while on the run. On 21 October, Susan too was arrested and, when interviewed, she confessed the whole truth of her dealings with Clive. Although Mark initially thought the case against her was dubious, the CPS decided to prosecute, and she was charged with attempting to pervert the course of justice. She was tried along with Clive at Felpersham Assizes on 23 December. Clive was given seven years, and – to the surprise and horror of her friends and family – Susan was sent to prison for six months. She was taken straight down from the court to the cells. With little prospect of an appeal, it was a bleak Christmas for the Carter family.

Making Babies

Early in the year Shula and Mark were unavoidably reminded of their failed attempts to start a family when David and Ruth's first child, Philippa – or Pip, as she soon became known – was born on 17 February. Shula was touched when they asked her to be godmother, and it made her ever more determined to have a baby of her own by whatever means possible. After talking to Ambridge's new GP, Richard Locke, she and Mark decided to investigate the alternatives. So Shula began the round of preliminary X-rays, scans and tests. These confirmed that her remaining fallopian tube was blocked, and so her only option was to try IVF. The couple went to counselling sessions, and by the summer she was ready for her first implant.

In late June, came the happy news that Caroline was going to marry Ambridge's latest vicar, Robin Stokes. A part-time non-

(THE DOOR CRASHES OPEN)

BETTY What on (earth)— ?
CLIVE Lock the door!
BETTY What's going (on)?
(DOOR SLAMS TO. LATCH DROPPED)
CLIVE Shuddup! This thing's loaded.
JACK (WITTERING) Oh good grief, oh good heavens…
BRUNO You. Fill this bag with money.
BETTY But…
BRUNO Move it!
CLIVE Now! Start filling it. Money. Fags. Move!
JACK Do as he says Betty.
BRUNO Fast!
JACK (FAINT) Oh dear, oh no…
CLIVE Fill it now! Or I'll blast your head off!
BRUNO Keep your hands above the counter!
CLIVE You, you old git. Move over there. Keep an eye on him.
BRUNO Come on, Missus! You can move faster than that!

4. INT. TELEPHONE BOX. 5.57
(DEBBIE'S HITTING THE TELEPHONE)
DEBBIE I don't believe this! Look at it! It's wrecked.
KATE (OFF) Just dial 999! You don't need to put money in!
DEBBIE There's no sound. There's no signal.
(A SIGH. SHE'S ALMOST CRYING WITH FRUSTRATION) This is ridiculous! Stupid (HITTING IT) bloody machine…

Ruth with her newborn daughter, Pip

Celebrity Appearance:
1993 – Anneka Rice
did a 'Challenge
Anneka' on the
village hall

stipendiary minister, Robin also worked as a vet, and had come to the village after the break up of his marriage. In spite of her avowed agnosticism, Caroline had started going out with him after her bruising encounter with Cameron Fraser, and soon fallen in love. Their wedding was set for spring the next year. By the time the engagement was announced, Shula and Mark had some triumphant news of their own: Shula's implant had been successful, and she was pregnant. But their joy was short-lived; just a few days later she miscarried. As they adjusted to yet another bitter disappointment, they were told that she should wait until the autumn before the next implant. As the year went on, they found reasons to postpone the decision, and it was only after Christmas that they resolved to try again.

Silver Linings

After the trauma of her abortion, it had taken Elizabeth a while to find her feet again. She was supported by long-time admirer Nigel, who'd been there

*Caroline and Robin
Stokes (Tim Meats)*

for her all the while and given her a shoulder to cry on during her worst moments. In spite of some friction with Nigel's hard-drinking mother, Julia, she was now firmly established as the marketing manager of the recently formed Lower Loxley Corporate Entertainments. At the end of September, she and Nigel resumed their much-interrupted romance. Phil and Jill were delighted, but not so Julia, who made it quite clear that a mere Archer was no fit girlfriend for a Pargetter. Cameron's abrupt departure also made way for a new arrival, when the Estate was sold to a 62-year-old former Suffolk landowner, Guy Pemberton. In sharp contrast to smooth-talking fraudster Cameron, his tenants were relieved to find him a patrician of the old school, full of mannerly charm. From the start, he seemed keen to put down roots in his new community; one of his first ventures was to go into partnership with Sid Perks and buy The Bull from Peggy Woolley.

1994

Death and Life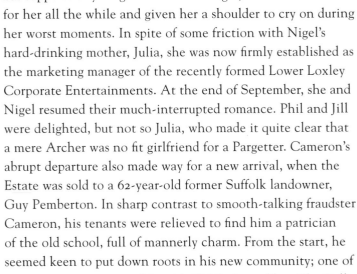

The year began full of hope and promise for Shula and Mark. Shula was to be Caroline's matron of honour at her marriage to Robin Stokes, which was set for 19 February. She and Mark also shared a closely guarded secret: just a few days before, Shula went to the fertility clinic in Borchester for her second round of IVF implants. Her sister Elizabeth, meanwhile, was holding on to a happy secret of her own. Her renewed liaison with Nigel had blossomed, and early in the New Year he'd gone down on his knees and made a thoroughly romantic proposal, which she'd accepted. Knowing that they'd face determined opposition from Julia, they decided to postpone the announcement until after Caroline's wedding.

But fate was soon to deal a shattering blow to Shula's life, and to the lives of all those around her. On the afternoon of 17 February, she was home at Glebe Cottage organising a modest hen party that she'd planned for Caroline, helped by Nigel and Elizabeth. Debbie meanwhile had persuaded Caroline to take a break from wedding plans and come with her for a ride. As the two of them rode down a narrow lane, a speeding car spooked Caroline's horse, and she was badly thrown. A moment later Mark, on his way home from work, swerved to avoid her, and his car hit a tree, killing him instantly.

Although the immediate sympathy from family and friends centered on the grief-stricken Shula, the tragedy had repercussions for many of those around her. Caroline

With this ring: Nigel and Elizabeth finally share their vows

was badly injured and lay unconscious in hospital for over a week, her marriage to Robin postponed indefinitely. For Phil it brought back painful memories of Grace's death, almost forty years before. As Shula's initial terrible shock and disbelief slowly faded into a sense of numb acceptance, she somehow found the courage to stay on alone at Glebe Cottage and try to rebuild her life. In a bittersweet twist of fate, she was sustained by the awareness that she was, at last, expecting the child she and Mark had so longed for – although he had died without ever knowing it. She also found increasing comfort in Nigel's loyal friendship and support. He and Elizabeth had shelved any idea of announcing their engagement, and Nigel became a frequent visitor to Glebe Cottage where he spent time keeping Shula company and doing odd chores. Elizabeth was at first understanding, but as time went on – well aware of the long history between her sister and her fiancé – she found it hard to take. When Nigel turned to Shula for advice over a medieval banquet, Elizabeth finally lost her patience and walked out on him. A week later, however, they were back together, and they were married on 29 September. Richard Locke was best man, Debbie, Kate and Alice bridesmaids, and the reception was at Brookfield. Julia remained haughtily disapproving right up to the end, but her snobbishness was rudely debunked by her sister Ellen, who turned up at the wedding and revealed

JILL	But look ... oh look Phil! (BABY CRIES) Isn't he just lovely?!
SHULA	I'd like to introduce Daniel Mark Archer Hebden. Weighing 7 pounds 12 ounces.
JILL	Daniel. (OVERCOME) Oh, Shula...
SHULA	Daniel, this is your granny and grandad.
PHIL	(LAUGHS) I think he's smiling.
JILL	(EMOTIONAL) Look at those little fingers. And hasn't he got a lot of hair!
SHULA	(HAPPILY) And blue eyes, like Mark.
PHIL	He's beautiful.
JILL	He's gorgeous. Aren't you, Daniel? (HAPPY NOISE) Yes you are! Oh Shula... I'm so happy for you! He's just... perfect!
SHULA	Yes... (CRIES) Yes Mum... he's perfect! (CRIES) And very precious!

the truth about Julia's own humble origins – her father had been a greengrocer, and her real name was Joan.

In contrast to Nigel and Elizabeth's happiness, there was to be no wedding for Caroline and Robin. As she began to recover, her agnosticism made it difficult for her to square Mark's apparently random and meaningless death with Robin's Christian faith, and this difference was a factor in their eventual decision to end the relationship.

By the autumn, although coping with the day-to-day business of life, Shula was still struggling to come to terms with her grief. On 14 November, with Caroline at her side, she gave birth to a baby boy, Daniel. Although her joy was inevitably tempered by the continuing sadness of her loss, she now at least had the consolation of being a mother to the son that Mark would never know.

TB at Brookfield

In the aftermath of Mark's tragic death, Brookfield was soon facing a very different kind of crisis. In March, Robin found a suspected TB reactor among the dairy herd. Although the tests were inconclusive, another reactor was confirmed in May. The infected cow was slaughtered, and a movement order imposed on the farm, which meant that none of its stock – including calves that would normally be sold – could leave the premises. So began a stressful few months for all at Brookfield. Phil, David and Ruth could only wait and pray that there would be no more reactors, but their hopes were dashed in July when another two were confirmed. There were also problems for Jill when some of her B&B guests, worried by the TB rumours, cancelled their bookings. Neighbouring farms were tested, including Tony's herd and Brian's deer, but were found to be clear. Meanwhile the steady toll of reactors mounted at Brookfield. By the time their last was confirmed at the end of the summer, they had lost eleven cows, or ten per cent of their entire herd. The Divisional Veterinary Officer suspected that badgers might have been the source of the outbreak, but this was impossible to prove. Although compensated for the slaughtered cows, the financial loss for the business was substantial. The movement order stayed in place until the end of the year, costing them £7,000 in feed and labour for the rearing of the fifty extra calves. All in all, 1994 was a year that all at Brookfield were glad to put behind them.

Cousin Trouble

After leaving Brymore School, Pat and Tony's eldest son John had shown himself determined to take charge of his own career. Instead of staying to help Tony at Bridge Farm, he'd turned his back on organics and signed up for a year's work experience at Home Farm, hoping to learn more about intensive farming. Keeping his options firmly open, however, he also began his own business rearing conservation-grade pork. Now just 18, he also kept up his on/off flirtation with 22-year-old Sharon Richards, who was working for Pat at the dairy. He was a big hit with Sharon's daughter Kylie, and gained further kudos by becoming the first winner of the single-wicket cricket trophy that Shula had donated in memory of Mark. As the summer wore on, Pat was worried that he was seeing too much of Sharon – a suspicion confirmed when she came home from a two-week holiday and discovered Sharon's knickers in his bed. Although Tony was more lenient, Pat was dead against her son getting involved with an older woman and single mum. John cheerfully ignored her and went on seeing Sharon. In October, there was a big row after John gave Sharon a driving lesson and she crashed into Peggy's car. As a result, he stormed out and moved in with Sharon on The Green. But this cosy co-habitation soon soured, and by the end of the month Sharon had left to take up a job in Leeds.

Not to be outdone, his cousin Kate Aldridge was also giving her parents a few sleepless nights. She skipped her GCSE revision to go to a folk festival where she fell in with a hippie crowd, and more trips to festivals followed. After predictably bad exam results, Brian talked her into retaking them next year at Borchester Tech. She reluctantly agreed, but on the August bank holiday she disappeared along with the day's takings from the riding course. Hearing nothing from her for several days, Jennifer called in the police, and so began her and Brian's long and heartbreaking search for their errant daughter. They heard some news of her movements from her traveller friend, Spike, and later in the autumn a girl called Zoe arrived at Home Farm, claiming she could help them find her. Zoe, however, turned out to be no friend of Kate's at all, but a hippie scamster who conned cash from them before disappearing. As the end of the year approached, Kate showed no signs of coming home. In December, after visiting the Smithfield show, Jennifer in desperation spent time searching the shabbier areas of Kings Cross in the vain hope of finding her missing daughter.

Sharon Richards and John Archer (Celia Nelson and Sam Barriscale)

Father and Son

After her break-up with Robin Stokes, Caroline had found herself attracted to the more mature charms of new estate owner Guy Pemberton. In spite of the difference in their ages – he was in his early 60s, she approaching 40 – romance soon followed, to the disappointment of Marjorie Antrobus, who had become rather fond of Guy herself. In January, after Guy had a bad fall on the Home Farm riding course and broke his pelvis, she moved into the Dower House to care for him. It was then that she had her first encounter with Guy's son Simon, when he came down from Leamington to visit his father. Never one for social niceties, Simon made it clear from the start that he resented her place in Guy's life. His distinct lack of people

1995

Profile
SUSAN CARTER

CHARLOTTE MARTIN, PhD, SIPS an Americano in a bustling coffee bar looking like the kind of woman that Susan Carter might aspire to be. She'd notice the crisp white blouse, the stylishly cut hair and the easy manner. Unlike Susan, Charlotte didn't just work for a doctor; she is a doctor. Not a GP, mind, but a research psychologist. She loves eating out at one or another of the restaurants on her doorstep – one of them with a Michelin star, if you please – and lives with husband Ian, a teacher, and their two daughters, 14 and 10, just down the road from a top-of-the-range supermarket. 'We call it the village shop,' she says with a chuckle.

What would Susan make of that?

'The knowledge that she was shopping in the kind of place where people like Jennifer Aldridge might go would appeal, even if the prices wouldn't.'

Perhaps you don't need a PhD in psychology to work that one out. But as someone who's been Susan's alter ego since the early 1980s, Charlotte knows her better than most. She's in her early 40s and therefore slightly younger than her character. A 'townie', what's more, living in a Victorian villa in a prosperous part of Birmingham.

'I know people criticise Susan for trying to better herself,' Charlotte muses, 'but she's doing it for the family, trying to give them the life that she never had. She's always had to fight to get away from her upbringing. What I don't like about her is that she's very judgemental. But again that's part of her upbringing. The scriptwriters understand that very well, and I've been very lucky with the storylines that have come my way.'

The biggest came in 1993. After trying to protect delinquent brother Clive from the consequences of an armed raid on the shop she managed (full-time in those days), Susan spent Christmas as a guest of Her Majesty. 'Radio can be challenging because the listener can't see your expressions and everything has to go into the voice,' Charlotte reflects. 'Joining *The Archers* was a massive learning curve for me. Before that I'd done mainly theatre and television.' *Crossroads*, since you ask. Oh yes, *Boon* and *Howard's Way* as well. She also played the voice of a spaceship computer in a sci-fi series called *Jupiter's Moon* and once appeared in a UB40 video.

None of which quite prepares you for playing a terrified mother-of-two facing a spell in choky. But, hey, she's an actress. That's what they do. She didn't feel the need to immerse herself in the role by spending a short holiday in Holloway. All the more remarkable, then, that while Susan was inside, Charlotte was invited to appear on a daytime chat show to talk about women in prison. She declined. 'Fantasy and reality were becoming too blurred,' she recalls. 'I didn't know anything about prison and felt I had no right to sit discussing the subject with women who did.'

Her own life experiences have been comparatively comfortable. She was born in Fontainebleu, near Paris. Her father

> 'Radio can be challenging because the listener can't see your expressions and everything has to go into your voice.'

was a naval officer attached to NATO headquarters but, when she was 2, he returned to the English Midlands to run the family building firm. Charlotte and her sister were brought up in a well-appointed semi in affluent Solihull. 'Mum and Dad had a lot of Shirley Bassey records and, as a child, I learnt them off by heart, dressed up and strutting around to them,' she recalls. 'I loved the theatricality of those songs. But when I started buying my own music, I was into punk. I remember trying to sneak out to a gig one night wearing a bin liner. My mum dragged me back in the house.'

Charlotte smiles at the memory and takes another sip of coffee before explaining why, five years ago, an established radio actress and busy mother-of-two should start a psychology degree at Birmingham University. With the doctorate under her belt, indeed, she's now embarked on NHS-sponsored research into psychosis. 'Don't forget that *The Archers* only takes up six days of the month,' she says, 'and that's when I'm in it. So I have time for other things. I think psychology and acting are closely related. In fact, I find it useful to be able to stand back and look at Susan from a different perspective,' she adds before draining her cup and setting off towards the upmarket emporium otherwise known as the 'village shop'.

Profile

CAMILLA FISHER

ARCHERS ARCHIVIST CAMILLA FISHER is a walking encyclopaedia on Ambridge, the characters who live there and the ones who died there. She can go back – way back – to the days when Tony Archer was knee-high to Tom Forrest's gundog. And even before that. What's not in her head can be instantly brought up on the computer system that she began updating soon after joining the programme in 1994.

Tom, his sister Doris and brother-in-law Dan are also embalmed in rows of drawers that open as smoothly as any pull-out mortuary slab. Storylines are neatly filed away in card indexes going right back to 1951. Here's one, plucked at random from 1968. It turned out to be a day of mixed fortunes for Dan Archer: first he jumped into a slurry pit to save a heifer that had fallen in; then a cow fell on top of him. Mercifully, he had recovered enough by the evening to receive, with his good arm, an award from the National Farmers' Union.

The drawers also harbour photographs of every character, living and dead. 'These are the very dead,' says Camilla, pulling open a black file. Out spill pictures of Gwen Berryman, who played Doris. Here's Gwen in her prime, treading the boards in Blackpool. (*Archers* actors have always had a life outside Ambridge.) And here's somebody – her father or grandfather? – in glorious sepia outside the family boot repairers in Wolverhampton.

Who could have imagined that the woman who transformed herself into the nation's best-known farmer's wife for nigh-on thirty years hailed from the Black Country? But then it's also a rum thought that Ambridge, the fictional heart of rural England, should be so meticulously catalogued, as though it were a real place, here in the Mail Box in the centre of Birmingham.

The daughter of a GP, Camilla was born and has lived most of her 56 years in the city. 'I'm a Brummie,' she beams in an accent that, nonetheless, veers more towards Caroline Sterling than Vicky Tucker. She lives in an upmarket suburb and comes to work most days in an inflatable boat with husband Tony at the tiller. Their garden backs on to the Birmingham-Worcester Canal. There's a picture of it over the archivist's computer, looking very rustic, like one imagines the banks of the Am.

The Am, Lakey Hill, Grange Farm and Grundy's Field are all mapped out in her head (as well as on the back of her door). Her job is to ensure that the programme is rooted in time and space. She sits in on the twice-yearly meetings where long-term storylines are discussed and is there to ensure that writers' flights of fancy don't take them too far from rural reality. 'That's what makes us different from other long-term series,' she muses. 'Stories become more believable because they're rooted in an area, rooted in a family, rooted in a character.'

Rooted, too, in the realities of rural England. It was Camilla's suggestion, for instance, to have a storyline around Helen Archer beating off fierce competition to move in to the flat over the village shop. 'In the real world many young people can't find places to live in the villages where they were born,' she points out. 'So this was a good way of bringing in an overlooked space that I was aware of and getting the writers to weave a story around it.'

She cites Helen's father, Tony, as an example of the need to remain rooted in character. 'It would be difficult to come up with a storyline that he had been transformed into a lothario like Brian.' The archivist pauses and ponders for a moment. 'I suppose he could have an affair, but listeners would find it difficult to believe because, in some cases, they feel as though they've known him all their lives. He's in sight of his 60th birthday, yet he's been with the programme since birth.'

Or at least since he was knee-high to Tom Forrest's gundog.

> 'Stories become more believable because they're rooted in an area, rooted in a family, rooted in a character…'

skills soon had wider repercussions around the village; although Guy and his son had strong issues of their own, he put Simon in charge of the Estate while he recovered. One of Simon's first moves was to consider suing Brian for Guy's fall on the riding course. Also in the firing line was Susan Carter, now back at the Estate office and struggling to rebuild her life after her release from prison the previous year. Simon was unhappy about her criminal record and critical of her administrative skills. He also made an enemy of the Estate dairy manager, Geoff Williams – who eventually resigned – and installed smarmy yes-man Graham Ryder as Estate Manager to cover for Shula's maternity leave. By late spring, Simon had become a figure of hate to Guy's tenants and generally disliked around the village. Relations with his father only worsened when, in May, Guy and Caroline announced their engagement.

One of the few people to sense a more sympathetic side to Simon's character was Shula. Although she was sceptical at first, when she returned to work at the Estate,

Guy Pemberton (Hugh Dickson) with fiancée Caroline

Simon turned out to have a surprisingly natural way with baby Daniel. He and Shula got on well enough for her to ask him over to dinner, and then to a barbecue at Brookfield (only for him to row with David). When Shula had a false meningitis scare with Daniel, Simon took her into casualty and supported her while her son was tested. They were soon close enough for Simon to confide some of the reasons behind his difficult relationship with Guy, saying that he'd always felt upstaged by his elder brother Andrew, who'd been killed in a car crash, and that Guy had never supported him in his chosen career as an engineer. She sometimes found his easiness with Daniel difficult – knowing he could never take Mark's place as his father – but when Guy and Caroline were married on 11 September, she was there to help him through what was a difficult occasion for him. Soon after, he took her out for a romantic dinner and when they got back to Glebe Cottage he kissed her – the first time she'd allowed herself to kiss another man since Mark's death. So it was understandable that she felt confused and let down when he announced a few days after that he was going to Dubai for a business trip. While he was away he kept in touch and sent her orchids, and – in spite of Jill's continuing doubts about his character – when he returned in December, Shula was there to pick him up from the airport. Before Christmas he asked her to spend New Year with him in Amsterdam. Shula thought hard for a few days, and then said yes.

Fascist Roy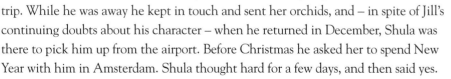

Much to the relief of her parents, Kate Aldridge eventually returned from her travels in March, fresh from an anti-road protest camp in Kent. Jennifer was so terrified of losing her again that there were few repercussions, in spite of Debbie's fury at the way she'd behaved. Although Kate had had a boyfriend, Luther, on her travels, she was now single again and in April her eye was caught by one of Ambridge's fittest lads, 17-year-old Roy Tucker. Roy quite fancied her too, and they started going out together, although it soon emerged that they had very different tastes in friends. He wasn't too sure about the flaky hippie types she hung out with, while she was correspondingly dubious about some of his shaven-headed, lager-drinking mates. In the event, both were proved right, but it was Roy's naivety that was to land him in the deepest trouble.

It all began in February, when GP Richard Locke was outbid by Usha Gupta for Blossom Hill Cottage. He took her out for a peacemaking meal, but on the way out she was mugged and her bag was stolen. Richard was there to rescue her and take her home, but this proved to be the first of several racist attacks she suffered. In early March someone threw a stone through her window; a week or so later her car was broken into, and then in April her house was trashed and smeared with racist slogans. By this time, she and Richard had grown closer, and he moved into her spare room at Blossom Hill. In spite of this, and the ongoing police investigation, the attacks continued. Dog excrement was pushed through her letterbox, and then – far more seriously – two lads on a motorbike threw acid in her face. Mercifully her injuries were superficial, but by this time she felt she'd had enough, and put the Cottage on the market.

Brian and Jennifer with troublesome teenager Kate (Kellie Bright)

While all this was going on, Kate was getting seriously worried about what Roy was up to at his mysterious meetings with his thuggish mates. He pretended they were planning minor burglaries, but the truth was that he'd got in deep with a right-wing crowd, led by a couple of violent racists called Spanner and Craven. It was this unsavoury pair who'd been responsible for the racist attacks on Usha. Disgusted by the reality of the attacks, Roy tried to pull out, but it was too late for that; the fascists trashed Mike's market garden at Willow Farm in retribution, doing several hundred pounds' worth of damage to his newly established pick-your-own business. After this Kate was finally able to persuade Roy to go to the police and come clean about the whole sordid affair. As a result of shopping his former mates, he was badly beaten up by some of their associates, and his motorbike wrecked. At the trial in October, Spanner and Craven were handed long prison sentences but, thanks to his cooperation, Roy was let off with a caution. He tried to apologise to Usha for his involvement, but – in spite of Richard's attempts to mediate – she found it hard to forgive him. Richard, however, told her he loved her and wanted to share his life with her, and she returned his feelings. Blossom Hill Cottage was taken off the market.

1996

Grief and Brutality

After their New Year's trip to Amsterdam, Shula and Simon seemed to be getting on as well as ever. In January they went to Derbyshire, where he taught her some of the basics of his rock-climbing hobby. Later in the month, however, he had to spend some time in London in connection – or so he said – with his irrigation business. Soon after, Guy overheard him on the phone to an old flame called Harriet. When challenged by his father, Simon claimed that her marriage had hit a rocky patch, and he was merely providing her with some emotional support. Caroline – who made no secret of her own loathing for Simon – was immediately suspicious. She wasn't convinced by Simon's excuses when he stood Shula up on Valentine's Day, and then found out that he'd lied to her about his reasons for breaking a dinner engagement. Guy continued to give his son the benefit of the doubt, however, and Caroline held back from sharing her suspicions with Shula. This became much harder for her when, towards the end of February, she saw Simon secretly seeing off Harriet at Hollerton Junction. When Guy went to confront his son at his flat in Leamington, there was a big row between them. Simon was unrepentant, admitting that he was still seeing Harriet, whose marriage was now on the point of breaking up.

Before Caroline could find a way to break the news to Shula, Guy had a sudden heart attack. Although he recovered, a week later he had another, fatal, attack. His marriage to Caroline had lasted barely seven months. In the aftermath, Caroline was too preoccupied with her own grief to worry about much else. Simon, while dealing with his own grief and guilt over his rift with his father, found secret consolation in Harriet's company. This didn't stop him overruling Caroline's plans for the funeral. She also blamed him for shortening Guy's life, and their relationship sank to a new low. When Shula tried to defend Simon's attitude to his father, Caroline finally lost her self-control and told her all about his affair with Harriet. Shula was slowly forced to face up to the truth about his deception, in spite of Simon's attempt to persuade her that he'd been innocently helping Harriet through her marriage break-up. When she finally confronted him he lost his cool and hit her in the face. Although the assault caused her no great injury, it gave Shula a glimpse of Simon's true nature and marked the decisive end of their relationship. In spite of this, she doggedly kept on with her job at the Estate, thwarting Simon's attempts to sack Susan, and mediating in his rows with his tenants, the Grundys.

She also found support in her friendship with Ambridge's new female vicar, Janet Fisher. A former nurse, Janet took on St Stephen's after a merger of the local parishes. Although she was generally a popular figure, not everyone in Ambridge was happy to worship under a female priest. It took Susan Carter a long time to get used to the idea; Peggy Woolley voted with her feet and began attending All Saints in Borchester.

Ambridge Brat Pack

Brian and Jennifer's year started ominously when, on New Year's Day, they found Kate unconscious at her cottage after overdosing on a mix of whisky and Temazepam. Although she recovered after a few hours in hospital, it was a salutory warning. The drugs were a Christmas present from her friend and lodger, Jolyon Gibson, ex-public schoolboy and small-time drug dealer. Although she insisted it was a purely platonic friendship, Gibson's arrival on the scene had caused trouble between her and Roy. She told him she accidentally OD'd after being left alone and depressed on New Year's Eve. Soon after she gave Gibson his marching orders, after making sure he'd paid his rent up to date. Not before time; a few weeks later he was arrested and charged for drug dealing. Kate and Roy soon made up, and in June went to a local Fleadh where they got interested in the alternative food scene. From this came the inspiration for their travelling falafel business, 'Pulsations'. Kate blagged a loan from Peggy, and in July she and Roy kitted out a van and set off on a tour of the music festivals. This idealistic venture collapsed in September when the van broke down and they couldn't afford the repairs. Roy's flirtation with the local counter-culture finally ended when he enrolled on an accountancy and finance course at Felpersham University. Over the autumn he and Kate drifted apart, and by the end of the year they had decided to end the relationship.

At Bridge Farm, John's love life was also keeping him busy. After his break-up with Sharon, he'd taken up with a lively Brummie called Hayley Jordan. A city girl to the core, Hayley's introduction to country life had not been painless; after learning the hard way what wellies are for, she'd then been chased by a heifer at Lower Loxley. She'd stuck with it all the same, and she and John were soon a fairly established item. Recently qualified as a nursery nurse, in the autumn she'd left Birmingham and begun her first child-minding job in Waterly Cross. Although very fond of John, she had few illusions about his capacity for everlasting fidelity. This being a leap year, on 29 February she ambushed him with a carefully staged – but mischievous – proposal. It didn't quite go to plan, as he was drunk enough at the time to accept, and it was a few days before the misunderstanding was cleared up. As the year went on, he took advantage of her good nature by getting her to look after his pigs while he was busy at Home Farm. Although she was willing to put up with this, she found his genetically programmed weakness for other girls harder to take. After a difficult holiday in Corfu, they had a big row and broke up, only to make up again two weeks later. After that he was more considerate, she stuck by him and they were still going strong at the end of the year.

The Evil Landlord

Over the past year, the Grundys' dire financial situation had reached crisis point. Eddie's attempt to make a quick buck selling personalised number

1997

Shula and Daniel

plates had backfired after one of them was linked to a forged registration document. Clarrie was exhausting herself by taking on as much extra work as she could find. Their landlord Simon Pemberton had already made up his mind that Grange Farm wasn't viable, and the sooner he could get rid of his feckless tenants, the better. His case was strengthened when a disastrous fire burnt down the Grundys' milking parlour, killing thirty-four of their cattle and destroying their tractor and other equipment. Joe and Eddie were under-insured, and in spite of Eddie's valiant attempts to restock with a dozen Jersey cows, their prospects were bleak. Simon had already decided that the fire was the result of their own neglect, and issued them with a notice to quit for breaching their tenancy. Eddie was determined to fight and the case was referred to the Agricultural Lands Tribunal. Shula finally gave up her job at the Estate (narrowly pre-empting Mr Rodway's decision to remove her) but continued in her unofficial support for the Grundys.

Simon – after the violent end to his relationship with Shula – began to pay attention to Debbie Aldridge. She had few illusions about his unscrupulous character, but admired his progressive attitude to farming. The physical chemistry between them proved stronger than her doubts, and they were soon involved in an affair. The Grundys' tribunal hearing was set for 1 April. They took advice from the Tenants Association and were pleased when Mike agreed to be their farming witness. The case was already leading to trouble between Simon and Brookfield. David still had the contract to farm the Estate land, but when he refused to give evidence against the Grundys, Simon promptly cancelled it. In spite of his underhand dealings, on the day of the tribunal the Grundys triumphed; the eviction notice was overturned and they kept Grange Farm.

This proved to be a turning point for Simon's fortunes. Furious with the result of the tribunal, he accused Debbie of siding with his tenants. She decided that she'd had enough of him, but the break-up proved even more traumatic for her than it had been for Shula. Simon lost control and beat her savagely. Although she was – at first – reluctant to report him, when Shula told her about Simon's previous violence to her, Debbie was finally persuaded to go to the police. Simon was arrested in Leamington and charged with the offence. At his trial in June he pleaded guilty. The court, however, accepted his plea that he was 'under stress' at the time, and to general dismay he escaped with a fine of only £200. It did nevertheless mark the end of his connections with Ambridge. Soon after, he left on a trip to the Middle East, and the Estate was put up for sale. It's safe to assume that no one was sorry to see him go.

The sale of the Estate was to have long-lasting repercussions. David and Ruth were keen to lease the non-tenanted land and expand the dairy herd. Phil was cautious, and while he hesitated, Brian trumped them all by purchasing the land in partnership with a mysterious consortium. Once again Pat and Tony faced the daunting task of raising a mortgage to buy Bridge Farm, but soon discovered that Brian's consortium – now established as Borsetshire Land – had also bought the tenanted farms. So Tony was faced with the depressing prospect of seeing a part of his annual rent go to line the pockets of his wealthy brother-in-law at Home Farm.

Ruth in the milking parlour

The Brat Pack Moves On

The year began with John and Hayley's relationship taking another step forward. On Valentine's night, John – in what was, for him, an unusually romantic gesture – took her out for a meal, told how much he loved her, and said that he wanted them to live together. Hayley didn't need asking twice and soon took a fancy to April Cottage which had been empty since the recent death of Martha Woodford. In spite of doubts from both his parents and his grandmother, Peggy, they persuaded Jack Woolley to lease them the cottage and they moved into their new love nest in March. Sadly their domestic bliss wasn't to last for very long. In August, shortly before John was to appear in Lynda Snell's open air production of *A Midsummer Night's Dream*, Sharon returned to the village and came to Bridge Farm to see him. In her shamelessly seductive presence, John forgot his loyalty to Hayley and was soon sneaking off for secret liaisons with his old flame. This diversion ended abruptly in November when Hayley surprised them together at the cottage. She knew better than to believe John's feeble excuses; she packed her bags on the spot and went home to Brum. Abandoned and remorseful, John went up there and made a pathetic attempt to win her back, but she wasn't having it. By Christmas, it looked as if he'd lost her for good. There were to be no more passionate moments with Sharon, either. Rejected by an angry John, by the following spring she had taken daughter Kylie back to Leeds. John never saw her again.

After their break-up before the previous Christmas, by the summer Kate and Roy had made up and were getting on well enough to play Helena and Lysander

Profile
ROY TUCKER

THERE AREN'T TOO MANY pubs with striking works of art on the walls. But there is one in Ringwood, Hampshire, run by a publican who once played Hamlet 113 times for the Oxford Stage Company and still found time to audition for the role of Roy Tucker in *The Archers*. Ian Pepperell is evidently a cultured man. Colourful abstracts by the French artist Pascal Magis adorn the front bar.

'I like these as well,' says Ian, pointing out works by a Portuguese sculptor who specialises in recycling French road signs of the 1950s. 'That's an old Michelin sign made into a star,' he adds before chuckling good-naturedly at the suggestion that it's the nearest his pub is going to get to a Michelin star.

Grey Gables it ain't. Instead it's a traditional 400-year-old inn offering 'Oriental cuisine' from two Thai chefs as well as an impressive range of real ales. As usual, Ian has been up since six cooking full English breakfasts for the guests occupying eight en-suite bedrooms. And what time does he usually get to bed? 'Around one o'clock,' he says nonchalantly. 'I'm always on the go. That's why I'm built like a racing snake – not much more than nine and a half stone ringing wet.'

He was born in Oxford forty years ago and grew up in Ringwood, the son of a company director and a nurse. He excelled in drama at the local comprehensive and won a place at the Webber Douglas Academy of Dramatic Art. 'I worked in this pub whenever I came back home,' he recalls. 'And when I left London for good around ten years ago, I was offered the chance to manage the place and then take over the lease.'

So how does he manage to fit in his other life as an actor?

'Well, it has put paid to my theatre work,' he concedes. 'But *The Archers* is far easier because you're up in Birmingham recording for only a few days a month when you're lucky enough to be in the script.' He has grown to love a programme with which he was barely acquainted when he first had the chance to audition for the role of Roy. 'I remember meeting Jack May [Nelson Gabriel] who asked me, "What else are you doing at the moment?" and I told him I was playing Hamlet. "Marvellous," he said. "Have a cigarette." We weren't supposed to smoke around the studios, but Jack could get away with most things.'

Ian evidently has an affectionate regard for the old troupers of the trade. 'Margot Boyd was fabulous,' he enthuses. 'She was over 90 when she finally bowed out as Marjorie Antrobus, and I used to push her around in her wheelchair. She said she liked playing opposite me because she could always hear what I was saying.' He pauses before adding: 'One of the great things about *The Archers* is the vast age range of the characters. We have a comparatively new Phoebe [Lucy Morris], aged 14, and she's brilliant.'

> 'One of the great things about *The Archers* is the vast age range of the characters.'

Ian and his wife Nikki don't have any children themselves, but they do have Basil, a somewhat boisterous dog that looks as though it might have come out of a subterranean lair in the New Forest. 'He's like a cross between a bat, a rat and a meerkat,' Ian laughs while Basil snuffles around our ankles. Nikki, meanwhile, is preparing for the lunchtime rush. *Archers* fans tend to visit the pub from all over the country and she has learnt to smile wanly when guests gush: 'Oh, you must be Hayley.'

Cast members come to visit as well when they happen to be in the vicinity. 'Terry Molloy [Mike Tucker] popped in for a drink the other day,' Ian confides before going on to recall their first meeting either side of a microphone. 'Bearing in mind that I'd never heard Mike speak before, I was taken aback when Terry went from his quite posh voice into this broad accent. I had to readjust very quickly and play Roy the way that country people talk around here. But I posh him up a bit when he's at Grey Gables.'

Like Roy, Ian knows all about the demands of paying guests. 'I think I'm like him in some ways,' the actor muses. After all, one manages a country-house hotel, the other a country-town pub – albeit one with French abstracts and recycled French road signs on the walls.

Profile
HELEN ARCHER

LOUIZA PATIKAS BECAME USED to village life from an early age. Greek village life, as it happens. 'We used to decamp to a village in the Peloponnese for weekends and holidays,' she says in the voice of the very English Helen Archer. 'It was pretty basic in those days. We had to go to the well to get water. But I'm really a city girl, brought up in Athens. The smell of car pollution laced with jasmine is heaven to me, and I can't sleep without the sound of honking car horns.'

Just as well, then, that she now lives in West London. Not much jasmine but plenty of traffic. Her father is Greek and her mother English. 'She's one of the few surviving fluent speakers of Esperanto,' the actress reveals after slipping into one of the few remaining seats in a bustling café just down the road from her flat in a road of substantial and elegant Victorian villas. Mum is looking after her baby in the meantime.

Little Demitri – 'he's named after my dad' – was conceived in the normal way with Louiza's husband Jonny, another actor who has been appearing in a Tom Stoppard play at the National Theatre. Demitri is only a few weeks old when we meet. 'I could count the hours of sleep I've had in the past fortnight on two hands,' confides the woman whose alter ego in *The Archers* is currently pregnant by an anonymous sperm donor. Well, at least she'll have some insight into how Helen might feel during the early stages of motherhood.

New Year, new Archer? 'Yes, there'll be no husband to give the baby another name. It's great to have such a storyline put my way,' she enthuses. What Dan and Doris would have made of it we can only speculate. Sixty years ago, the first episode of *The Archers* opened with Dan fretting over another imminent birth. Whether Daffodil was pregnant by artificial insemination is another matter for speculation. Certainly it was not a procedure considered for human beings. Not in Ambridge anyway.

All Louiza knows is that Helen has 'pressed what my friends call the baby button'. In other words, she wants a child desperately – 'and she's very determined'. At the same time, Helen is not exactly enamoured with men right now. 'She certainly seems to pick them,' the actress says, shaking her head and rolling her eyes. 'Greg and she were essentially well suited, but he was a problematic man.' Indeed. 'As for Ross and Leon, they were absolute duds. I'd like to think that my radar is slightly better than hers.'

But are there any similarities between actress and character? 'I'd like to say the cleanliness,' she laughs, 'but you'd be horrified if you saw my flat.' And do you enjoy food and cooking? 'Oh, yes. But I'm quite chaotic in the kitchen. Jonny is far more efficient.' She pauses for a moment before going on to say: 'Like Helen, I'm very loyal to my family, but we don't have much else in common. The scriptwriters have created quite a complex character. She can be quite

> 'The scriptwriters have created quite a complex character. She can be quite gauche, not at all cool.'

gauche, not at all cool. But however vulnerable she is in her personal life, she can be tough in business and quite brusque at times.'

Certainly Helen brusquely showed Hayley the door to Bridge Farm when she came back from college to join the family business. 'You can't blame me for that,' Louiza insists. 'I wasn't playing Helen at the time. But whenever I meet listeners, they still bring up the eviction of Saint Hayley.'

As it happens, she's a close friend of Lucy Davis, Jasper Carrott's daughter, who played Hayley before her screen commitments took her out of *The Archers*' orbit. Louiza has other acting commitments, too. But, like the farmers she has encountered at events organised through the organic movement, she has felt the need to diversify. Travel writing is something of a passion. She speaks fluent French and Italian, as well as Greek, and writes for the British Airways magazine *Highlife*, among others. 'I've also taken a course on fashion journalism,' she says. 'I had my first spread in the *Telegraph* the other day and I'm into styling.' Come again? 'I'm a personal shopper for people who want advice on how to re-style their wardrobes.' A bit like Trinny and Susannah? 'Yes, only I hope I'm a bit nicer about it.'

That's not difficult to believe.

Proud parents Ruth and David at Josh's baptism with vicar Janet Fisher (Moir Leslie)

1998

in Lynda's production. But Kate had more important things on her mind than amateur dramatics. In July she joined a protest camp with her friend Spike and other eco-warriors who were determined to stop a wood being felled to widen the Borchester bypass. This wasn't really Roy's scene, and he kept his distance as Kate and her comrades dug in and built tree houses. He was also unsettled by the arrival of Kate's old traveller friend, Luther – in spite of Kate's insistence that he was only there to fight for the cause. The protesters found some support in Ambridge, most notably from seasoned campaigner Lynda Snell. When a big protest demonstration got out of hand, both Lynda and Marjorie Antrobus found themselves whisked off in police vans along with the rest, to be let off with a caution. Although the road scheme went ahead regardless, Kate was satisfied that the protesters had fought valiantly and made their point. But the strain of it all proved too much for her relationship with Roy, and they parted again. Luther moved on to carry the fight to Manchester airport, and Kate was single again – but not quite alone. Late in November she shared an uneasy secret with Debbie: she was pregnant.

Bridge Farm Tragedy

In the first few weeks of the New Year, rumours of Kate's pregnancy began to spread. Jennifer's first reaction was to suggest an abortion, but Kate angrily insisted that she wanted to keep the baby. When Hayley let slip the news to Roy, he went straight round to see Kate, but she told him that he wasn't the father – it was Luther. Roy didn't see how she could be so sure. He demanded a DNA test when the baby was born, but she insisted it wasn't his, and told him to get lost. Roy did, but stayed convinced that he was the father, whatever she claimed.

John, meanwhile, had spent Christmas pining for his lost love Hayley, who still hadn't forgiven him for his two-timing with Sharon. But when Roy took Hayley out for Valentine's Day, she spent the whole time talking about John. When John heard about this he found the courage to take her out on Shrove Tuesday, when he presented her with a ring and asked her to marry him. Confused about her feelings, she said she did still love him, but gently turned him down. She never had the chance to change her mind. The day after, Tony rowed with John after he was late back to feed the pigs, and still had a fence to mend. As their main tractor was out of action, John set off in a huff on their old cableless Fergie. A short while later – after he hadn't turned up for his brother Tommy's 17th birthday tea – Tony and Tommy found him underneath the tractor, which had rolled over and killed him.

His death was a stunning blow to the whole family. Although the official verdict confirmed it as an accident, Tony blamed himself for the row. John's sister Helen bottled up her grief, and after the funeral she returned to her farming course at Reaseheath. But it was perhaps Pat who found it hardest to take. Although she threw herself into her work, as the summer approached she was still struggling to come to terms with the tragedy.

The accident left Hayley devastated; she felt guilty too, worrying that by turning down his proposal she'd somehow been responsible for his death. Determined to keep his pig business alive, she helped to persuade Tommy to join with her and take it on, and he dropped out of his A level course to sign up instead at the local agricultural college. Kate and Roy made a temporary truce, but it didn't last for long, as Roy still refused to accept that the baby wasn't his. Kate blithely went on with her birthing plans. She talked to Richard about a home birth, but when she eventually went into labour, it wasn't in her cosy cottage at Home Farm – it was in a tent at the Glastonbury festival. Her daughter was born there on 28 June, safely delivered by Kate's midwife friend, Morwenna. After she came home, however, Kate refused to let Roy even see the baby. Roy went to Usha and applied for a Parental Responsibility order, which would force Kate to let her child – still unnamed, and known as 'Baby' – have a DNA test to establish paternity. Kate's response to this fascist establishment pressure was to take her daughter and hit the road to France, but she was furious when she was stopped by a court order. After Roy won the court case, she had no choice but to allow the test. Roy was vindicated and jubilant when it confirmed that he was indeed the father. Kate, however, still wouldn't let him near 'Baby', and he threatened her with more court action; but in the end Debbie helped convince her that it would be better all round to reach an amicable agreement. With Jennifer and Betty's help, she and Roy managed to work on an access arrangement and, in October, Baby was officially named Phoebe at a suitably pagan-esque ceremony on Lakey Hill. This event was quite a novelty for both families, especially grandfathers Mike and Brian.

TOMMY	It's turned over in the ditch.
TONY	Don't move. (RUNNING) John! John!
TOMMY	(OFF. RUNNING AFTER) What's happened?
TONY	(RUNNING) I told you not to move.
TOMMY	But Dad...
TONY	(ON. STOPS) Don't come any closer.
TOMMY	(OFF – STOPS) Dad—
TONY	Go straight back to the house. Ring an ambulance and then Richard Locke—
TOMMY	Is he hurt?
TONY	Go and ring an ambulance now.
TOMMY	Yes. OK. (HE RUNS OFF)
TONY	And tell your mother to stay at home. Do you hear me? Whatever you do, don't let her come up here. You can tell her there's been an accident but when the ambulance gets here everything's going to be fine. Do you hear me?
TOMMY	(FAR OFF) Yes, Dad.
TONY	Oh, John. (PAUSE) John! My boy! What have you done? (PAUSE) (BENDS DOWN AND TOUCHES JOHN) You're cold. (BEAT) You're so cold. (TAKING OFF JACKET) Take my jacket, it's warm... (PAUSE) I'll stay and talk to you until someone comes. (STARTING TO CRY) Talk to you – what do I say? (PAUSE) (TONY CRIES) Oh John! John! (TONY CRIES)

Kate headlines at Glastonbury Festival with newborn Baby

Love and Betrayal ⌀

It was a romantic start to the year for Shula. On New Year's Eve she was kissed by a good-looking 35-year-old, Alistair Lloyd, who'd recently set up a veterinary practice in Ambridge. It was a slightly complicated situation, as Alistair had been going out with her friend Caroline, but his attraction to Shula proved stronger

Shula and Alistair (Michael Lumsden)

and they began a full-on relationship. The couple seemed well suited: Alistair was kind and sensitive, and tried hard with young Daniel. But when Daniel fell ill with an inherited form of juvenile arthritis, this set in motion an unstoppable series of events that was to shatter their relationship and cause a major scandal in the village. Although Daniel slowly recovered from his illness it was serious enough to cause him a lot of pain, and Shula turned to her GP Richard Locke for comfort and support. Although Richard was still Usha's partner – and one of Alistair's closest friends – he and Shula fell in love and began a secret and passionate affair. Richard left Usha, telling her there was another woman in his life – but not revealing who. Guilty and emotionally torn, Shula confided in her parents, but couldn't find the courage to confess all to Alistair; it was David who finally told him the devastating truth. Now the affair was in the open, Richard tried to persuade her to move with him to Manchester. Still torn apart, she decided she wasn't prepared to leave Ambridge for him and so ended the relationship. After his deception, there was no way back for Richard and by the end of September he'd left, never to return. Bitterly angry, Usha blamed Shula for wrecking her life. Although Shula's reputation around the village was in tatters, there was one person who stood loyally by her. Alistair had been deeply hurt, but still loved her in spite of all. Over the autumn he helped her face up to the gossips and piece her life together again. When, in October, he asked her to be his wife, she was happy to say yes. They were married at Borchester registry office on Christmas Eve.

Nelson's Last Mystery ⌀

The last two years had seen the transformation of Nelson's (now slightly outdated) Wine Bar into a more modish and contemporary café-bar complete with cappuccino machine. Nelson, however, had found it hard to adjust to the new ambience and its associated trendy young patrons, preferring to pass his free time in the more sophisticated company of Nigel's mother Julia, and her younger sister Ellen. When they asked him out to Spain for Christmas, he happily accepted, and while there decided to permanently sever his ties with Borchester High Street and opt for a place in the sun. He never returned to England. Most of the proceeds of the café-bar sale went to the receivers, his cottage was repossessed, and his remaining possessions shipped out to Spain. The last any of his Borsetshire friends heard from him was in April, when he called Elizabeth to wish her a happy birthday. Soon after that, he disappeared quietly off the Ambridge radar, no one knew where. Three years later, Elizabeth was to receive another call from Ellen, to say that Nelson had succumbed to a mysterious death in Argentina. His body was shipped back home and, on 6 April 2001, he was buried in St Stephen's churchyard, beside his father and mother. The official certificate put the cause of death down to simple heart failure; but true to form, his life remained an enigma right up until the very end.

Ambridge Eco-wars

1999

In February, the anniversary of John's death found Pat still struggling to come to terms with her bereavement. Her moodiness and low spirits led to tension between her and Tony, and with Clarrie at work in the dairy; in March she went down with a bout of flu, which left her very low and run-down. Things reached crisis point after a big row with Tony, in which she blamed him for John's accident. When the row brought on a panic attack, she went to newly arrived local GP Tim Hathaway, who diagnosed depression. She was prescribed a course of anti-depressants and counselling, and so began the slow road to recovery.

But there were more worries in store for the Bridge Farm Archers, after the news came out that Brian was growing a trial crop of genetically modified oilseed rape on the Estate. Tony was appalled at his brother-in-law's cavalier disregard for organic principles, and was concerned that the risk of cross-contamination might compromise Bridge Farm's organic status. He soon became a leading figure in a campaign to force Brian to stop his flirtation with the so-called 'Frankenstein foods'. In May, Brian found himself under siege at a big public meeting in the village, where Tony spoke up strongly about the unknown risks of GM technology. Embarrassingly for Brian, his daughter Kate also heckled him. He did, however, find himself with a few supporters, including Susan and Mike Tucker. True to form, Brian determined to press ahead in spite of all the opposition. Tony and Janet Fisher organised a parish referendum on the issue, but others were prepared to take more direct action. Two weeks after the meeting, Ruth and David disturbed a group of masked saboteurs who'd been trashing the GM crop. As they ran off, David was punched in the face. Although they weren't able to positively identify any of the group, Ruth saw the number plate on their van and told the police. In the eyes of the village gossips, Kate's reputation as an eco-warrior placed her high on the list of suspects; but this theory took a knock when, at the beginning of June, the police went to Bridge Farm and arrested her cousin Tommy. One of the saboteurs had identified him as driver of the van used in the attack, and when the police searched his room, they found an incriminating balaclava. Although Tommy's first instinct was to put up his hands, he changed his mind after talking to some fellow activists, who persuaded him to plead not guilty, on the grounds that the trashing of a potentially dangerous crop was in the public interest. This was a high-risk strategy as, if it backfired, he could face a possible prison sentence; but it also meant that the important ideological issues would be aired in a high-profile court case. Tommy determined to press ahead, and Usha helped him to prepare his defence on the grounds of 'lawful excuse'. The publicity ahead of the trial led to a big rift between Tony – who was solidly behind Tommy's brave stance – and Jennifer, with Peggy caught uncomfortably in the middle. At the trial in October, Usha called a number of expert witnesses to support Tommy's case, and – to the immense relief of his family – the jury returned a verdict of 'not guilty'. A jubilant Tommy was free to go, leaving a thoroughly disgruntled Brian facing the end of the Estate's involvement with GM crops – and Peggy wondering if the two sides of the family would ever talk again.

Kate's Dilemma

Apart from the occasional tensions, Kate and Roy's truce over the care of Phoebe held for most of the year. However, as the autumn nights lengthened, Kate was getting bored and depressed with her job at the shop, and began to yearn for new horizons beyond the cosy confines of Ambridge. At the end of November, Roy was horrified when she announced that she was heading off to Morocco in a minibus with her friend Spike, and taking Phoebe with her. Only a week later, however, she had to fly back after Phoebe went down with gastroenteritis. But the trip had only fired Kate's wanderlust, and as Christmas approached she felt ever more trapped in her life as a single mum out in the sticks. On 13 December, after much heart-searching, she bade a tearful farewell to her daughter and flew back to resume her travels, leaving Phoebe with Roy. A few days later she called from Morocco to say she might be away for a few months; but it was to be another year before she was seen again in Ambridge.

Return of the Exile

It was definitely a case of mixed emotions for Debbie, when – eight years after he'd left for Canada – her ex-boyfriend Simon Gerrard called her out of the blue to say he was back in the country, with a teaching job at Felpersham University. She stalled him for a few days, but he eventually persuaded her to meet him. Full of contrition, Simon claimed to be a changed man, and admitted that he'd treated her badly in the past. They met up again, and Simon's charm offensive slowly won her round. Trouble soon flared, however, when Brian found out the identity of her mysterious new boyfriend, and banned him from coming to the farm. Debbie's response was to spend more time with Simon at his flat in Felpersham, where they soon resumed their old passionate affair. A few weeks of stalemate ended when Jennifer – who was by now a growing fan of Simon's – finally persuaded

Brian to let her ask Debbie and Simon around
for a meal. The rather less-than-convivial
dinner that followed left Brian convinced that
Simon was a shameless gold-digger who was
chasing Debbie to get his hands on a share
of Home Farm. Another row ensued and this
time Debbie stormed out on him and moved
in with Simon. So began another stalemate,
with Debbie coming in to work on the farm,
but hardly communicating with Brian. By the
end of the year – as the village made plans for
its Millennium celebrations – the deadlock
had eased enough for Simon and Debbie to
spend Christmas at Home Farm. Brian's views
on his character looked like being justified
the following spring, when he was accused of
sexually harassing a student. For a short time
Brian hoped that Debbie would finally see the
light and dump him, but he was disappointed:
the charges were dropped. Debbie stood by him
and, on 12 May, she and Simon were married.

*Troubled times ahead for
the Grundys*

Disturbing Omens

Towards the end of the old century the Grundys' dire financial situation had gone
rapidly from bad to worse to desperate. Their milk production had been hit by an
outbreak of BVD in their dairy herd (a virus infection, causing diarrhoea) and they'd
run up a big debt to their feed company, Borchester Mills. The bank refused to
extend their overdraft and at the end of December they had been given three weeks
to pay their debt or face bankruptcy. There seemed no hope of them raising the
money in time, and their future looked bleak. As the rest of the village welcomed
the arrival of the new Millennium, the Grundy family had little to celebrate.

In 1999, Carole Boyd wrote *Lynda Snell's Heritage of Ambridge* 'totally tongue in cheek'. Then she recorded it as an
audiobook. 'It's sometimes difficult to know where fiction ends and reality begins,' the actress ponders. 'That's why
my agent came up with *Life's a Soap Opera* as a title for my stage show.'

Profile

EDDIE GRUNDY

T REVOR HARRISON'S INSTRUCTIONS SEEM somehow appropriate for the actor who has been the voice of Eddie Grundy for over thirty years. 'You'll find me behind the hedge opposite the village pub,' he says. The Harrison homestead, however, is not at all how *Archers* listeners would imagine Keeper's Cottage. It's surprisingly modern, comparatively spacious and uncluttered by empty cider bottles, metal detectors or dog-eared magazines on ferret-breeding.

But there are some green wellies in the hall and a selection of gnarled walking sticks. 'I'm very keen on bird-watching,' Trevor confides. 'We've got kestrels and buzzards round here and I've even seen a breeding pair of red kites.' Now 53, he's evidently a countryman at heart who relishes living in deepest rural Worcestershire with his second wife, Annette, a support worker with West Mercia Police. 'We've been here thirteen years and it's made me realise how true to life the *Archers* storylines are,' he says.

There's a certain Eddie-ish quality in the story he tells about his encounter in the pub with someone from the local shoot. 'He asked me if I wanted a brace of pheasants and said he'd leave them on a table outside the pub. Well, I had a couple more pints and forgot all about them. Until I woke up in the middle of the night, that is, and suddenly thought: "Pheasants". Then I thought: "Foxes. They'll make a terrible mess if they find them." So I got up and went to retrieve them. Walking back across the road, it struck me that I was wearing nothing apart from a pair of wellies and a Barbour. I began to wonder what my story would be if a police car happened to be passing.'

Which is what might well have happened had it been Eddie rather than Trevor. But in that case the pheasants might well have been poached from under the nose of the Grundys' eldest son, the local gamekeeper. Trevor wouldn't poach any more than an egg. Apart from anything else, he's an MBE. It was for 'services to radio drama, especially *The Archers*,' he explains, shaking his head. 'It came totally out of the blue and I still don't know who put my name forward. The letter from the Prime Minister's office informing me about it was the last one I opened that morning. Like all freelancers, I look for cheques first.'

Who can blame him? Most actors lead financially perilous lives. 'Eddie has been my mainstay since 1979,' he says. His only regret is that his grandmother died just before she could hear him in the role. 'I spent a lot of time with her as a child and I was always being told to shut up and listen when *The Archers* was on.'

Shutting up and listening did not come naturally to a boisterous lad who was often in trouble with the teachers at Grange Secondary Modern in Stourbridge. One staff member, however, was shrewd enough to spot his talent. His performance as Mr Toad in a school production impressed her so much that she managed to get him an audition at the Birmingham Theatre School. Roles in repertory and small parts in television followed before Eddie Grundy became a household name. He even had his own fan club, founded by the late John Walters who produced the John Peel show on Radio 1.

'When Walters introduced me to Peel, *he* asked for *my* autograph,' grins Trevor. 'It was all very tongue in cheek.' But it led, eventually, to the droll, deadpan DJ making an appearance on *The Archers* in 1991.

Sadly, neither of the two Johns is with us any longer. But Trevor is still in demand to make personal appearances. Indeed he has become something of a Cyril Fletcher *de nos jours*, writing odd odes and then reciting them at festivals to celebrate, say, Vale of Evesham asparagus or Pershore plums.

'I did my Ode to the Great Pershore Plum live on BBC Breakfast,' he recalls. 'Afterwards, [presenter] Bill Turnbull said: "So that's what Eddie Grundy looks like."' Obviously he had never seen one of the great country and western singer's albums. Trevor disappears into the kitchen and reappears with a signed copy of *The World of Eddie Grundy*, which contain such gems as 'A Pint Of Shires' and a song comparing Clarrie favourably with Venus de Milo. 'We put this album on when guests have overstayed their welcome,' the actor confides.

What's he trying to say?

> 'When Walters introduced me to Peel, *he* asked for *my* autograph.'

Profile

JOLENE PERKS

THE ACTRESS BUFFY DAVIS plucks a framed cartoon from a shelf at her home in a leafy part of South London. A rustic-looking character is staring at a village road sign on which is written: 'Ambridge, twinned with Sodom and Gomorrah'. A Sunday paper published it soon after *The Archers* announced its arrival in the new century with a scene in which the landlord of The Bull was enjoying a post-coital rub down in the shower with a not-so-little madam called Jolene.

Buffy smiles, as well she might. She was that singer in the shower. 'In reality there were three of us,' she recalls. 'In the studio with us was a spot-effects girl rubbing baby oil into her arms and dangling plastic bags over the microphone to sound like a shower curtain.'

Ten years on and Jolene is the landlady of The Bull, albeit recently widowed and understandably depressed. Buffy is an actress, however. Still smiling, she replaces the cartoon, sits cross-legged on the sofa and reminisces about the extraordinary furore that the shower scene caused. 'I remember driving up to Warwickshire to see my dad on the Sunday after it went out. The headline on the front of his newspaper [the *Telegraph*] read: "Sex in Ambridge Brings Disgrace to *The Archers*". I thought, "Wait a minute; that's me."' And what did Dad think? 'He just laughed, but my mother-in-law didn't approve. It's a subject we've avoided ever since.'

Buffy's husband, Derek Pearce, is a sculptor and musician. Beyond their back window is an enormous trampoline that takes up most of the garden. 'That's not mine; it's Luke's,' she confirms, referring to her 12-year-old son. He was still at nursery school when the shower scene was broadcast. 'I remember turning up with him one morning to find the other mothers giggling. One of them asked: "Did you know you're the sex symbol of Middle England?" That's how they'd billed me on one of those tacky daytime television shows. The publicity at the time was quite full-on. It felt quite strange, to be honest, because we'd played it as comedy.'

Equally strange to Buffy was playing any scene with Alan Devereux who played Sid Perks until the character's death. 'I was a bit awestruck,' she confides. 'Sid was already a big character in *The Archers* when I first came to England and tuned in.' It was the early 1970s, and she was 15. The family had moved to Manchester from Vancouver after her father's business had gone bust. For a girl used to the wide-open spaces of Canada – 'I loved to skate and ski' – it was quite a culture shock to feel crammed into a terrace not too much different from Coronation Street. She rebelled and, at one point, set fire to her school desk. 'What saved my life was being sent to a residential drama course in Anglesey for disruptive pupils,' she recalls. 'Almost immediately I began to think that maybe I could do this.' Soon she was playing Lady Ann in *Richard III* at Chester and eventually she won a place at the Guildhall School of Music and Drama.

Even before she went to drama school, she was an accomplished mimic. In the course of an hour's conversation, she slips effortlessly into one accent after another. 'It's funny,' she muses. 'Canada's a huge country but there's hardly any variation in voices from coast to coast. Yet in this small island they change almost from town to town.'

She does a particularly impressive impersonation of Prince Charles whom she met ten years ago when he hosted a fiftieth-anniversary party for the *Archers* cast at St James's Palace. 'It wasn't too long after the shower scene and his entourage were desperate that we shouldn't be pictured together,' she reveals. 'But he was insistent and quite sweetly flirtatious. The equerries kept shooing the photographers away.'

Buffy's real voice carries traces of a transatlantic drawl which seems ideal for a village publican's wife with country and western connections. Does she like that kind of music away from *The Archers*? 'Well, I didn't pre-Jolene. But I've got into Dolly Parton and Patsy Cline since then. My tastes are quite eclectic really – everything from opera to pop via the music hall. I really like big, powerful voices, be it Pavarotti or Gracie Fields.'

The kind of songs, in other words, that anyone might let rip with in the shower if they're not otherwise engaged.

'I really like big, powerful voices, be it Pavarotti or Gracie Fields.'

Profile

KENTON ARCHER

I T'S NOT EVERY ACTOR who gets to play his own grandfather on a BBC television drama about Dunkirk. 'I've played him on the radio as well, and that was more satisfying because I had more to say,' Richard Attlee confirms. Recognise the surname? Yes, that's right. The actor who plays Kenton Archer, Phil and Jill's oldest if not wisest son, is descended from the most celebrated of Labour prime ministers.

Clement Attlee was his mother's father, he points out. 'My real name is Richard Harwood. But when I joined Equity they said I couldn't keep that name because another member was already using it. Attlee seemed the obvious choice.' And the hereditary peerage that goes with it? 'My cousin John has taken that.' No lunch at the Lords then with 'Dave' Archer, as Kenton delights in calling his on-air brother, otherwise known as Tim Bentinck, the 12th Earl of Portland? 'Alas, no,' he beams from under a baseball cap that seems very Kenton.

While the character he plays is '52 going on 22', as he puts it, Richard is 46. 'I suppose there is a bit of Peter Pan about me,' he ventures after some consideration. 'I like to go out with the younger members of the cast if I'm on tour.' That was true even when he was playing Napoleon in a touring production of *War and Peace* and had to remove a glued-on hairpiece every night before hitting the town. 'I used to call it the ferret,' he says. No hairpiece necessary when he played Roy Jenkins in *Longford* on Channel 4 or, indeed, Clement Attlee.

He has only the vaguest memories of his grandfather visiting the family home in Beaconsfield. After all, Richard was 4 when Clement died in 1967. But is he proud of what Attlee's administration achieved between 1945 and 1951? 'Very. I'm no Peter Hennessy [the eminent historian], but I've read the biographies and I believe that he was an amazing man.'

At this point, the window of the café where Richard is sipping an un-Kenton-like hot chocolate is lit up by a flurry of flashbulbs. 'Look at that,' he marvels as the paparazzi pass by in pursuit of a starlet on her way to one of the nearby theatres here in London's West End.

Well-known radio actors, of course, pass among us unnoticed. Starlets come and go in the public eye, but Kenton goes on. 'Hopefully so,' says Richard tentatively. 'I was a bit in and out of *The Archers* at first. In fact, the first role I played was as a bus driver on a hen do. Debbie's, I think it was. Then Kenton was going backwards and forwards to Australia for a while.'

Now, though, he's a prominent and popular character. Popular with the listeners anyway. What about the actor who plays him? 'When he first came into the programme, everything he touched fell apart,' Richard recalls. 'Now he's become more three-dimensional and an intriguing character to play.'

If his recent split with on-air partner Kathy had happened on screen, he accepts that his life wouldn't have been

> '… he's become more three-dimensional and an intriguing character to play.'

his own. 'It's nice to be part of something that a lot of people love without feeling that you're owned by it, as the cast are in shows like *EastEnders*. If I'm at a party and somebody finds out that I'm an actor, the next question is: "What are you in?" And if you say "something by [the theatre company] Cheek by Jowl", they look blank. But if I reveal that I'm Kenton Archer, they say, "Oh my God. Let me close my eyes and then talk to me again."'

Richard travels further than most to attend recordings at the BBC's Mailbox Studios. He lives with wife Miranda and children Grace, 11, and Harry, 8, in deepest Sussex. 'The four of us were bursting out of our little flat in London and we wanted to move to somewhere with an identity of its own,' he says. It's a long way from Birmingham, but he knows the city reasonably well, having been to university there to study Drama and Russian. 'I had an inspirational Russian teacher at school [Merchant Taylors'], but it suffered a bit at university where the drama rather took over. The accent was good enough, though, to get me a couple of roles playing Russian billionaires.'

What his grandfather would have made of those phenomena of post-cold war global capitalism we can only speculate.

Profile
JAZZER McCREARY

JAZZER McCREARY WOULD ALWAYS keep one eye on his beer, whatever else he was getting up to in a nightclub. Ryan Kelly, the actor who plays him, did much the same in his clubbing days. The difference is that Ryan did it all too literally. He used to remove one of his glass eyes and place it carefully on the rim of the bottle. 'Nobody touched it,' he deadpans in that familiar Glaswegian brogue.

Ryan has been blind since he was born, thirty-three years ago, in Glasgow's Drumchapel, a housing estate that makes Meadow Rise and its immediate environs in downtown Borchester seem like Belgravia by comparison. He rarely bothers with the glass eyes these days. 'I never liked wearing them much,' he shrugs. On radio, after all, voice not visual appeal is the gateway to the imagination.

To say that Ryan likes playing Jazzer is putting it mildly. 'I love it,' he emphasises, 'because I'm living the dream.' Which dream? 'Me and two pals dreamed of being on the radio. We were always playing different parts from BBC educational stuff when we were at school.' By that time his mother (a fork-lift truck driver, incidentally) had moved him to Corby in Northamptonshire. A fair number of aunts, uncles and cousins moved south with them. 'I've got about sixty assorted relatives,' he grins. 'That's not counting the distant ones. Some people count sheep to get to sleep. Well, I've never seen a sheep, so I count relatives instead.' And do any of them listen to *The Archers*? 'Some of them do. Even the ones who still live in Glasgow. My Uncle John's dead chuffed when he hears me, and I've got a cousin who listens in prison.'

Ryan himself first became absorbed by the programme when he was 14. 'I've always loved it,' he says. 'It's the way they can put things across with radio. I even managed to get hold of some of the archive stuff.' So he's aware of former Scottish characters, like nasty Cameron Fraser. 'He was posh Edinburgh,' the Glaswegian sniffs. 'When I went for my audition, I offered two different voices – my own and some country bumpkin type. Two days later they rang and said they really liked the Glasgow Jazzer.'

And what does he, Ryan, think of Jazzer?

'His heart's in the right place and he's very loyal to his friends,' he ponders. 'But he can be a dunderhead, a complete idiot.' So is it brawn, not brain that so many women find irresistible?

'Well, he's developed as a character and the milk round has given him a lot more opportunities to socialise.' That's one way of putting it. 'Don't forget that Jazzer is clean now, completely off drugs apart from beer and cigarettes,' Ryan goes on before lighting up and inhaling deeply. There's a full ashtray near at hand here at the family semi-detached on a private housing estate in Nuneaton.

It's his wife Sonja's home town. She, too, is blind. They met at a nearby special school when they were 14 and started going out two years later. After A levels, Ryan moved south once more. Against all the odds, he completed a course in drama at the Bristol Old Vic. 'It was the first time I'd lived independently,' he explains. 'I had to find digs that would take my guide dog, find my way to the shops and then to the theatre.'

He and Sonja stayed in touch, however, and nine years ago she gave birth to their daughter Bethany, who is sighted. 'I got the role in *The Archers* five months after she was born,' Ryan recalls, still relishing a memorable year in a life that has been anything but easy.

With all the problems he's had to overcome, learning his lines is not difficult, he maintains. How does he absorb them? Not by Braille apparently. 'The mic would pick up my fingers moving over the script. So I use this,' he says, bounding from his armchair and moving across the room to his computer with surprising swiftness. 'They email me the script in audio form.' What comes out is a monotone. It's up to Ryan to put in what he thinks should be the right intonation. But he has to be open to suggestions when he gets to the studio. And his guide dog, Hadley, has to stay in the green room while his master's voice is recorded for the cocked ears of millions.

> 'I've always loved it … It's the way they can put things across with radio.'

Chapter Six 2000s

The new millennium was barely a year old when UK farms were plunged into crisis. Within two days of foot-and-mouth disease being discovered at an abattoir in Essex, the government and the European Commission had banned the export of animal products from the UK. By the end of August, 3,750,222 animals had been slaughtered. The funeral pyres were particularly prevalent in Cumbria and the West Country.

In *Archers* country, meanwhile, David and Ruth weren't taking any chances. They were now running Brookfield, since Phil had reluctantly taken a back seat and, rather than risk their expanded dairy herd and their prime Herefords, they decided to barricade themselves and their family inside the gates.

The Herefords provided high-quality beef. Once the all-clear sounded, it would be sold online and at the farm gate. Like Hassett Hills lamb, it was part of Ambridge's reaction to the growing demand from discerning customers for better quality food. Tom Archer's organic sausages were targeted at a similar market, as indeed was his sister Helen's cheese and his mother Pat's ice cream and yoghurt.

On the Land...

- Second-home owners and wealthy commuters in counties like Borsetshire expected their food to be 'locally-sourced' and 'seasonal'. Hence the market for shops like Ambridge Organics and boxed vegetables delivered from the farm to the back doors of restaurants, barn conversions, old rectories and former pubs.
- The supermarkets developed their own organic and upmarket ranges while remaining fully conscious of the demand for cheap food from the other end of the social scale.
- Competition became more cut-throat and farmers' margins tighter. Accordingly, intensive battery farming continued on an industrial scale to meet the requirements of the mass market.
- Milk rounds were almost an endangered species as they struggled to compete with plastic one- and two-litre cartons sold at rock-bottom prices. But small-scale farmers like Oliver Sterling were prepared to invest in niche markets.
- Control of Grange Farm's high-quality Guernsey milk was handed over to Oliver's former herdsman Ed Grundy and his partner Mike Tucker. Vicky Tucker provided further finance and Brenda Tucker marketing expertise while Jazzer McCreary chatted up potential customers.
- The single payments scheme of 2003 finally severed the link between production and subsidies across Europe.
- Across England's green and pleasant land, meanwhile, poly-tunnels spread rapidly as farmers such as Adam Macy sought to extend the growing season. Environmentalists like Lynda Snell had to be appeased.

... And in the Land Beyond the Farm Gate

- The Prime Minister's son, Euan Blair, was arrested for being drunk and incapable – a high-profile example of youthful binge-drinking which became an issue in country towns like Borchester as much as big cities as the decade wore on.
- British troops were embroiled in wars in faraway countries after the attack on the Twin Towers shook the western world to its foundations.
- London came under terrorist attack in 2005, drilling 7/7 into the national consciousness alongside 9/11.
- Pub closures became commonplace in villages where there were no other community facilities. The Cat and Fiddle duly closed in 2000, but The Bull remained viable largely thanks to the enterprise of Jolene Perks and her daughter Fallon.
- It became increasingly difficult to imagine Jamie Perks or Phoebe Aldridge travelling to Borchester Green School without being plugged into an iPod or MP3 player.
- Couples like Roy and Hayley Tucker struggled to find accommodation in villages like Ambridge as property prices soared. The crash of 2008 reduced the demand for second homes in the country, but they remained out of reach for many first-time buyers.

2000

Doom at Grange Farm

After the Grundys' bankruptcy ultimatum, Eddie spent the first few weeks of the new millennium in a desperate attempt to raise funds, by whatever honest means available. But it was all to no avail: he and Joe were finally declared bankrupt at a hearing in February. Their livestock and equipment went under the hammer at a farm auction in March. But – as with the Tuckers before them – worse was to follow for the Grundy family. A week after the sale, Eddie was shocked to receive a notice to quit the farm from their landlords, Borsetshire Land. The real villain behind the eviction turned out to be BL's chair and strong-arm man, Matt Crawford. On 30 March, he sent them a letter giving them a month's notice to move out. So on top of losing their livelihood, the whole family faced the very real prospect of becoming homeless. William – now working as an under-keeper to Greg Turner at the Estate – was offered a room at the Dower House by his godmother, Caroline. There was nothing for Clarrie and the rest of the family but to apply to the council and wait to be housed. So it was that at the end of April they left Grange Farm for the last time and moved into a council flat at Meadow Rise, a notorious Borchester sink estate. These were desperate times as they struggled to adapt to their cramped and basic accommodation. It all got too much for young Edward, who sought refuge with his new mate Jazzer McCreary. But it was perhaps Joe who suffered the most. After being forced to kill Eddie's three ferrets, he disappeared for a couple of days and was found back in Ambridge, dehydrated and suffering from hypothermia. This prompted Eddie to take some drastic action: he bought a caravan, and moved the whole family out to a quiet spot on Estate land. Their refuge there was short-lived, however, as Matt Crawford moved to evict them. It was Betty Tucker who came to their rescue, and they hauled the caravan up to the yard at Willow Farm. But as winter approached Clarrie wondered how they'd cope, and feared that they'd end up back at Meadow Rise. The answer to her prayers came when Eddie persuaded Jack Woolley to lease them Keeper's Cottage, and the family moved into their new home at the end of October.

EDDIE	(SLAMS VAN DOOR) Right. (PAUSE) Well. (AT A LOSS) We might as well go, then.
CLARRIE	I suppose so. (BEAT) Do you… do you want to lock up, Joe? (PAUSE)
JOE	No. You do it, Clarrie.
CLARRIE	All right then. (GOES TO BACK DOOR) (ALL STAND SILENT AS CLARRIE LOCKS BACK DOOR, OFF A BIT. BIT OF SKYLINE. THEN:)
WILLIAM	(GENTLE) Come on Grandad, in you get.
EDDIE	(CHOKED) That's right.
JOE	(SMALL) Eddie.
EDDIE	Go on, Dad.
WILLIAM	Come on.
JOE	Ar. Right you are. (HE AND WILLIAM GO TO PASSENGER SIDE OF VAN) (EDDIE SIGHS)
WILLIAM	(ODD, UNDER, AS JOE GETS IN) That's it. OK?
CLARRIE	(APP BACK) William, you'll have to drop these keys to the Estate office tomorrow.
WILLIAM	(APP BACK) Yeah no problem.
CLARRIE	(KISSES WILLIAM) You'll remember to eat, won't you love?
WILLIAM	(HUGS CLARRIE) Don't you worry about me.
CLARRIE	I can't help it.
EDDIE	Come on, love, he'll be all right.
JOE	(CALLS FROM OFF) Are you coming, Clarrie?
CLARRIE	All right, Joe…

Sunny Ormonde (Lilian Bellamy) has known Kim Durham (Matt Crawford) since they were both in an actors' co-operative. 'We used to act as each other's agent,' Sunny recalls. 'We've done lots of plays together and we usually have lunch when I'm down in Bristol. Kim lives there and I do some teaching at the Bristol Old Vic. It was great when they paired us together in *The Archers* – although I found doing those slanging matches quite exhausting.'

Troubled Times at Brookfield ❧

The birth of the new millennium also heralded life-changing events at Brookfield that touched the whole Archer family. As spring approached, Phil – now in his early 70s – began to talk to Jill about finally stepping back from the farm and moving out of Brookfield. After talking to their accountant, they broached the subject with David and Ruth. If they were to move out, they would need to release enough money from the business for them to buy another house, and to provide them with a retirement income. This would end up costing David and Ruth around £35,000 a year, but the farm would be theirs; Shula and Elizabeth would inherit half of Phil and Jill's retirement house on their death. Kenton – who had used his inheritance to buy the antiques shop – would get nothing. This was OK by Shula, but when Elizabeth found out she was furious. Twins Lily and Freddie Pargetter had been born on 12 December, and she was unable to see why she and her two children should inherit nothing from Brookfield. This led to weeks of bitter disagreement between David and his younger sister. Elizabeth reversed her decision to make David and Ruth godparents to the twins, choosing instead Debbie and Simon Gerrard. Things came to a head at the christening party, which descended into in an undignified yelling match between David and Elizabeth. The row was soon to include the family black sheep, Kenton, who'd abandoned the antiques business several years ago, and was now back in Australia, where he'd married a local girl, Mel. Elizabeth gave him a call and quickly got him on her side. Together they bluntly rejected David's compromise suggestion that they become sleeping partners in the farm.

The row was still simmering when it was overtaken by another, more sinister, crisis. In May, Ruth found a lump in her breast, which turned out to be cancerous. The cancer was multi-focal, and she was told that she would need a full mastectomy, followed by a course of chemotherapy. The family put its quarrels aside to support Ruth as she prepared for her operation. Her mother, Heather, came down from Northumbria, and her close friend Usha helped to talk her through her fears and worries. In July she had the operation to remove her breast, and was home again a week later. The next month was spent in a slow process of recovery, and in coming to terms with her changed appearance; it was a while before she'd even let David see her operation scar. In August she began her first punishing course of chemotherapy, which carried on at intervals through the autumn.

Meanwhile, the problems over the inheritance hadn't gone away, and resurfaced at a family meeting in October. Kenton – whose wife Mel was expecting a baby any day – came over from Australia, and he and Elizabeth pushed hard for a better deal. David refused to back down, and the family reached another unhappy stalemate. It wasn't until the end of November that Ruth and David's life began to turn a corner. After her last chemotherapy, Ruth was gradually able to get back to her work on the farm, and in December she was given the all-clear from the cancer clinic; she would still have to go back for check-ups, but the cancer cells hadn't returned. Elizabeth wasn't about to let the inheritance issue drop, however. After an outbreak of Leptospirosis in the dairy herd, she used it as an excuse to question David's managerial ability and persuaded Phil to bring in a farm consultant. It was left to Phil to finally assert his authority and break the deadlock by deciding to turn Brookfield into a limited company; if Ruth and David ever sold up, the other children would get a share of the proceeds, but otherwise the farm would pass on to them and to their descendants. Elizabeth and Kenton may not have been happy, but they would have to swallow the bitter pill.

Cheating Hearts

Over the previous autumn, Eddie's ex-singing partner Jolene Rogers had been a regular visitor to The Bull, where she was holding weekly line-dancing classes.

*Sid and Jolene
(Alan Devereux and
Buffy Davis)*

She and Sid also shared an interest in keeping fit and had begun attending the same gym together. It wasn't long before this mutual interest led to more intimate sessions in the bedroom – and shower – at Jolene's flat in Leyton Cross. Their secret affair continued throughout the spring, but Jolene's daughter Fallon soon caught on and leaked the news to young Edward Grundy, who wasn't so good at keeping secrets. In June a drunken Eddie finally told Kathy that her husband wasn't, as she thought, at a meeting of the Licensed Victuallers Association, but in the arms of his buxom lover. She and Sid made a brief attempt to repair their marriage but, by the end of July, Kathy had had enough and took Jamie down to Bridge Farm, where Pat had offered them John's old room. She told Sid she wanted a divorce and asked for a £60,000 settlement for her share of The Bull. To pay her, Sid was forced to ask Caroline – who'd inherited her own share of The Bull from Guy – to increase her investment in the business. He also faced a tough fight to get a reluctant Kathy to agree to reasonable access arrangements for Jamie; but at least he was able to share his life with the woman he loved. Jolene moved into The Bull, where she has pulled pints and graced the bar ever since. The following summer, she and Sid were married at Borchester registry office, to the accompaniment of Tammy Wynette's 'Stand By Your Man'. They went back to a reception at The Bull in a pink Cadillac, and soon after left for a honeymoon in Nashville, Tennessee.

2001

Fortress Brookfield

Now that Phil and Jill had finally settled the inheritance row, they were faced with the problem of finding somewhere to live when they retired and moved out of Brookfield. But as luck would have it, a happy solution soon emerged. While the family had been arguing over the farm, Phil's sister Christine had also decided to retire from the Stables. She and George offered to sell the house and business to

Shula and Alistair, who decided to go for it. Now Daniel was growing up, they'd need a bigger house; Shula would run the Stables full-time and Alistair could convert the outbuildings for use as his surgery. The move would leave Glebe Cottage empty. Although Chris and George quite fancied it, Shula decided to give first refusal to her parents. Jill and Phil were delighted to accept, and plans were made to carry out the swap in the autumn.

But these plans soon paled into insignificance in the face of a looming agricultural disaster. On 19 February, a case of foot-and-mouth disease was confirmed in Essex. By the middle of March, the disease had swept through most of the country. Although the Ambridge area was spared at first, Brookfield joined the rest of the farming community in enforcing a strict hygiene regime. All livestock movements were banned, disinfectant dips were placed at all entrances to the farm, and the whole family changed clothes whenever they went in

Will and Ed Grundy (Philip Molloy and Barry Farrimond)

or out. As with the countryside nationally, hunting was banned, some footpaths closed, and people were discouraged from walking over farmland. Local businesses dependant on tourism, including Grey Gables, were hard hit.

In mid-March, a case was confirmed at the nearby village of Little Croxley. In a last-ditch measure to prevent infection, David and Ruth decided to close down Brookfield completely. Bert Fry came to stay at the bungalow, and for six weeks – as smoke from burning livestock pyres darkened the skies around the country – the family lived in a state of virtual siege, isolated on the farm, with friends and family delivering groceries at the gate. But in spite of these precautions, two weeks in came the news they'd all been dreading: David found suspicious-looking sores on a cow's foot. There followed a few hours' agonising suspense until Alistair was able to confirm that it was only dermatitis, not foot and mouth.

It was a relief all round when, at the end of April, they decided it was safe to open 'fortress Brookfield'. Thereafter the number of cases nationally gradually began to fall, and life for all the Ambridge farmers slowly returned to something approaching normal. Although the village farms mercifully escaped infection, the costs in lost production were high, and it wasn't until early the following year that Ruth and David were able to sell a bunch of heifers at Borchester market.

In September, as planned, Phil and Jill finally left Brookfield and moved into Glebe Cottage. For Jill – as for Doris before her – it was a bittersweet occasion as she walked away from over thirty years of memories. At the same time, Chris and George moved into the Lodge (until work was finished on the Police House, which was to be their new home) while Shula and Alistair began their life at the Stables. Although David, Ruth and the kids were delighted with their new home, Jill couldn't help but notice that the microwave was seeing rather more use than her faithful old Aga.

Brotherly Love (Part 1) 🔊

Over the summer a fierce rivalry developed between the two Grundy sons, Will and Ed. Will was now well established in his job as assistant to Estate keeper Greg Turner, while his younger brother was more of a worry to his parents. Ed was more interested in doing odd jobs for the new owner of Grange Farm, divorced ex-farmer Oliver Sterling, than in his schoolwork and, after skipping a few exams, he'd flunked his GCSEs. What both brothers shared was attraction for pretty, 17-year-old Emma Carter. In June, Ed made Will jealous by snogging her after a dance at Ambridge's hottest (and only) club venue, The Bull Upstairs. She seemed to regret it afterwards, however, and in September she agreed to go to a gig in Borchester with Will. Ed was there too and, when both he and Emma got bored, he pinched Will's car and drove her home. On the way a deer jumped out in front of them, Ed swerved and the car crashed. Ed was unhurt, but had to drag an unconscious Emma away from the burning wreck. She was rushed to intensive care with concussion and a badly broken leg. The injury was slow to heal, and she spent several weeks in hospital, worried that she might never walk properly again. Will was bitterly angry with Ed for what he'd done; Neil blamed both the Grundy boys and a big rift developed between the two families. He tried to ban Ed from visiting Emma in hospital, but when he sneaked in Emma was happy to see him, gave him a fond hug and thanked him for saving her life after the crash. She eventually came home at the end of October, but was told she'd have to spend another eight weeks on crutches. Ed was by now beginning to suffer the full consequences of his actions. He was charged with taking Will's car and with dangerous driving, and began to worry about being sent to prison. In the end, he escaped with a year's ban and 120 hours' community service. He was also told to write a letter of apology to Emma, which went some way to healing the rift between the Grundys and the

Carters. The feud between the Grundy boys proved less easy to heal. By early December, it was clear who had the upper hand: a depressed Ed was picking up litter and working at the canning factory, while Will was happily treating Emma to tea at Grey Gables.

Out of Africa

Kate Aldridge's long absence from her home and daughter Phoebe had taken her about as far south from Morocco as it's possible to get: to Cape Town, where she'd met and fallen in love with a young radio journalist, Lucas Madikane. Over the previous summer she'd become pregnant, but then later in the year she and Lucas had clashed over his decision to make a career move to Johannesburg. So it was that in early January Kate – now heavily pregnant – finally arrived back at Home Farm. Roy, meanwhile, had paired up with Hayley Jordan, who was already becoming something of a surrogate mother to Phoebe. In spite of the inevitably sticky atmosphere between Roy and Kate, warm-hearted Hayley did her best to build bridges, and was with Kate when her daughter, Noluthando Grace, or Nolly, was born early at Borchester General on 19 January. If not the first mixed-race baby ever to be brought home to Ambridge, little Nolly was almost certainly a first for both the Aldridge and Archer families, and was doted on by her grandmother Jennifer. Nolly's arrival was shortly followed by that of her father, Lucas, from South Africa, anxious to see his child and persuade Kate to take her back to Johannesburg. Once again, Kate found herself terribly torn between her love for Phoebe and the prospect of a new life with Nolly and her father. It was only when Roy agreed to bring Phoebe out to visit that she finally decided her future lay not in Ambridge but in South Africa, with the man she loved. Not long after their return, she and Lucas were married.

Return of the Native

2002

As the last of the spring lambs were put out to grass, David and Ruth celebrated the birth of their third child, Ben. His arrival was soon followed by the return of black sheep Kenton from Australia, still smarting from the break-up of his marriage to Mel and his subsequent separation from his daughter, Meriel. Unsure of his welcome at Brookfield, he was taken in by his little sister Elizabeth at Lower Loxley. Although offering to work for his keep, he was still perhaps Borsetshire's least reliable employee and was easily distracted by the more mature charms of Lower Loxley's new shop and restaurant manager, Kathy Perks. He was soon spending time with her and Jamie at April Cottage, and planning his next business venture – a cyber café in Borchester. In spite of his enthusiasm, Shula resisted the temptation to invest in the scheme, but Kenton wasn't going to let his dire business record and complete lack of capital stand in his way. By November, still undaunted, he was scouring the side streets of Borchester for suitable premises.

Profile
MATT CRAWFORD

MATT CRAWFORD IS HARDLY one of life's *Guardian* readers. 'Definitely not,' smiles the actor Kim Durham, folding up his own copy before strolling to a nearby tapas bar. On the way, we speculate about which paper Matt might browse through over breakfast at the Dower House. The *Telegraph*, perhaps? 'A bit too county,' Kim muses. 'I think he'd have the *FT* [*Financial Times*] and sneak a glance at Lilian's *Daily Mail*.'

In the restaurant, he orders the fishcakes and nothing else apart from a glass of water. Admittedly, it's lunchtime but recording is over for him today and all he has to do this afternoon is stroll down to New Street Station and catch a train home to Bristol. He lives in a rented flat near the river and cycles around town. One of his other jobs outside *The Archers* is teaching drama students at the Bristol Old Vic. 'It's a vibrant city and I find it more manageable than London,' he says.

The voice is a slightly softer version of Matt's. So did he have anyone in mind when it came to playing that abrasive and expansive son of Peckham? 'I modelled his voice on Sir Philip Green's,' he confides. The billionaire retailer? 'That's right. I heard him interviewed and he came over as gruff, sharp-witted and pugnacious. I'm only talking here about what he sounds like, you understand.' Quite so. 'I'm sure he's a lovely man,' he adds before taking a quizzical nibble of a fishcake.

When he first came to play the part, he was recovering from bronchitis. 'Matt wasn't required for another six months when, by chance, I had a scratchy throat again,' the actor recalls. 'The third time I played him, I was told that I didn't quite sound the same, so I had to gravel it up a bit. Since then I've softened the voice slightly as Matt has become a more rounded character and less of the pantomime villain.'

Not too soft, mind you. 'I'm glad he hasn't come out of prison a reformed character,' Kim goes on. 'It would be too easy, living in the bucolic idyll of Ambridge, to have the sharp edges rubbed off you completely.' So Matt won't be entering the single-wicket competition? The actor pulls a face before adding: 'And I certainly won't be playing Baron Hardup in one of Lynda Snell's pantomimes either.'

Like Lynda, Kim came originally from Surrey, albeit Farnborough rather than Sunningdale. 'My dad was from quite humble origins but, through the RAF, he worked his way up to become a senior radio engineer. He was very keen on Harold Wilson's white heat of technology. In fact, I remember going to the marginal seat of Reading with him to canvas for Labour in the 1964 election. As I got a bit older, though, I started to think for myself and we'd have some lively arguments about politics. I was further left than he was.'

Now 62, the same age as Matt, there's still a bit of the old hippy about his appearance. Or at least there was on the day we met. The rear fringes of his

> '**It would be easy, living in the bucolic idyll of Ambridge, to have the sharp edges rubbed off you completely.**'

receding hairline were long enough to form a greying ponytail should he have felt so inclined. 'Don't be fooled by that, or the moustache,' he insisted. 'I've grown them for a part in a play at the Gate [Theatre] in Dublin.'

It's a reminder, yet again, of the versatility required by the jobbing actors who make up the cast of The Archers. He and his on-air partner, Sunny Ormonde, (Lilian) are both vastly experienced in various forms of their trade and have been friends for many years. Does that make them prone to sharing the occasional giggle in studio? 'Yes, but it's tended to happen when giggling is required – like the time that we first looked around the Dower House. We sampled the double bed and Caroline Bone, who owned the place at the time, caught us at it.'

In real life, Kim has two grown-up daughters, one of whom gave up a burgeoning acting career to become a financial adviser. 'I'm useless at anything like that,' he confesses, 'so it's very useful to have someone to tell me where I ought to be salting away any spare cash.' And does she fill in your tax returns?

'Oh, I couldn't ask her to do that,' he beams before tucking The Guardian under his arm and setting off for New Street Station.

Profile
VANESSA WHITBURN

SOMETIMES AN EDITOR'S GOTTA do what an editor's gotta do. Godfrey Baseley notoriously did it in 1955 when he killed off the character of Grace Archer on the evening when ITV had been hoping to beguile television owners with the counter-attractions of its brand new channel. Not for nothing was Godfrey known as 'God'. Nearly fifty years on, Vanessa Whitburn reluctantly visited terminal cancer on Siobhan Hathaway as a dramatically tear-jerking way of moving on a storyline that had kept listeners enthralled for eighteen months.

'You just get to a point where a decision has to be made,' Vanessa reflects in her office in Birmingham's BBC studios. 'By removing the character of Siobhan, the drama would shift to the dilemma that Jennifer was facing over whether or not to stay with Brian and take in the son he had conceived with his mistress. I remember big arguments between the writers at the time.' Comparatively polite arguments, mind you. Vanessa had come to *The Archers* from Channel 4's *Brookside* where passions could become so heated that, on one occasion, the contents of the fruit bowl flew to and fro across the table. She arrived in the comparatively civilised atmosphere of Ambridge-creation almost 20 years ago, making the name of Whitburn second only to Baseley in terms of longevity in the post.

Her enthusiasm for the work and the pride with which she talks about her 'team' is infectious. But, as with any job, there are downsides. One is the relentless workload. Another is the occasional requirement to ring actors and tell them that they are no longer needed. 'The tough calls are down to me and I don't enjoy it,' she admits. 'Caroline Lennon [Siobhan] was terrific. Luckily, she had plenty of work elsewhere at the time.' But no actor likes to lose a regular role in a long-term drama and some become wedded to their parts to the point where they become synonymous with the character. 'Norman [Painting] always made it plain that he wanted to play Phil as long as he could,' Vanessa recalls. 'He was a very sick man for a long time and I was so glad that he was able to be in the studio just two days before he died. I really didn't want to have to make one of those calls to Norman.'

Writing Phil out of the programme presented her with another dilemma. He had, after all, been one of only two surviving actors from the small cast with which Baseley launched The Archers on 1 January 1951. There were no more than ten actors in the show in the early 1950s, compared to over sixty today, around thirty to forty of whom are regulars. 'But now we are focused on the whole village rather than just the Archer family,' Vanessa points out, 'and we weave in eight or ten stories a week compared to three in the 1950s. Audiences can take in far more information these days. They're used to a lot of media.'

Accordingly they would have read or heard about Norman Painting's death on the day it happened or the morning after. The temptation for an editor could have been to interrupt the cycle of Archers stories with what's known as a 'topical insert' – the emergency rewriting and re-recording sometimes required to take account of unforeseen events. 'But I didn't want to cram in Phil's death,' she explains. 'Norman wouldn't have deserved that. We wanted to give the story sufficient weight and time.'

And so it came to pass that the figurehead of the Archer family eventually passed away in his armchair to the strains of Elgar's Dream of Gerontius. Very English. Very pastoral. Very Phil. The jaunty rum-ti-tum of the 'Barwick Green' signature tune was respectfully kept off the air at the end of that episode. But The Archers goes on. 'Onward and upward,' as the editor puts it. 'Many of our stories these days are about the younger characters.' As Phil departed, his granddaughter Pip moved centre stage. The little girl with whom he once shared a piano stool is now a feisty teenager who has been giving her

> 'Audiences can take in far more information these days. They're used to a lot of media.'

father the sleepless nights that Shula and Elizabeth once gave him.

Keeping tabs on a programme with such longevity means that writers have to be kept constantly aware of family history. So the *Archers* archivist Camilla Fisher attends every monthly script meeting. At the same time, research producer Rosemary Watts has to ensure that storylines are rooted in the real world of today. It's down to her to find out, say, the length of time that Matt would spend in prison for the offence he committed, the kind of prison he would go to and the likelihood that he would remain tagged if let out early. 'We have a Radio 4 audience and there are a lot of experts out there,' Vanessa insists. 'They soon let you know when you get anything wrong.'

She must sometimes feel like a juggler struggling to keep innumerable balls in the air. But she prefers to think of herself as the conductor of an orchestra, harnessing and harmonising the talents around her. And she has done it well enough for *The Archers* to win no fewer than three Television and Radio Industries Club Awards during her editorship. Not to mention the Radio Personality Award from the Royal Variety Club of Great Britain and three Mental Health in the Media awards.

There were two writers when Godfrey Baseley launched the programme. Today there are ten. 'I increased it by two when I took over because I'd seen how well that worked on *Brookside*,' Vanessa confides. All the writers are now invited to the script meetings with the producers, Camilla and myself. It means that we have an engine room of thought that pumps through the programme and they're fully up to speed when they come to write their month's worth of scripts.'

Actors are rarely invited to these meetings. One exception was June Spencer who was able to bring her personal experience of coping with a partner with Alzheimer's to advise on how to write for her role as Peggy trying to cope with a gradually deteriorating Jack Woolley. 'Sometimes an actor's performance can affect what we do,' Vanessa goes on. 'Carole Boyd, for instance, brought in what I call an aggressive sniff to encapsulate how Lynda feels when her back is against the wall. It's now written into the scripts.'

Lynda, of course, likes to project herself as the protector of the Borsetshire wildlife against the inroads of venal farmers. And while *The Archers* long ago shed its obligation to be a government mouthpiece on matters agricultural, rural issues are rising up the news agenda and need to be regularly reflected in a drama set in the countryside. 'The debates are becoming fiercer and more complex than they ever used to be,' Vanessa muses. 'And there are more vested interests. It's exciting but rather daunting to be running a show that deals with so many conflicting points of view.'

The most daunting period of her editorship, however, came nearly ten years ago when that foot-and-mouth outbreak left the stench of burning animal carcasses hanging heavily over the British countryside. In Birmingham, the editor of *The Archers* was pondering how to reflect a national story that was not going to disappear in a hurry. A major rewrite was required. 'I remember going for a long walk in the park to clear my head,' she recalls. 'When I came back, I rang Jenny Abramsky's office [she was director of BBC radio at the time] and asked for money. Then I divided the writers and producers into two teams, one of which would concentrate on the hole that was opening up. The atmosphere in the studio was like a hothouse newsroom. Scripts were being broadcast sometimes two days after being written.'

Some parts of the country were hit far worse than others. And *Archers* country, on the borders of Worcestershire and Warwickshire, was still waiting for its first case. 'We heard that a few farmers were barricading themselves in to keep the disease at bay,' she goes on. 'So we decided that's what must happen to David and Ruth and their family.' A hothouse atmosphere was developing in Brookfield as well as the studio.

Vanessa, meanwhile, was acutely conscious of the devastation being wreaked in her native West Country. 'I was brought up in Exeter and my grandmother was from farming stock. She and my grandfather, who was a plumber, lived just round the corner from my school and I used to go there for lunch. They insisted on total silence while we listened to *The Archers*. That's how I was intravenously fed the programme.'

Little could she or her grandparents have known then that she would one day ascend to the metaphorical throne of 'God' and go on to orchestrate events in Ambridge over two turbulent and dramatic decades.

Old Habits

Since his recovery from his post-traumatic epilepsy, Brian had shown little enthusiasm for extra-marital adventures, channelling his energies into building up the farm and expanding his business interests. In the previous year, he'd decided to invest in a farm in Hungary, and found himself in need of a skilled linguist. So it had seemed only natural for him to consult GP Tim Hathaway's wife, Siobhan, who was now working as a freelance translator. Tim and Siobhan's own marriage was under strain, and Brian found the temptation of Siobhan's dark-haired Irish beauty too much to resist. She was equally seduced by his charm, and in December they'd met in Brussels and begun a secret affair. What had started as a casual diversion for Brian soon became a tangled web of lies and secret liaisons. Whatever Brian's true feelings, it was certainly the real thing for Siobhan, and she wasn't able to keep it a secret from Tim for long. In February, he found an empty earring box and a love-note in her room. Just two weeks later he surprised her and Brian together at home, and the truth was out. Mercifully for Brian, Tim didn't broadcast the news to the whole village but, by the end of March, he and Siobhan had given up any hope of repairing their marriage, and Siobhan moved to a flat in Felpersham. A few days later she broke the news to Brian: she was pregnant, and yes, it was his, and yes, she wanted to keep it. Brian's reaction wasn't quite what she'd been hoping for. Although he promised to stick by her and support her and the baby financially, he made it clear that there was no question of him ever leaving Jennifer and starting a new life with her. Siobhan loyally put aside her dreams and accepted that this was the best offer she was going to get.

Jennifer, meanwhile – although aware of the gossip surrounding Tim's break-up with Siobhan – had otherwise remained in a state of blissful ignorance. In a moment of anger, Tim had told his friend Alistair, who'd confided in Shula, but they were so far the only two to know Brian's secret. The next to find out was Siobhan's friend and confidante Elizabeth, who'd guessed she was pregnant, but was suitably shocked when she discovered that the father was her Uncle Brian. As summer approached, other people began to have suspicions; when

BRIAN	I never did that. If I was with you I never thought about Siobhan.
JENNIFER	But when you were with her – well, you really don't need to answer that, do you?
BRIAN	Jenny, you and I were happy. I never faked that.
JENNIFER	My birthday. You sent me off to a health farm so you could be with her.
BRIAN	No, no. She was at a conference.
JENNIFER	(HALF SOB HALF LAUGH) How inconvenient. I was so touched – such a thoughtful present – I couldn't wait to get back to you to – (SHE CAN'T GO ON) I'm sorry, Brian – I'm afraid the best health farm in the world couldn't make me twenty years younger.
BRIAN	Jenny, it wasn't like that.
JENNIFER	What was it like then?
BRIAN	I'm sorry. I'm so sorry.
JENNIFER	(OUT OF THE BLUE) Do you love her?
BRIAN	(FATAL PAUSE) Well—
JENNIFER	You do, don't you?
BRIAN	I love you too, darling. I do.
JENNIFER	Do you?
BRIAN	Yes!
JENNIFER	That's unfortunate, Brian. Because you can't have both of us, can you? (MUSIC)

Technical broadcast assistant Sarah Morrison once spent a freezing November night in Hanbury churchyard, Worcestershire (deepest *Archers* country). Well, somebody had to record the sound of bells for New Year's Eve at St Stephen's. On another occasion she found herself in a tattoo parlour in Leamington Spa recording the buzzing noise that accompanied Christopher Carter's encounter with an artist of the flesh. There were no screams.

Kate came over for a visit with Lucas and Nolly, she glimpsed her father with Siobhan in a hotel in Felpersham, and drew her own conclusions, which she kept from her mother, but hinted at to Lucas. Still Jennifer suspected nothing; and besides, she soon had other things on her mind. Late in the summer, cracks began to show in Debbie's marriage to Simon Gerrard. In August Debbie had been feeling stressed and overworked, and they fell out over plans to start a family. She could feel her biological clock ticking, but Simon made it clear that he was in no hurry at all. A few weeks later, she came across his mobile phone bill, which showed a lot of calls to Brenda Tucker – now a local radio journalist – who'd been attending a course of his evening classes. He managed to persuade her that it was all purely innocent, but then – at the end of November – she caught him in an embrace with his work colleague Jeanette. This was the last straw for Debbie, who walked out on him and began divorce proceedings.

While all this was going on, Siobhan had given birth to a baby boy on 14 November.

Siobhan Hathaway
(Caroline Lennon)

Brian risked discovery by rushing to her bedside, but Jennifer was to discover the truth about his affair soon enough. Throughout her traumatic break-up with Simon, Debbie had been harbouring suspicions of her own about her stepfather. Simon had reported seeing him alone with Siobhan, and Debbie herself had spotted Siobhan using Brian's handkerchief. She'd then asked Elizabeth, who'd told her yes, it was all true. This was the breaking point for Debbie. She and Brian had a highly charged confrontation where she made him face up to the consequences of his year-long betrayal of her mother. She also warned him that if he didn't tell Jennifer, she'd do it herself. The next day a shaken Brian finally confessed all to Jennifer, who discovered that not only had her husband been involved in an affair with Siobhan, he was the father of her baby. Devastated, she presented him with a stark ultimatum: either he ended all contact with Siobhan and his son, or their marriage was over. It cost Brian a few days of agonised soul-searching before he reached his decision. On 30 December he bade a painful farewell to Siobhan and his son Ruairi at the airport, before they flew back to her family in Ireland. Brian went home to Jennifer.

2003

Celebrity Appearance:
2003 – Alan
Titchmarsh was a
celebrity judge on the
'Open Gardens Day'
in Ambridge

Coming Out ❧

After Siobhan's departure with Ruairi, Brian faced the uphill task of rebuilding his marriage and proving to Jennifer that he'd put the affair behind him. Jennifer's tightly controlled anger erupted on her birthday – 7 January – when his present of perfume ended up scenting the carpet, and she let loose all her pent-up bitterness at his betrayal. After that, things cooled down a little and they managed to co-exist, leading parallel lives in the same house; this frosty standoff thawed only just a little when she accepted his Valentine's Day gift of roses. Brian's relationship with Debbie, however, only seemed to get worse. Still depressed after her break-up with Simon, she found it impossible to forgive her stepfather for the way he'd behaved.

In early March there was a welcome distraction for Jennifer when her first-born Adam finally returned from Africa after a ten-year absence. He was vague about his reasons – hinting at an unhappy love affair – but very keen from the start to play a full part in the running of the business. Brian was glad to oblige, appreciating his fresh take on farming and his enthusiasm for new ventures. By April, Adam had persuaded him to diversify into a venison-rearing enterprise, and a month later he planted out 25,000 strawberry plants, ready for their first crop later in the year.

Although Debbie got on well enough with her long-lost brother, it did little to lift her mood, or heal the rift with Brian. Her divorce was finalised in April, coinciding with a debilitating bout of flu. In the meantime, Brian and Jennifer's marriage was making a slow recovery. On their wedding anniversary at the end of May, he took her out for a meal, where they were both mellow enough to talk it through properly for the first time; Jennifer remembering her own fling with Roger and accepting that her own record wasn't entirely blameless. When they got home, some of their old affection returned and there was a full reconciliation.

Just a few days later, however, things reached a crisis between Brian and Debbie. Siobhan had emailed photos of Ruairi's christening, which Brian had printed out but then nobly binned. Debbie came across them and accused him – quite wrongly – of betraying them all and keeping up a secret contact with Siobhan. It proved a breaking point for Debbie and – in spite of all attempts to dissuade her – just a few days later she left to begin a job with a seed manufacturer in France. As Brian struggled to cope without her, his life was about to be further complicated by a confession that Adam made to Jennifer: the person who'd broken his heart in Africa wasn't a she, but a he. Jennifer quickly adapted to the discovery that her eldest son was gay, but it proved to be a much steeper learning curve for alpha-male Brian. Although he attempted to keep up a normal working relationship with his stepson, his traditional prejudices were never far below the surface and it was a difficult time for both of them.

Worse still was to follow for Brian, however. In the autumn Siobhan made a secret visit to her close friend Elizabeth at Lower Loxley, bringing Ruairi with her. She arranged to meet Brian, still clinging on to the hope that he might leave Jennifer and start a new life with her and Ruairi. Brian picked her up in his car, intending to tell her once and for all that this wasn't to be. As they argued, the car skidded and crashed, and Brian was seriously injured. Siobhan was unhurt, and he told her to leave the scene, after making an anonymous 999 call. He was taken to hospital with concussion and a punctured lung. Jennifer rushed to be at his side, and as he slowly recovered he was able to hide the fact that Siobhan had been with him at the time of the accident. Siobhan then secretly visited him in hospital, and finally accepted that they could never be together. She took Ruairi back to Ireland, leaving Jennifer none the wiser.

The Ambridge Slasher ⌘

Late in the summer, Shula was shocked to discover that one of her horses had been badly cut by a mysterious attacker. She called the police, but there was no clue as to the identity or motive of the culprit, and a few days later another of her livery horses was slashed. As the news spread, she began to lose her much-needed livery clients, and the slasher was still at large. As part of a drive to increase their security measures, she and Alistair found themselves a guard dog, Scruff, but this wasn't enough to prevent a third, and even more horrific, attack. This time the victim was Caroline's beloved old horse, Moonlight, who broke his leg and had to be put down. Oliver Sterling – the new owner of Grange Farm, who'd recently become Caroline's partner – helped Alistair organise farm watch patrols and, after another attempted attack in early September, Neil Carter recognised the slasher as he fled the scene: it was the Ambridge post office robber, Clive Horrobin. After his release from prison in 1997, Clive had been involved in a series of local burglaries, and it had been thanks to evidence from George Barford that he had been re-arrested and given another five-year prison sentence. Now back at large again, Clive had targeted the Stables in a twisted revenge attack, unaware that George and Chris had retired to the Police House. Once again, Susan was left in despair of her wayward brother. Clive pleaded guilty to the attacks, and after psychiatric reports was jailed for another four months. This seemed all too lenient to Shula, who was left with the traumatic memory of the attacks, and the difficult task of rebuilding her livery business.

Clive's imprisonment was only a temporary respite for Chris and George. Soon after his release the following spring, Clive reappeared in Ambridge, broke into the Police House and held Chris and George at gunpoint, then escaped after being disturbed by Phil. Just a week later he came back and torched the house, which

The slim, finely chiselled features of Tom Graham (Tom Archer) can sometimes be found among the raucous crowd at the York Hall in London's Bethnal Green. Tom has been a boxing fan from an early age. 'I used to go with my Dad [a photographer] to see the likes of Nigel Benn and Chris Eubank,' he says. 'These days I'm a keen fan of Carl Froch. Apart from being WBC super middleweight world champion, he comes from Nottingham where I grew up.'

burnt to the ground. This time Susan refused to cover for him and shopped him to the police. Clive was given a twelve-year sentence for the arson attack.

Over the next year, Chris and George took up temporary residence at Woodbine Cottage while their house was rebuilt. Sadly, however, they never had the chance to move back to their old home. Early in 2005, when the building work was all but completed, George died from a heart attack, his death perhaps hastened by the stress of Clive's vendetta. At his funeral the Hollerton Silver Band played 'Abide With Me'. An old wooden footbridge over the Am was rebuilt and named in his memory.

Farming Blood

After the Grundys had finally found refuge at Keepers Cottage, Clarrie now had a steady job at the Bridge Farm dairy, while Eddie was kept busy selling concrete ornaments and compost for local gardens. Early in the year, fortune smiled on them for once when a cheque for £7,000 dropped through their door, in compensation for their lost milk quota. At about the same time a small paddock came up for sale near Grange Farm and soon Joe and Eddie were the proud owners of the three-and-a-half acre field. They lost no time in installing one of Ed's calves (an 18th-birthday present from Oliver Sterling) and then put up a pole barn. It wasn't long, however, before Lynda Snell – now herself the proud owner of two llamas – reported them to the council on the grounds that the barn had no planning permission. Joe wasn't about to be browbeaten by any council order, and began a spirited resistance which ended in victory when David agreed to 'lease' them a token few acres, so putting them over the legal threshold for agricultural outbuildings.

There was less good news as far as Joe's grandson Ed was concerned. Over the summer he was involved in a series of petty thefts with his mate Jazzer, which ended up with a hundred hours of community service, plus a rehabilitation order. So it was that over the autumn Ed found himself gardening at a local nursing home while attending regular sessions on Enhanced Thinking Skills. His brother Will, meanwhile, continued his ongoing courtship of Emma Carter. She was now working as a waitress at Jaxx, Kenton's newly opened café, which had been generously financed by Jack Woolley, now his business partner and landlord. On her birthday, Will took Emma for a romantic balloon ride and proposed. Emma – although secretly still carrying a torch for his brother, Ed – said yes.

Souad Faress is one of several *Archers* cast members to take up writing in one form or another. After taking a course at an adult education college near her home in London, Souad published several short stories and finished up reading one on Radio 4 in the voice of Cleopatra. In 2004, her play *Seed* explored the experience of women in colonial India and toured theatres to much critical acclaim. She is currently working on a play about gun-running.

Desperate Measures

Over the past year or so, Helen had been involved in a growing relationship with the Estate's head keeper, Greg Turner, and had moved in to live with him at his cottage. As with George before him, Greg was known as something of a surly introvert, although Will had a great respect for him as a keeper. As Helen had got to know him better, she discovered that he'd been involved in a difficult divorce, and his ex-wife, Michelle now lived in France with his two daughters, Annette and Sonja. Although Greg visited his girls occasionally, it wasn't easy for him, and the girls suffered too. The previous summer, Sonja, his eldest, had gone off the rails, and Michelle had sent her over to visit. Helen had done her best to befriend her and smooth over her difficult relationship with Greg. Both girls came over again for Christmas and the New Year. The visit didn't go well: Sonja rowed with Greg over her friendship with Jazzer, and vegetarian Annette was upset by the more gruesome realities of a keeper's life. After they left, Greg became depressed by his continued separation from the girls, and by what he saw as his failures a father. His troubles worsened after Jack Woolley was shot in the leg by a careless gun on one of Greg's drives. It took Jack several weeks to recover; Brian blamed Greg, and from then on both he and Matt made his life difficult by picking him up on every small mistake. Greg's depression quickly spiralled out of control, in spite of Helen's attempts to get him to see a doctor. At the end of April, he walked out on his job after a row with Brian over his decision to visit Sonja, who'd been caught shoplifting. When he returned, Helen found his black moods and outbursts of temper impossible to live with, and moved out to stay with Kirsty. Over the next few days, she tried to get him to talk rationally about his problems, and was upset when he told her he'd applied for a job elsewhere. Helen realised she still loved him and hoped for a reconciliation, but Greg was already beyond help. On 7 May, Will and Brian discovered his body in a hut on the Estate: he'd shot himself.

His death drove Helen into a state of bottled-up grief and despair. Her mood swung between anger with Greg over what he'd done, and her own sense of guilt. Pat and Tony soon became worried when she stopped eating proper meals and began to lose weight. In spite of all her friends and family could do to help, her eating problems developed into full-blown anorexia. She eventually collapsed in September and was admitted as an in-patient at a clinic for eating disorders. This marked the start of a slow recovery; by Christmas she was able to spend some time back at home, and was slowly coming to terms with her past traumas.

Brotherly Love (Part 2)

2004

Although Emma was seduced by the prospect of a securely married life with the dull but steady Will, in her weaker moments she still found herself irresistibly drawn towards his wild younger brother. Ed was now back working for Oliver at Grange Farm, using some of his spare time to customise his car in Tony's barn, while sharing a cannabis-growing sideline with Jazzer in the loft – until Tony caught on and made

Profile

ED & WILL GRUNDY

THE GRUNDY BROTHERS ARRIVE separately. No surprises there. *Archers* listeners know that they can't be in the same pub without exchanging glares, glowers and sometimes clenched fists. But we're not in The Bull in Ambridge, needless to say. We're in a street-corner Victorian local in Birmingham, tucked away behind the designer shops of the Mailbox and conveniently close to the BBC studios. And this is not Ed and Will; it's Barry and Phil.

Barry Farrimond has spent the afternoon recording as Ed. Later this evening he'll head off home to Bristol where he lives with his fiancée Jo – 'she's British Chinese, born in Northern Ireland' – and their 3-year-old son Akiro ('it's a Japanese name'). Philip Molloy has not been required to transform himself into Will today. But he has popped into town from a few miles down the road. He lives on the edge of the green belt with his partner Laura, daughter Ffion (10) and son Ethan (5). Phil is a Brummie, born and bred. But then his father, Terry, was a Birmingham-based actor for many years, combining theatre work at the Rep with radio work as Mike Tucker.

Phil has been Will since he was 8, over

twenty-one years ago. Although he's not Jewish, he went to a Jewish primary school which meant that he had Fridays off. Where better to kick his heels than in the green room when Dad was required for recording? Mum, too, on occasions. His mother, Heather Barrett, played Dorothy Adamson, wife of a former vicar of St Stephen's. 'I remember one of the producers coming in and asking me if I wanted to come through into the studio and say a few words,' Phil recalls. 'I guess it was an informal audition because two weeks later I had a phone call asking if I wanted the role. The answer was "Yes, please". Apart from anything else, I got paid as a BBC child actor.'

Twenty miles or so down the road in his native Stratford-upon-Avon, where his father was a restoration builder, young Barry was finding work as a child actor for the Royal Shakespeare Company. 'I had three roles before I was 16 and you could say that I died on stage a few times,' he smiles. 'In *Macbeth*, I had my throat slit as one of Macduff's sons. In *Tamburlaine the Great*, I was murdered and thrown into a fiery pit.'

Before he can go on, his fictional brother drums his fingers on the table and beams happily: 'I can see a pattern emerging here. *The Archers* is the only drama you've not been killed in.' Mind you, he has come close, as you know

'... I didn't want to hurt you too much. I'm quite a passive guy really.'

only too well, Phil. As Will, you nearly strangled him. As Ed, that is. By now both young men are grinning at the memory of taking part in one of the most dramatic scenes in *The Archers*' history. 'I'd never done anything quite like it,' says Phil.

'Apart from that scene on the river bank where we had a fight after you found out about Emma and me,' Barry reminds him. 'You and I were locked in this moment when we looked up and saw the spot-effects girl punching a cabbage.'

'How could I forget? It was difficult to keep a straight face at that point.'

'It made just the right kind of sound, though,' Barry concedes and Phil nods in agreement. 'Before we got to that bit of light strangulation,' he goes on, 'I was supposed to slam you against the wall. But I didn't want to hurt you too much. I'm a quite a passive guy really,' he says as an aside.

'Julie Beckett [senior producer] came in to demonstrate and nearly put me through the wall,' Barry reflects ruefully. 'Then she said to you: "That's what we're after."'

Phil duly obliged. After which the least he could do was to buy Barry a pint. The pub where we're sitting is evidently a bolthole at the end of emotionally draining recording sessions. 'It's much quieter at lunchtimes,' says Barry who doesn't much like the evening background music. Well, he is a musician when he's not acting. After studying at the Sylvia Young Theatre School in London, he did a course in creative music technology at Bath Spa University. His favourite instrument is the didgeridoo, which he plays rather differently from Rolf Harris.

It's a talent that could come in useful if ever he falls on hard times and feels the need to take up busking again. 'I used to do a bit of fire juggling on the streets of Stratford,' he confides. 'I'm also into rock climbing and bush craft, Ray Mears style. In fact, I invented a knot for the International Guild of Knot Makers.'

'You're having us on,' says Phil

'I'm not. It's called the Farrimond Friction Hitch. Look it up if you like.'

Phil reaches for his iPhone, goes into Google and there it is – 'quick release and adjustable for use on lines under tension,' apparently. Phil shakes his head in disbelief, drums his fingers on the table again and grins: 'It must be the Grundy entrepreneurial spirit. We just can't help it.'

That 'we' is revealing. As they chat away amicably, comparing mobiles and checking one high-tech feature against another, it's a scene that would warm the cockles of Clarrie's heart. But drama requires tension, and both actors relish their roles in providing it. 'I've got no illusions about how high my acting career can go,' says Phil. 'To me *The Archers* is the pinnacle. It's really intelligently written and the friction between Will and Ed is going to keep ticking away as young George gets older.'

Phil has another job in the audio-visual department at a Birmingham grammar school, having studied television production at Bournemouth University. When it comes to TV soaps, he prefers to be on the other side of the camera from the cast. (He has worked as a camera assistant on the likes of *EastEnders*, *Brookside* and *Hollyoaks*.) And when it comes to leisure activities, he's into skiing, fencing and clay-pigeon shooting. So could he ever kill live birds? 'Not for fun,' he says. 'And certainly not grey partridges,' he adds with a wink. He is, after all, a gamekeeper every time he reimmerses himself in the role of Will. 'I feel as though I know him so well now that I could wake up in the night and know what he's thinking,'

And what does he think about Will as a man?

'He's a great guy but overburdened with common sense, bless him.' Until the red mist comes down, that is. 'Well, he has had some knocks that have put him back a bit. He's suffered a lot of heartache.'

'Dry your eyes, mate,' Barry puts in.

'Not many of us could keep our lives in check if they'd suffered what he has,' Phil insists.

Barry takes the point. 'If it had been me, Ed would have finished up in that river,' he declares.

Despite their animosity on air, both actors evidently feel themselves to be part of a fictional family that has been through a lot together. Both remember warmly their all too brief brotherly rapprochement on the sand dunes of the east coast. 'I really enjoyed doing that scene,' says Barry. 'Trevor [Harrison, also known as Eddie Grundy] was amazing.'

'Trevor's always amazing,' Phil concurs.

They're equally impressed by Edward Kelsey, who plays their grandfather Joe. Not because of his vague resemblance to Sean Connery in later life, but because his was the voice of Baron Greenback in *Danger Mouse*. 'I only discovered that a couple of years ago and it blew me away,' says Phil.

'Too right,' Barry agrees. 'He gave me a little signed *Danger Mouse* book for our little boy.' He pauses for a minute before asking Phil: 'Did you know he did Colonel K as well?' Apparently so. Both young actors launch into a series of impressions.

They may have arrived at different times, but they leave the pub together, chatting happily and slapping each other on the shoulder. Clarrie would have loved to see it.

> 'I feel like I know him so well now that I could wake up in the night and know what he's thinking.'

Celebrity Appearance:
2004 – Griff Rhys
Jones was staying at
Grey Gables when
Lynda approached
him about the *Cat and
Fiddle*, which she felt
was an architectural
jewel that deserved
saving for the village

them burn the whole crop. Will had chosen his boss Greg Turner to be best man, but after Greg's tragic suicide, he bowed to pressure from Clarrie and asked Ed. As the wedding approached, so Emma's doubts grew. When Ed offered her a ride in his newly souped-up Escort, she allowed herself to be persuaded, and found the old chemistry between them still as strong as ever. After a difficult hen night it all got too much, and she went down to Grange Farm – where Ed was house-sitting for Oliver and Caroline – and they slept together one last time. The next day, however, she told him it was all a big mistake, and she was still going to marry Will. Ed was gutted and threatened to spill the beans to his brother. While Emma worried, Ed confessed to Oliver that he was in love with her, and that he couldn't face staying around for the wedding. Oliver took pity on him and offered him a farm labouring job in Hungary, where he shared a business interest with Brian.

Although Will was oblivious to Ed's true motives for taking the job, he was angry with his brother for letting him down, and had to ask George to be best man instead. When Emma heard, she went into a state of deep denial, thanking Ed for what he was doing, but still insisting that she was going ahead with the wedding. Deeply hurt and confused, Ed left for Hungary. But his departure was only the start of an emotional roller coaster for Emma. Just two weeks before the wedding, she confessed to Tom's girlfriend, Kirsty Miller, that she was pregnant – and that she thought the baby was Ed's. She briefly considered an abortion, but decided to keep the baby, thinking that Will would never know who the real father was. Will, however, was shrewd enough to pick up that something was amiss, and on his wedding day, he asked her if she really did love him. She swallowed her doubts, and told him she did – and that she was pregnant with his baby. The wedding celebrations went ahead as planned. Soon after, the couple moved into Greg's old cottage, which they refurbished and christened Casa Nueva. In November, Ed returned, sun-tanned and self-assured after his travels, sporting a glamorous American girlfriend called Beth. Although this reawoke all of Emma's feelings for him, she was forced to play it cool, and hold on to her explosive secret: the baby she was carrying might not be Will's, but Ed's.

Kathy's Nightmare

Towards the end of the year, Kathy's relationship with Kenton deteriorated after a difficult visit from Kenton's young daughter, Meriel. Perhaps as a distraction from all this, as Christmas approached, Kathy took on a part in Lynda's production of *A Christmas Carol*. After one of the cast dropped out, leaving Lynda with no Mr Fezziwig, Kathy encouraged Owen, the chef at the Lower Loxley Café, to take over the part. Her motives were purely innocent: Owen was a shy loner with a notable lack of social skills, and she thought it would do him good to get out and socialise. Little did she realise what a grave mistake this was. Right from the start, Owen misinterpreted her kindness, assuming it was Kathy's roundabout way of coming on to him. As she supported him through some difficult rehearsals, he became ever more obsessive. Finally, after the two of them were left alone in the village hall, he raped her.

Shocked and traumatised, she shut herself away for a few days, unable to face telling anyone – let alone reporting the attack to the police. It was only when Sid called round and realised what a terrible state she was in that she was able to say what had happened. Sid's furious response was to punch Owen in the face and threaten him with dire consequences unless he packed his bags and left the area. Owen got the message, and by Christmas he was gone; but Kathy's long struggle to recover from her emotional scars was only just beginning. Over the following months her reliance on Sid led to problems between him and Jolene, who – like most of the community – had no idea why Owen had left the area in such a hurry. Kenton, too, was upset and bewildered by her behaviour, and it wasn't until the following April that she finally found the strength to tell him the whole disturbing truth. With his support, she slowly recovered her self-confidence, and they were able to start rebuilding their relationship.

Brotherly Love (Part 3) ⏎

2005

Over the winter, Emma faced the double whammy of sharing her shifts at Jaxx with Ed's lithe and glamorous American girlfriend Beth, while becoming ever more heavily pregnant. It was some relief for her when, in March, Beth broke the news to Ed that it was all over, and she was going back home. Alone at Casa Nueva while Will was at work, Emma was only too happy to offer Ed some friendly tea and sympathy, and it was on one of his visits that she went into labour. So it was that Ed took her to hospital and stayed with her until Will arrived, and her son was born on 7 April. Ed was one of her first visitors. When she gave him the baby to hold, and told him he was to be called George Edward, he assumed that the middle name was after his father, Eddie. She let him believe it was.

Although she was a proud and happy mother, as the weeks went by she confessed to her mum that she was beginning to suffer from cabin fever at their isolated home. So when Ed called round and offered to help her learn to drive, she was only too pleased. Over the summer – whenever Will wasn't looking – he took her out for the odd driving lesson, and Emma found it hard to hide her guilty pleasure in their meetings. It was a strain for Ed, too, and by the end of the summer he was talking to Oliver about going travelling again. But at the same time, Will and Emma's relationship was heading downhill. Emma was feeling increasingly trapped and claustrophobic at Casa Nueva; Will was already wanting another child, and suggesting that Emma needn't be in

	6. EXT. CASA NUEVA 12-05AM.
	(CAR PULLS UP, ENGINE RUNNING)
WILL	Please – don't go now! Go in the morning—
ED	(CALLS – OFF FROM CAR) Emma? Are you OK?
EMMA	(CALLS) Stay there! I'm coming.
WILL	(LAST DESPERATE PLEA) Emma! You can't – you and George – you're all I've got! He needs me – he's my son!
EMMA	(BEAT) No, Will.
WILL	I'm his dad – it's not fair on him!
EMMA	You've got to know this – just, you've got to try to understand…!
WILL	What—?
EMMA	Will – George isn't your baby – he's Ed's.
WILL	(LONG PAUSE) (COMPLETE DENIAL) No…! No, that's—
EMMA	Please – you gotta believe me. You're not his dad. I'm sorry. It's the truth.
WILL	(BEAT – AN EDGE OF DESPAIR) No…!
EMMA	You see…? Do you understand? That's why I can't stay here with you. I'm going with Ed. (BEAT) I'm so sorry Will…! (MUSIC)

Emma Grundy (Felicity Jones) with baby George, caught between warring brothers Ed and Will

any hurry to go back to work. In September it all came to a head in a big row, and when Emma heard about Ed's plans to go travelling it was more than she could take. She begged him to take her with him, and told him that George was his baby. This was enough for Ed, and the two made plans to escape Ambridge and start a new life together. Before they could make a move, Will caught them in a passionate embrace at Ed's 21st birthday party, and their secret was out. Emma defiantly told Will that Ed was George's father, and she loved him. Will's instinctive response was to lay into his brother and beat him up. But by the time he got home Emma was already packing to leave, telling him that their marriage was over. Emma went back to Ambridge View, her parents' newly built house at Willow Farm. Neil refused to let Ed in the house, so he, Emma and George moved into a caravan on Neil's land. Will wouldn't accept that George wasn't his son, and tried to coax Emma to come back again. When this failed, things turned nasty. Will started divorce proceedings and a custody battle, and forced Emma to allow George to have a DNA test. The results vindicated his belief that he, not Ed, was George's father. Although a bitter blow to Emma, Ed stood by her and promised to care for her and for baby George, whoever his father was. So the young family began their life together in the Carter's caravan. Neil relented enough to let them spend Christmas Day in the house; but in spite of her father's low opinion of Ed, as the cold winter weather set in, Emma seemed as devoted to him as ever.

Pusscats and Tigers

At the start of the previous year, Lilian had finally abandoned the golf-and-gin-palace set in Guernsey and returned to settle in Ambridge, where she'd bought Nightingale Farm. Never one for the solitary life, she was soon involved in an amorous intrigue with Borchester Land's top dog, Matt Crawford. This somewhat volatile relationship was further complicated when Matt became involved in a no-holds-barred divorce battle with his wife, Yvette. After a few months of open hostility, involving hidden paintings, changed locks and some deft money-laundering by Matt's henchman and 'financial consultant', Stephen 'Chalky' Chalkman, Matt emerged bruised and quite a lot the poorer, but single. Once the dust had settled, 'Tiger' Matt moved into Nightingale Farm, where he didn't have to try too hard to get a purr out of his 'Pusscat' Lilian.

Love and Faith

After the ugly series of racist attacks, Usha had now been living peacefully at Blossom Hill Cottage for several years. In spite of various attempts by her family – principally her redoubtable Aunt Satya – to find her a suitable partner, she was still very much single. Recently, however, she'd become friendly with Ambridge's new vicar, Alan Franks. A widower with a teenage daughter, Amy, Alan was by now a familiar sight as he hurried between his various local parishes on his motorbike. In May he encouraged Usha to take part in a multi-faith charity race, and her work colleagues upped the stakes by sponsoring her to dress as a chicken. A chance combination of events led to the *Borchester Echo* running a front-page photo of Alan giving chicken-Usha a lift home on his bike. After this ice-breaking event they jitterbugged together at the village fete dancing contest, and Alan took her on a day trip to Hereford Cathedral.

Alan and Usha (John Telfer and Souad Faress)

Buffy Davis (Jolene) is a member of a rowing club on the Thames. 'Apart from keeping you fit,' she says, 'it switches off the mind like meditation. All you can think of is whether your oar's going in and out in time with everyone else's.'

Not content with having a first in French and Drama as well as being fluent in Italian and Greek, Louiza Patikas (Helen Archer) has set her sights on doing A level Latin. 'I've always wanted to study it,' she says. 'My Uncle Ray took up philosophy at 91, so why not?'

Celebrity Appearance:
2005 – Stephen Fry
appeared as himself in
the Red Nose Day spoof
of *The Archers*

By the autumn their ecumenical friendship was heading towards a romance, but
this was interrupted when a visit by Amy's grandmother, Mabel, coincided with
one by Usha's Aunt Satya. With her strongly traditional Jamaican heritage,
Mabel shared Satya's disapproval of the couple's growing attachment. They didn't
let this put them off, however, and they were soon happily intimate. Although
their relationship had Amy's blessing, some of Alan's parishioners were less open-
minded. After Susan Carter had seen them kissing on New Year's Eve, she made
no secret of her disapproval, condemning the relationship as inappropriate. In
spite of her respect for Alan, Shula found herself in agreement. As time went on,
she was still unable to overcome her scruples. When Usha and Alan eventually
decided on a colourful part Hindu, part Christian wedding three years later,
Shula and Alistair politely excused themselves from both ceremonies.

Letting Go

Since Peggy Woolley had finally persuaded Jack to hand over the management
of Grey Gables to Caroline, the couple had been enjoying a peaceful retirement
at the Lodge. Now well into his 80s, over the past year or so Jack's sharp business
mind had begun to lose its edge, and he'd become muddled and forgetful at times.
In the spring it got to the point where Lilian suggested to Peggy that he should see
a doctor. Peggy was reluctant, insisting that there was nothing wrong with Jack;
he just got a little confused when he was tired. By the end of March, however, she
was forced to accept it could a sign of something more serious. Jack was referred to
a memory clinic, and was eventually diagnosed with the beginnings of dementia.
Now realising that his condition was only likely to get worse, Peggy encouraged
him to offload some of his business interests. Although Jack was reluctant to let go,
by the end of the summer he'd agreed to sell his shares in the *Borchester Echo*, and
– to Kenton's alarm – was also planning to sell Jaxx Caff. Kenton scrabbled around
trying to raise a mortgage, but failed, and the café was sold to another buyer, who
kept him on as manager. By the autumn Peggy was thinking about getting Power
of Attorney to manage Jack's affairs, but her negotiations were interrupted when
Jack's adopted daughter Hazel got wind of his illness and arrived at Grey Gables.
Jack was – as ever – delighted to see her. Peggy, however, was deeply suspicious of
her motives, and rightly so. Hazel found out about Peggy's plans to take Power of
Attorney, and after a big showdown she threatened to stay on for good unless Peggy
persuaded Jack to leave her Grey Gables in his will – and give her a half a million
pay-off. Peggy was about to give way when some swift detective work by Lilian
revealed that Hazel had invented a new husband and stepchildren to win Jack's
sympathy. Confronted with the truth, Hazel saw the game was up and left clutching
a rather more modest cheque from Peggy. Yet again Jack was sad to see her go,
but this time – after Peggy hinted at the truth behind her sudden departure – he
accepted that it was probably for the best.

2006

Brotherly Love (Part 4)

As the winter dragged on, Emma and Ed were struggling to cope with the harsh realities of life with baby George in the caravan, but there seemed nowhere else for them to go. Things weren't helped when Will announced that he wanted to take George on a week's holiday to Tenerife. Although Emma eventually gave way, she resented being bullied by Will over access and an acrimonious custody battle developed, with both sides threatening legal action.

Meanwhile, Mike Tucker was grieving after Betty had died suddenly of a heart attack the previous autumn. Although he was now over the initial shock, and kept on with his milk round, Roy and Hayley worried about his continuing depression. Over the spring, however, his mood gradually improved, and Oliver began to interest him in a scheme to produce old-fashioned quality milk at Grange Farm for doorstep delivery. Ed – who was still working part-time for Oliver and was desperate to provide for Emma and George – picked up the idea enthusiastically and ran with it. By early summer they had bought in a small herd of Guernseys, and were planning to start production when the first calves arrived in the autumn. But – as was often the case with Ed's ambitions – it wasn't to be so simple.

Will and Emma's custody battle reached a crisis when Will pushed his luck by abusing his access arrangements once too often. When he eventually turned up at the caravan, there was a violent scuffle between the two brothers which resulted in George falling and cutting his head. This was a breaking point for Emma, who walked out of the hated caravan and took George to live with her parents in Ambridge View. When Ed pleaded with her to come back she refused, saying that from now on she'd do whatever was best for George. Ed stormed out, saying that it was all over between them. Still banned from the Grundy household, it soon turned out that he'd disappeared completely, leaving Emma desperately worried, and Oliver wondering if he'd ever get the milk business off the ground.

For much of the summer Ed was a missing person, in spite of all attempts to trace him. It was only at the end of July that Oliver got a call from a hospital A&E where Ed had been taken after being found beaten up in a doorway. Oliver took him back to Grange Farm and attempted, with Caroline, to nurse him back to health. Ed, however, was by now heavily into drink and drugs. He upset Emma by refusing to talk things through with her, and following a row with Eddie he went on a major binge, ending up unconscious and back in A&E. This proved to be the low point in his brush with substance abuse. Oliver took him back in, on condition that he stayed clean and went to regular sessions at the local drugs clinic. Over the autumn, the counselling had its effect, and he gradually pulled his life back together. He made up with Eddie, and after Mike and Oliver's milk scheme finally overcame its teething troubles and gained official approval, he started to show an interest in the Guernseys. By the end of the year, he was back milking regularly at Grange Farm; but he and Emma remained as far apart as ever.

'In Character':
Over the years some
famous thespians have
appeared in *The Archers*
in character parts,
including:
DAME JUDY DENCH
TED MOULT
BALLARD BERKLEY
RICHARD GRIFFITHS

Profile

LILIAN BELLAMY

SUNNY ORMONDE IS WEARING sharply pointed boots with a high-ish heel and a leopard-skin pattern. 'Believe it or not,' she purrs, 'they're very comfortable.' They're also very Lilian Bellamy, the character she has been playing since that nicotine-coated, gin-soaked voice proclaimed its comeback to Ambridge with the immortal words: 'What does a girl have to do to get a drink around here?'

In other respects, Sunny is not very Lilian at all. For a start, she hasn't smoked since 1980. She doesn't drink either. Well, not much. 'I like wine, but if I have more than one glass I feel as though I've had two bottles the following day. And I really like beer.' Real ale? 'Ooh, yes.' But she only runs to a couple of halves in the Dirty Duck after watching a performance by her beloved Royal Shakespeare Company in Stratford.

She lives not too far away, sharing a large semi with her partner, her 14-year-old son, Jake, and a three-legged Labrador called Cindy. How did the other leg go missing? 'Not sure. We got her from an animal rescue place,' she says, flopping down on the settee next to the dog and under the gaze of various ornamental buddhas and other beatific figures.

Sunny is into matters metaphysical as well as what she calls 'alternative issues'. She took up astrology when she was in her 20s. 'It was either that or psychology,' she muses. 'I wanted to understand the two very different parts of my personality – the outgoing part that loves putting on a performance and the reclusive part that's happy with my own company.' So what star sign is she?

'I'm a sun Gemini but I have Leo ascending and a moon in Cancer.' And what on earth does that mean? 'Well, the Gemini part explains the split personality, the Cancer bit means that I'm quite homely, wanting some security, and the ascending Leo is the outgoing performer in me. In fact, my stage name came from someone in the astrology group pointing out that I was quite a sunny sort of person. My original name was Pat Wainwright.'

A farmer's daughter from Cheshire, as it happens. Yes, Sunny knows more about sheep and cows than Lilian ever would. Indeed she can relate to stories about outbreaks of bovine TB at Brookfield because her father's herd was decimated by the disease and he had to give up. By that time, she had already left home, inspired by the English Literature teacher who first took her to the RSC. 'We saw Eric Porter's Shylock and David Warner's Hamlet, and they seemed to burn into my consciousness.' So she didn't need much persuading when the same teacher suggested that she apply to join a drama course at Stratford's College of Education.

It was 1969 and she was sweet 16 when she arrived in the town that would become her permanent home. Eventually, that is. First came three years' further training at the Guildhall School of Music and Drama in London, followed by a lengthy trawl around the repertory theatres. She was playing in *The Threepenny Opera* in Ipswich when she met Nawal Gadalla,

> '...I just decided to throw caution to the wind and have a good time...'

who would one day become an *Archers* scriptwriter. They formed a lifelong friendship and, back in London, shared a flat on the Holloway Road. 'Every night, before we went out, Nawal insisted on listening to *The Archers*,' Sunny recalls with a smile. 'I think it reminded her of home and security, and I could relate to that.'

Many years later, Nawal would write the script for which Sunny auditioned as Lilian. By that time, she had over 400 radio plays under her belt, some of them directed by *Archers* editor Vanessa Whitburn. 'When I expressed an interest in doing Lilian, Vanessa rang me and said that I was welcome to try but wondered whether my voice would be harsh enough. Not expecting to get the role, I just decided to throw caution to the wind and have a good time – which was, of course, the quality they wanted for the character. Since then I've had some cracking storylines that have allowed me to play alongside my old mate Kim Durham [Matt Crawford] and develop Lilian to someone more multi-dimensional.'

Does she like her character? 'I do. She's very vulnerable and I feel rather protective of her.' As for Lilian, she'd probably like the outgoing, Leo side of Sunny. And she'd certainly like those 'leopard-skin' boots.

Profile
TOM ARCHER

IT'S DIFFICULT TO IMAGINE the slightly built Tom Graham imposing his will on a recalcitrant sow or shifting heavy pig arks about. But appearances can be deceptive. The actor who plays organic sausage entrepreneur Tom Archer has, at one time or another, tried his hand at canoeing, scuba-diving, fencing, kick-boxing and snowboarding.

'It's mainly snowboarding these days,' he confides, 'but the other activities have been useful to put on my CV.' Indeed his prowess at diving helped to land him a role in making a music video for the rock band McFly. 'It entailed pretending to have an argument with a girl while we were in a truck that swerved off the road and finished up in a river,' he recalls. 'We managed to free ourselves, kiss and make up while still underwater. It was done at Pinewood Studios with a huge tank that had been used in *The Bourne Identity* and the James Bond films. Divers with respirators had to be standing by to give us oxygen at regular intervals because we were there all day. It was scary but really exciting,' he adds before taking a sip of his Americano.

It's mid afternoon in Birmingham and his part in recording is over for the day. Tom has been the other Tom for fourteen years. 'It's great being able to come up here regularly and slip into a fantasy life,' he says. Soon he'll be off back to South-West London to slip back into his home life with the actress Fiona Sheehan, who has been understudy for Keira Knightley in the West End. 'I met Fiona at the Globe [Theatre] when she was playing in *The Fitzrovia Radio Hour*, a pastiche of 1950s plays on the wireless,' he explains. 'I liked the look of her and managed to get to see her after the show. We had an immediate common point of understanding when I told her that I was in *The Archers*.'

Tom was just 17 when he took the role of… er, Tom. For three years before that, he had been polishing his budding acting skills by attending twice-weekly sessions at ITV Junior Television Workshops in Nottingham. He was brought up in a village seven miles south of the city where commuters far exceeded farmers. His mother taught children with special needs and his father was a freelance photographer. Official photographer, indeed, for Notts County FC. 'I still support them,' Tom maintains doggedly.

Everyone in Ambridge called him Tommy during his early years in the role. 'Charles Collingwood [Brian] still does off air,' he grins. 'He called over to me the other day: "Have you bought my book yet, young Tommy?" And when I did buy it, he wrote in the fly leaf: "To Tommy. Read and learn."' He takes another swig of coffee before chuckling: 'I really like Charles.'

Regular listeners will be only too aware that Brian is not exactly Tom Archer's favourite uncle when they're in character. His devious dealing behind his nephew's back brought an end to their ill-starred business partnership after a lengthy whinge from the junior partner that made

'It's great being able to come up here regularly and slip into a fantasy life.'

his father Tony seem like a little ray of sunshine. 'He's a bit more idealistic than I am,' Tom Graham says of his alter ego. 'But he's had some hard knocks and he seems to be growing up a bit.' So do the two Toms have anything in common?

He ponders for a while before responding: 'We're both very determined. But he's much better at getting up in the mornings.' Well, that tends to be the way when you compare actors with farmers. It's difficult to imagine two more different professions.

Not that Tom is confining himself to acting. He has a first-class honours degree in Psychology from Manchester University and is currently embarked on a PhD that could eventually lead to him setting up as a counsellor. Luckily, he hasn't yet had to grapple with the psychological complexities of someone like his fictional sister Helen, embarking on single motherhood in her early 30s with the help of an apparently anonymous sperm donor. 'She had a rough time with Leon and Annette, and she'd definitely benefit from some counselling,' he ventures when pressed. 'But it would have to be non-judgemental of course.'

Of course. It would be difficult to imagine a psychologist being able to impose his views on Helen any more than her father could impose his will. Or her brother for that matter.

David at Brookfield

Ruth's Temptation ∽

With young Ben now approaching his 4th birthday, Ruth was more than ready to ease back on the childcare and take a more hands-on role on the farm. For the past year and a half the day-to-day running of the dairy herd had been the responsibility of their contract herdsman, Sam Batton. A young Devonian with a taste for adventure sports, Sam had been instrumental in introducing a more efficient grazing regime, introducing Ruth to the high-tech intricacies of his plate meter. He'd also found enough spare time to lead a full social life; after splitting up with his long-distance girlfriend, Fliss, he'd moved on to Tom's now-ex-girlfriend, Kirsty Miller, who became a frequent visitor to Sam's digs at Rickyard Cottage. Over the spring, as Ruth started to do more around the farm, she and Sam spent time together on routine dairy jobs, and collaborated on a clover survey of the pasture. When Sam began to have some doubts about his relationship with Kirsty, he found a willing confidante in Ruth, who was by now starting to appreciate him for more than just his skill with a plate meter. When Sam and Kirsty left for a two-week holiday in Gozo, Ruth couldn't quite surpress a few pangs of jealousy. But after Sam's return, it was his turn to feel jealous when Ruth and David spent a romantic night in the kids' treehouse – which Sam had helped build. This simmering mix of sexual chemistry approached boiling point when David's old flame Sophie Barlow returned to the area to attend her mum's charity fundraising event. David found that his rather dippy ex-girlfriend had blossomed into a glamorous divorcée with her own small chain of fashion outlets. It was almost as if the last nineteen years had never happened. A resentful Ruth struggled to bite her tongue as David cleared his diary to help the lissom Sophie organise a charity fashion show at Lower Loxley. After a week or two of this Ruth was feeling thoroughly stressed and insecure, and found a waiting sympathetic ear in Sam. Her emotional confusion only increased when he told her that he and Kirsty were now history. Soon after, she caught David lying about a liaison with Sophie. Convinced that her husband was having an affair, she rushed into Sam's arms and they ended up kissing passionately. Although David insisted – quite truthfully – that nothing had happened between him and Sophie, Ruth was by now in a state of emotional turmoil and when Sam pushed her to spend the night away with him, she finally surrendered. So one night early in November – after telling David she was meeting an old college friend – she drove to meet her lover at a hotel in Oxford. For a few moments the whole future of her marriage hung in the balance; but Ruth found herself unable to take the fatal step, and went back to spend the night

SAM	(ON PHONE) David was OK? He didn't suspect anything?
RUTH	No.
SAM	Where did you tell him Laura lives?
RUTH	I don't know where, but said Oxford.
SAM	It's simpler that way.
RUTH	That's what I thought.
SAM	And you're supposed to be with her till when tomorrow?
RUTH	I don't know, I didn't say when I'd be back. He didn't ask.
SAM	Great. The longer the better, eh?
RUTH	(SICK) Yeah.
SAM	Just try and get here as quick as you can.
RUTH	(PRICKLY) I'm doing my best!
SAM	I know. Everything'll be ready and waiting for you when you get here anyway.
RUTH	What will?
SAM	The room and everything. And me.
RUTH	Oh, right, Oh, we're starting to move again.
SAM	Great. See you soon. Very soon I hope. Love you.
RUTH	You too. Bye. (PHONE CALL ENDS AS SAM HANGS UP. HANDBRAKE OFF, GEAR ENGAGED, CAR MOVES) (SIGH)

at Usha's. The next day Sam shocked David by walking out on his job with no real explanation. David soon found out the truth, however, when he confronted a tearful Ruth, who confessed all. Angry and betrayed, David was at first unable to forgive her, and over the next few weeks Ruth wondered if their marriage would survive. But a long heart-to-heart with Usha helped David gain a sense of perspective on the whole not-quite-affair. After that, things got easier; by the time Christmas arrived, they had agreed to call a truce and give their mutual wounds time to heal.

Wedding of the Year

Soon after Adam had braved coming out to his friends and family, he'd begun a relationship with the head chef at Grey Gables, Ian Craig. The previous year – to Brian's mild discomfiture – the couple had bought Honeysuckle Cottage and set up home together in the heart of the village. Now happily settled with the man he loved, Adam was more than a little fazed when Ian's old friend Madeleine – aka Madds – asked him to father a child with her. Although Ian was very keen, Adam struggled with the whole idea, and took some persuading before he reluctantly came into line. But just when Ian was ready to start the whole process, Madds fell for another man and decided to start a more conventional family. Adam supported Ian through his disappointment, and in the autumn they decided to formalise their own commitment to each other in a civil partnership.

Adam and Ian (Andrew Wincott and Stephen Kennedy)

Although most of their friends and family were naturally delighted, Brian struggled once again with his knee-jerk prejudices. The ceremony went ahead as planned at Lower Loxley on 12 December. Brian announced that he would boycott the whole proceedings; but at the last minute he relented, after Ian's father, Glen – who'd never come to terms with Ian's sexuality – overcame his doubts to be there and support his son on his wedding day. Somewhat shamed by Glen's example, Brian arrived at the reception, where he shook Adam's hand.

Vintage car enthusiasts can be as keen-eared as twitchers and train-spotters. So studio manager Michael Harrison went to great pains to ensure that the recording of Jim Lloyd's vintage Riley was exactly as Jim described it. Not just any old Riley but a 1948 Riley RM. 'With a hard top,' Michael emphasises. 'It's important that we get that right.' Cows can be rather more troublesome to record than cars. 'If you stand in a field full of them, it's silent most of the time,' Michael points out. 'We have to exaggerate the amount of mooing slightly and, at the same time, ensure that we match the right breed to the right farm.'

2007

End of the Affair ✍

It was now more than three years since the near-disastrous car accident that had ended Siobhan's last attempt to lure Brian away from his marriage. This hadn't quite put an end to their relationship, however. Although Siobhan had settled in Germany with her new partner, Dieter, Brian had made the occasional clandestine visit to see her and his son Ruairi. On his most recent trip – made under the cover of visiting Debbie, who was now looking after his farming interests in Hungary – Brian was concerned to find her looking tired and stressed. She passed it off as overwork; but then in April she came over and called him, asking him to meet her at a local hotel. Brian was shocked to see how ill she looked, and she told him the sombre truth: she was suffering from a malignant form of cancer that had spread to her liver. Her relationship with Dieter had come to nothing, and she'd come to see Brian to ask that if the worst happened, he'd take care of Ruairi.

When a stunned Brian went back and told the whole story to Jennifer, he received no sympathy at all. However sad it might be for Siobhan, there was no way Jennifer would ever contemplate taking on her child. Unable to stomach this, Brian went back to Siobhan and told her the opposite – that he and Jennifer would be happy to have Ruairi. This flagrant lie was quickly exposed when Siobhan tried to thank Jennifer for her kindness. Jennifer, as a result, became even more entrenched. Although Adam was broadly behind his mother, he managed to persuade her to meet Siobhan and talk it through with her. It was a difficult meeting, but in spite of herself Jennifer was moved by her illness and her general predicament. As Siobhan explained, her options were limited. Her only close family were her 80-year old mother and her sister, Niamh, a single career woman – neither of whom were ideal candidates to care for Ruairi. Nevertheless, Jennifer felt she could never love Ruairi, and that the only answer was for him to go to Niamh. Siobhan went back to continue her treatment with her family in Dublin, leaving Brian still desperately hoping that Jennifer would change her mind. Once again it was Adam who helped her talk through her confused emotions, reminding her of how when she'd married Brian, he'd been such a good father to Adam and Debbie.

In May there came the news they'd all been fearing: Siobhan's condition had sharply deteriorated, and she was unlikely to survive for long. Brian rushed to be at her side, leaving Jennifer facing the real possibility that he might choose Ruairi over his marriage, and she'd lose him for good. In a mêlée of confused emotions, she flew over to be with him, and met Ruairi, but came home still as undecided

SIOBHAN	It's all right, Brian. I've come to a decision.
BRIAN	Oh?
SIOBHAN	It's time I did. After all, it's me causing all the trouble.
BRIAN	(OVER) No, you're not.
SIOBHAN	And there's a simple answer. (ATTEMPTING TO BE LIGHT) I've decided not to die. How about that?
BRIAN	Oh, Siobhan.
SIOBHAN	Solves everything, doesn't it?
BRIAN	That's what I want. More than anything. And Ruairi. All of us. You must keep fighting.
SIOBHAN	I'm going to. With everything I've got. I have to for his sake… But… (TRAILS OFF
BRIAN	(UNDERSTANDS) Yes.
SIOBHAN	In case the miracle doesn't happen… I suppose I'd better talk with Niamh again.
BRIAN	What for?
SIOBHAN	Tell her how things are. Warn her she'll maybe have to take Ruairi.
BRIAN	No!
SIOBHAN	Be realistic, Brian.
BRIAN	I am being realistic. Don't talk to Niamh. I can make Jenny change her mind.
SIOBHAN	(NOT CONVINCED) You think so?
BRIAN	Yes. I'm sure of it. Please, Siobhan. Believe me…

as ever. A few days later – on 1 June – Siobhan died. Jennifer's sympathy for the bereaved child finally overcame what was left of her doubts, and soon after Brian returned to Home Farm, bringing Ruairi with him.

The arrival of Brian's 4-year-old love-child quickly became the talk of Ambridge. And it wasn't only the village gossips who made Jennifer's life difficult. As she tried her best to take Siobhan's place as a mother to Ruairi, her own daughter Alice – appalled by what her father had done – refused to stay in the house with her new half-brother, and went to live with her friend Amy at the vicarage. Over the summer, as Ruairi gradually settled into his new home, Alice stuck doggedly to her guns, ending up with Adam and Ian at Honeysuckle Cottage. After getting a string of top grades in her A2s, she also surprised her parents by deciding to try for a place in the RAF, who'd sponsor her engineering degree. As she set off for her gap year in South Africa in September, she could barely bring herself to say goodbye to Brian.

Kathy's Revenge

In the autumn the police paid a surprise visit to Lower Loxley, after a man called Gareth Taylor was suspected of assaulting a girl in Bournemouth. When shown a photo of the suspect, Elizabeth and Nigel were shocked to discover that he was none other than their former chef, Owen. This news came as less of a surprise to Kathy, of course: it was now approaching three years since Taylor – aka Owen King – had raped her in the village hall, before comprehensively disappearing from the district. To hear that he'd now gone on to find another victim reawoke memories of all the terrible trauma that she had suffered, and she felt guilty that she hadn't reported the assault at the time, so leaving Taylor at large to attack some other poor girl. With Kenton's support, and determined to make amends, Kathy now bravely went to the police and told them her story. Taylor was arrested in Bournemouth, charged with both offences, and held on remand. So with the trial set for April, Kathy spent the last few weeks of the year knowing she'd have to face Taylor in court, and terrified that he might be given bail before the hearing. Nigel, Pat, Sid and Kenton were all called as witnesses for the prosecution. Elizabeth, however, was shocked to be called as a witness for Taylor's defence, after admitting in her statement that she'd thought at the time that Kathy and Taylor had become close friends. This led to some understandable tension over Christmas with her brother Kenton, only made worse when she let slip to Shula about the whole affair, which remained a secret from most of the community.

'We're always positioned between long-running radio drama and soap opera. I'm happy to call *The Archers* either. It's good: that's the point.'

Editor Vanessa Whitburn

Kathy takes the stand against Owen

The pressure on Kathy increased early in the next year when Taylor was granted bail. Although the conditions should have prevented him from coming anywhere near Ambridge, Kathy's sense of paranoia steadily increased. At the end of January her worst fears were realised when Taylor appeared outside her cottage, grabbed her and tried to bully her into withdrawing the rape charges. Luckily, Kenton arrived in the nick of time and chased him off. Taylor then gave himself up to the police, and spent the rest of the time before the trial in custody.

On 7 April, Kathy stood up to face her persecutor across the courtroom. A tough and searching cross-examination from the defence council left her feeling emotionally drained and sure that she'd messed it up. Pat, however, proved a strong prosecution witness as she described just how upset and traumatised Kathy had been in the aftermath of the assault; Elizabeth managed to take the stand without giving too much help to the defence. But the jury were in no hurry to end the suspense. After a long and difficult deliberation they reached a majority verdict: Taylor was found guilty on both charges, and – to the immense relief of Kathy and her supporters – sent down for fifteen years. Kathy's brave stance was vindicated, and her long nightmare finally came to an end.

Tom, Helen and Brenda

Since recovering from Greg's suicide and her subsequent anorexia, Helen had stayed resolutely single, dedicating herself to her work for the Bridge Farm shop, Ambridge Organics. Her brother Tom, meanwhile, had moved his pig business up to Home Farm, after Brian had rescued him from near-bankruptcy in the wake of a disastrous supermarket deal. He'd also fallen in love with Brenda Tucker, now on a Marketing and Business course at Felpersham University, and the couple had forged a close relationship.

Over the past autumn – encouraged by her friends and family – Helen had begun to get out more, and had launched into a full-on fling with Ross, an uber-trendy local journalist, only to be unceremoniously dumped by him at the end of November. Never one for half measures, she'd reacted by throwing herself into a life of serious partying and binge drinking, which had reached its inevitable crisis on New Year's Eve. After getting half-wasted at a club, she insisted on driving Tom home, and hit Mike Tucker as he walked down a lane near the village. Tom – well aware what a conviction for drink driving might do to his sister's state of mind – loyally covered for her, and told the police he'd been driving at the time. Mercifully, Mike's injuries were only superficial, and Tom was lucky to escape with a fine and a few points off his license; a repentant Helen began a course of counselling to help with her drinking problem and emotional hang-ups.

Later in the spring, Tom and Brenda moved into 'The Nest', a small holiday cottage at Home Farm, and when her term ended Brenda began to help Tom with his mobile catering business, Gourmet Grills. This cosy collaboration was soon threatened when Brenda had a vacation job offer from the Borchester Land supremo, Matt Crawford. Matt (who'd bought the Dower House from Caroline and was now living there with Lilian) was impressed by Brenda's lively mind and marketing skills, and took her on as a temporary PA. Although instinctively Tom mistrusted Matt, Brenda took readily to her new role, helping him through a tricky planning application. At the end of the summer Matt was impressed enough to offer her a regular vacation internship, with the prospect of a full-time job at the end. Tom could hardly object, although he remained deeply cynical about Matt's character and business methods.

It wasn't long before Matt's alpha-male instincts also began to worry Lilian. The prospect of a juicy property deal led Matt into close consultations with Borchester Land's new legal adviser, glamorous 45-year-old Annabelle Schrivener. Their business meetings led to flirtatious sessions in the bar, and the attraction seemed to be mutual. By the end of the year, Lilian began to suspect that she had a serious rival.

Tamsin Greig (Debbie Aldridge) is used to being well received on stage and screen. She won an Olivier Award for her portrayal of Beatrice in the Royal Shakespeare Company's *Much Ado About Nothing*. Her engaging character, Alice, was the star of *Love Soup*, David Renwick's TV follow-up to *One Foot in the Grave*. And she stole the show in *The Little Dog Laughed* at the Garrick Theatre, causing *Evening Standard* critic Henry Hitchings to gush: 'Her diction and poise are razor sharp. When she's off-stage, the audience longs to have her back.' Debbie, alas, is largely exiled in Hungary these days. But she does make the occasional return to the Home Farm kitchen where Tamsin played out that extraordinary show-down with Charles Collingwood as her adulterous step-father Brian. The late Ned Sherin compared the ten-minute scene to Chekhov.

2008

Power Struggles ❧

As the year began, Matt found more perfectly excusable business reasons to spend time with Annabelle. When Pip led vocal opposition to the proposed destruction of skylark nesting sites on the Estate, it was Annabelle's diplomatic skills that suggested a face-saving compromise. But Lilian's suspicions were proved only too right when she surprised them in a compromising clinch in Matt's office. Deaf to Matt's excuses, she walked out on him and went to stay with Sid and Jolene at The Bull. Matt – who was never that serious about Annabelle – saw the error of his ways, and faced the long task of winning Lilian back again. Being temporarily single, however, didn't deter him from the serious task of getting rich. Over the following months his hard-headed approach to profit-making was to touch the lives of both the Archer and Aldridge families.

At Brookfield, Ruth finally laid the ghost of her cancer to rest in January, by having a successful breast reconstruction operation. Meanwhile, Brian's wish for Ruairi to inherit part of Home Farm led to a row with Debbie and Adam, worried about the possible break-up of the business. It was eventually settled when Brian agreed to step back from the management of the farm and go into semi-retirement. Adam and Debbie would both become full directors, each taking a thirty-three per cent share of the profits; Adam would manage the soft fruit and livestock, with Debbie taking on the arable. Ruairi would then inherit a third of the whole when Brian died, but Adam and Debbie would at least have the chance to build up enough capital eventually to buy him out.

Adam at Home Farm

As Ruth recovered from her operation, she and David joined forces with Home Farm to develop plans for an anaerobic digester plant, which would use farm waste to produce methane-generated electricity. This had the dual attraction of reducing their carbon footprint by producing green energy, while bringing in a healthy profit from the subsidised electricity sales. When Matt discovered their plans he was unhappy at the way the Estate had missed out on the scheme, but Adam shared Ruth and David's reluctance to bring him on board. By April, however, they were forced to reconsider when it turned out that, for the scheme to be viable, they would need another partner. They went back to Matt, who typically made them sweat for a while before agreeing to a 60-40 partnership in the newly formed Ambridge Heat and Power. This still left them facing fierce opposition from many villagers; two lively public meetings left David in particular feeling bruised and disheartened. But it was Matt's own subterfuge that finally pulled the rug from under AHP. Deciding that the Ambridge scheme was too puny for his expansive ambitions, he jumped ship and joined with a much larger consortium in the north of the county. Minus one of their major investors, Brookfield and Home Farm were left high and dry and – after months of hard work and controversy – were forced to abandon the whole scheme.

If that wasn't enough, Matt had also been making life difficult for the Archer family at Bridge Farm. After a failed attempt by Borchester Land to convert their vegetable packhouse into a residential unit, Tom – fed up with being at the mercy of an apparently unscrupulous landlord – persuaded Pat and Tony to try and buy the freehold of the farm. They set about raising a mortgage, and after some tricky negotiations – and a discreet intervention from Lilian – Matt agreed on a fair price. Tom showed his commitment by agreeing to bring part of his pig business back from Home Farm, and start producing organic sausages alongside his existing range. So the family united to begin the momentous change from humble tenants to proud landowners.

Throughout all this, Matt had embarked on a personal journey of his own. After Lilian finally forgave him for his fling with Annabelle, she discovered that he'd been adopted as a child and had never known his real mother. She then persuaded him – somewhat against his own better judgement – to do some detective work. So it was that in September Matt went to a nursing home in Walthamstow to visit his birth mother, Louise. Although she was mildly intrigued to see her long-lost son, she made it clear that – for her, at least – Matt belonged to a part of her life that she'd put behind her, and she'd no wish to awaken the ghosts of the past. It was an atypically subdued and introverted Matt who came back to Lilian, convinced that the visit had been a failure. Lilian was soon to have another cause for concern about her Tiger. In the late autumn he showed signs of stress over his property business, C3PL, which he said was having minor cashflow problems. More worrying still, as Christmas approached, be began to spend a lot of time in huddled conference with his business partner, Steve Chalkman.

The saga of the Ambridge community shop has helped to fuel a boom in similar ventures in the real rural world. Some forty new ventures opened for business in 2010 – more than double the opening rate for 2008. 'The *Archers* storyline is definitely contributing to high levels of interest,' says Mike Perry of the Plunkett Foundation, which advises on community enterprises.

Louiza Patikas passes the time between recording scenes as Helen Archer by pitting her wits at Scrabble against her fictional grandmother. June Spencer (Peggy Woolley) is, apparently, still a formidable player at 90. 'If one's in the studio and the other is hunched over the board in the green room, we trust each other not to cheat,' Louiza assures us.

*Will the keeper
with Brian*

Brotherly Love (Part 5)

Ed Grundy had now put his drug habit well behind him, and was making a success of running Oliver's small dairy herd at Grange Farm. There'd been no happy reconciliation with Emma, however, who was still very much single and living with George at Ambridge View. With her safely off Ed's radar, Jolene's daughter Fallon had fallen headlong for him and the two were now an established item. Will, meanwhile, had met up with single mum Nic and her two young kids, Jake and Mia. Although they were soon pretty much a steady couple, there was something about Nic that made Clarrie distrust her – and all the more so when it turned out that Will's Aunt Hilda had left him a substantial legacy. Whatever Clarrie's doubts, early in the New Year Nic and her children moved in to Casa Nueva and she and Will set up home together. Soon after, Will used his inheritance to buy No. 1 The Green as an investment, but saw no reason to move out of his rent-free tied accommodation. As the weeks went by, Nic – like Emma before her – began to feel lonely at the isolated cottage. Will's long hours also meant that she was often left with the care of George on his regular access visits. Although Emma wasn't too happy with this, she couldn't really object. But when Ed saw Nic lose her cool with George outside the shop he began to worry. There was a big row when he challenged Will about Nic's parenting skills, and Ed then confided in Emma, who was quite happy to believe that Nic was a bad mother. Will by then was having a few sneaking doubts of his own, which came to a head when he caught Nic smacking George. The resulting run-in led to Nic taking her kids and going back to her Mum's, leaving Will to his solitary life at Casa Nueva.

From here on, things went downhill fast for Will. After being falsely accused of poisoning a red kite, he almost came to blows with Ed in The Bull. Ed, meanwhile, was drifting apart from Fallon, who was busy doing summer gigs with her band, Little White Lies. Emma had never stopped loving him, and he soon realised he was still in love with her, too. When, in July, they got back together, it came as another blow to Will, who'd been nursing his own secret hopes for Emma. It all came to a crunch in a vicious fight at Keeper's Cottage, in which Will half-strangled his brother. After that, he disappeared. A week or so later he was traced to a boyhood haunt on the Norfolk coast, and in a touching irony it was Ed who managed to persuade him to come back – for George's sake. But he didn't stay for long; unable to stomach seeing Ed and Emma back with George, he left Ambridge to start a temporary job on a shoot near Gloucester. Clarrie nobly took George down on visits to see him, and in November, Nic went to see him too. Although still very wary of any relationship, Will agreed to meet her again, and she managed to persuade him to come and see George in Ambridge. As Christmas approached, Will surprised his family by coming to help with the annual turkey pluck. Although he went back to his job in Gloucester, he left Clarrie and Eddie hoping that the worst might be over.

Jack and Peggy

At the Lodge, Jack's mental state had continued its inevitable decline, and Peggy – although she would be the first to deny it – was finding it ever harder to cope with his forgetfulness and erratic behaviour. There was an upsetting incident in September, when he locked her out of the house, and she had to be rescued by Tom and Brian. The family then managed to persuade her to take on a part-time carer; but the whole situation became more urgent when, in October, Peggy had a stroke. She was in hospital for two weeks while she recovered. In the meantime the family struggled to care for Jack, and ended up finding him a temporary place in a nursing home – much to Peggy's dismay, when she found out. Although her stroke wasn't as bad as it might have been, it left her weak and tired and – more seriously – partly blind in one eye. In spite of this she was determined to get back to the Lodge as soon as she could, and to keep Jack there with her. Knowing better than to argue, the family arranged a rota to help her cope, and so they struggled on through the autumn, while the search went on for a reliable carer. Although far from the perfect solution, they all knew that Peggy would fight to the last rather than let Jack move into a residential home.

Matt's Downfall

2009

As the year began, so Matt and Chalkman's problems with C3PL were getting deeper by the day. This wasn't a great time to be in the property business, and – unknown to Lilian, or to anyone else – they had financed bad debts, and as clients failed to repay them, so they themselves couldn't repay their own borrowings. By early February they had secretly thrown in the towel, and C3PL was under administration. This was bad enough news in itself, but it was about to have serious knock-on effects for Tom Archer. In January, he had a major bust-up with Brian, who'd tried to involve him in a big supermarket deal. Tom had already had his fingers burnt once by a supermarket and, after the row that followed, he found himself desperately looking for £50k to buy himself out of his partnership with Home Farm. Encouraged by Brenda – who was still doing occasional work for Matt around her uni studies – Tom approached Matt. He was in for a disappointment, however: with his own secret financial problems,

JUDGE	… I am therefore going to impose an immediate term of imprisonment. Reports will serve no useful purpose in the face of such an inevitable sentence.
	CROSS TO:
	8B. INT. COURTROOM, PUBLIC GALLERY, CONTINUOUS.
LILIAN	Immediate? How immediate?
JENNIFER	(REALISING) Oh Lilian.
	8C. INT. COURTROOM, CONTINUOUS
JUDGE	Mr. Chalkman, I sentence you to a term of three and a half years, of which you will serve a minimum of twenty-one months. Mr. Crawford, in view of your full co-operation, I sentence you to a term of eighteen months, of which you will serve a minimum of nine months. There are to be confiscation proceedings in this case which will be adjourned to a later date. Take them down.
	CROSS TO:
	8D. INT. COURTROOM, PUBLIC GALLERY, CONTINOUS
LILIAN	(LEAPS TO HER FEET, WAIL) No! Matt! Matt!
	(RUMBLE OF SURPRISE FROM OTHERS IN THE GALLERY)
JENNIFER	Lilian, please! That won't help.
	CROSS TO:
	8E. INT. COURTROOM, CONTINUOUS
LILAIN	(OFF) Matt, please…
MATT	(BEING LED OFF, LOOKING BACK) Can I speak to her? Please?
ESCORT	(HUSTLING HIM DOWN STEPS, MATTER OF FACT) Sorry. This way.

Matt gave him short shrift. A week or two later, Brenda overheard Matt and 'Chalky' Chalkman in a fraught conversation about C3PL, in which Matt hinted at some behind-the-scenes dodgy dealings. When Matt realised she'd listened in, he tried to buy her off by offering to help Tom after all. Knowing how desperate Tom was, Brenda agreed – but didn't tell Tom why Matt had suddenly changed his tune.

But Tom was never to get a penny from Matt. Just a few days later, the police made a dawn raid on the Dower House, and Matt was hauled off for questioning by the Serious Fraud Office. As a shocked Lilian was soon to discover, Matt's problems were more than just financial. He and Chalky had given false information to secure a £5 million loan from a local bank, and were both facing serious charges. Lilian was in for an even worse shock when she found out just how serious the charges were: even if Matt took his lawyer's advice, and cooperated with the SFO, he could still end up facing a prison sentence.

Rumours of the raid and of Matt's arrest were soon flying around the village. When Tom found out the truth about Brenda's surreptitious deal, they had a serious row, which ended in Brenda walking out and going to stay with Mike at Willow Farm. But there were more repercussions to come for Brenda. A few days later she was called in for questioning by the SFO about her involvement with Matt and C3PL. Although she was only interviewed as a possible witness, and couldn't tell them much, it did nothing to lift her mood, or stop her from missing Tom.

Matt, meanwhile, had bravely decided to bite the bullet, come clean to the SFO, and face the consequences. His position was made all the more uncertain by the fact that Chalky had slipped the police net and done a runner. It wasn't until a month or so later that he secretly got in touch with Matt, and tried to get him to fight the case, and go back on his statement to the SFO. Matt refused, and things turned nasty when a mysterious intruder broke into the Dower House, and a frightened Lilian began to suspect that Chalky was stalking her. Soon after, however, they heard that he'd taken his lawyer's advice and turned himself into the police. This was only a mixed blessing, as Matt began to worry that his former business partner would now do his best to incriminate him to try and save his own skin.

Matt was now facing business problems closer to home, as well. In May he was voted out of his position as chair of Borchester Land, to be replaced by Brian. A furious Lilian saw this as an act of family betrayal and for the next few weeks she and Jennifer were hardly on speaking terms. At the same time, Matt's mood began to darken. Lilian found him restless and uncommunicative, and he disappeared for hours at a time on mysterious trips in the car. Concerned and suspicious, she eventually made him take her with him, only to discover that Matt had been seeking respite from his troubles in aimless high-speed drives. Frightened by his reckless speeding she forced him to pull over, only to be abandoned in a layby as he drove away. When he eventually returned a couple of days later, she told him she'd had enough, and went to Home Farm to stay with Jennifer, the feud between the two sisters now forgotten.

While Lilian worried, Matt brooded on alone at the Dower House, largely indifferent to the few friends who took the trouble to visit him. He was formally charged for the C3PL fraud in September. After discovering that he could end up with a maximum ten-year stretch, he went on a drinking binge at Grey Gables. Loyal to him in his hour of need, Lilian was there when he sobered up, and took him home to the Dower House, where she stayed to care for him. But even with her support, Matt was still haunted by the threat of a long prison sentence. Just two weeks before the trial, he reached breaking point and

Matt (Kim Durham) arriving at court

took a flight to Costa Rica, a frantic Lilian beside him. In spite of all her attempts to persuade him to see sense, he seemed determined to start a new life as an exile. It wasn't until the day before the trial that he finally gave up the fight and flew back with her, arriving at the court the following morning with minutes to spare. As the trial began, Chalkman surprised them all by changing his plea to guilty. The same day, he was sentenced to three years, while Matt – as the minority shareholder – was given eighteen months. He was taken straight down from the court, and Lilian, shocked and distraught, went home with Jennifer, leaving her Tiger alone in the cells.

Mike's New Love

*Famous folk who
opened the village fete:*

ANTONY GORMLEY,
2009

The year began with builders still busy at Willow Farm, after the Tucker family had agreed to split the house into two units. Roy, Hayley, Phoebe and her little sister Abbie – born in July the previous year – were to take over the larger part, with a small extension built to house a new kitchen and bedroom for Mike. The conversion work was finished in the spring, and the extended family duly took up residence. Happily settled, Mike began to renew his much-neglected social life, and in April met bubbly and vivacious dental nurse Vicky Hudson at his dancing class. The couple hit it off right from the start and were soon acting like love-struck teenagers, to the dismay of Brenda, who – still loyal to the memory of her mother – disliked and mistrusted Vicky from the first time they met. But if she hoped that her dad would see the light and dump her any time soon, she was in for a shock.

In May, after making up their quarrel over Matt and his loan, Tom and Brenda announced their engagement. But this happy event was soon to be dramatically upstaged. After his daughter's engagement party in June, Mike proposed to Vicky, who didn't need asking twice. Almost before the rest of the family could catch their breath, they'd jumped the queue at the local Registry Office and the wedding was booked for mid-July – just four weeks away. Dazed by the speed of it all, Brenda went to her father and told him just what she though of his bride-to-be – that she was a shameless gold-digger who'd used her seductive charms to get her hands on Mike's property. Understandably, this led to a cooling of the father-daughter relationship, but Brenda relented enough to come to the wedding on 15 July. After a honeymoon on the Isle of Wight, Vicky and her large collection of teddy bears moved in with Mike at Willow Farm. Another honeymoon followed in Brittany, Vicky coming home this time with an all-over tan after discovering the local nudist beach. As the summer ended, she cemented her ties with country life by offering to loan Ed the cash to run a few more cows at Grange Farm, so that Mike could expand his milk round. Ed took the money gratefully, but a few alarm bells began to ring when Vicky showed more interest in the Guernsey's cute eyelashes than in the high butterfat content of their milk.

*Mike and Vicky
(Rachel Atkins)*

'Some of the biggest arguments between our writers are over the characters. Take Vicky for instance. Is she a complete nightmare or does she have a heart of gold? She winds us up just as much as she divides the listeners, and that's fine. The big 'no-no' is for an audience not to care either way. Lynda's another one who writers and listeners either love or hate. I happen to love her. Yes, she gets things wrong but she'd do anything for that community. Others would quite happily leave her hung out to dry.'

Editor Vanessa Whitburn

The Odd Couple

Jazzer (Ryan Kelly) riding a quad bike

The end of the old year saw Helen still single and still living at the family home. In February, she made a break for independence, and moved into the newly renovated flat over the shop; but she wasn't to be there alone for long. In April, Greg's younger daughter Annette turned up out of the blue and ended up staying in Helen's spare room. Although at first she claimed to be passing through on her way to stay with her gran, Helen soon discovered that she was homeless and vulnerable after being chucked out by her mum's new boyfriend, and so she took the 18-year-old girl under her wing. Annette seemed in no hurry to move on, getting herself a part-time job in the shop, and then falling for local wild boy Jazzer McCreary. Protective Helen soon put an end to this relationship, worried that Jazzer was leading the poor girl on. But it wasn't long before Helen became involved in an unequal relationship of her own with handsome Australian barman Leon. Although all went well at first, after her close friend Ian met him on a double date, he warned her that Leon was a serial womaniser. This wasn't what Helen wanted to hear, but then over Christmas she caught him flagrantly snogging another girl, and dumped him on the spot. What Helen didn't know was that Annette had already shared a guilty night of passion with Leon behind her back. This was a one-night stand that Annette was already beginning to regret. As 2010 was ushered in and the shops reopened after the New Year break, she went to the chemist and bought herself a pregnancy test.

'A good friend of ours has the perception to know that she's just like Lynda Snell. I also know two others who are just like her but don't know it. They're completely deluded. When I do my one-woman show at festivals or book promotions, I tell the audience: "Lynda Snells are everywhere. There might even be one in this room." That always gets them laughing.'

Carole Boyd [Lynda Snell]

Profile
VICKY TUCKER

S HE WAS A PAINFULLY shy little girl. Wore plaits at school and blushed a lot. Who would have imagined that Rachel Atkins would grow up to play the brash and breezy Vicky Tucker? Come to think of it, she wouldn't be the first shrinking violet to blossom through drama. 'It's a way of expressing yourself while not being yourself,' she suggests.

The voice has Vicky's warmth minus her full-on brand of Brummie, although Rachel was born in Birmingham forty-two years ago. 'My partner tells me that I sound my Gs when I'm particularly tired,' she smiles. She was brought up in upmarket Edgbaston, a mile or two from the BBC's Mailbox studio from which she has just slipped out for lunch – a cup of coffee in her case. Her mother came from France and her father from Smethwick, making her heritage a rare combination of the Gallic and the Black Country. 'There were lots of books in the house and education was cherished,' she recalls.

She went to a convent school and then to an all-girls' grammar. 'It meant that I played quite a few male parts in drama productions,' she says. 'But when we reached the sixth form there was more mixing with the boys' school. Together we created a revue that we took to the Edinburgh Festival. I was 17 or 18, doing comedy at night and playing Hedda Gabler during the day.'

Her route from Ibsen to *The Archers* spanned over twenty years, during which time she went to drama school in Cardiff before moving to London and gaining invaluable experience in theatre, on television and, above all, in her favourite medium: radio. 'My first radio role was done in a studio in Wales,' she says. 'I played a sheep.' Not the kind you find grazing on a Welsh hillside or the pastures around Brookfield, apparently. 'No, this was a political satire about the parliamentary process. I had to say more than "Bah".'

Why does she like doing radio so much? 'Because you depend solely on your voice to feed the listener's imagination. You can't rely on gestures, dress or physical looks.' Certainly the actress doesn't conform to this listener's vision of Vicky. Today she's wearing a dark sweater, blue jeans and flat heels. Only a bright pink scarf might match a Vicky-ish shade of lipstick.

Rachel had appeared in *The Archers* long before she took on the role of Mrs Tucker mark two. Back in 1999 she was one of the jurors who acquitted the youthful Tom Archer of trashing genetically modified crops. 'I think that episode was unique insofar as it featured no regular member of the cast,' she points out before going on to reveal that she also auditioned for the part of Sophie. Sophie? Oh yes. She was the dishy-but-dim dress designer who came back to fluster and flatter David Archer, thereby setting in motion a chain of events that almost ended his marriage. 'Then the actress who played Sophie in the 1980s [Moir Leslie] came back and obviously it made sense to go with her.'

'...I get to share a studio with actors I've been listening to for years.'

The part of Vicky has been more than adequate compensation, she feels. 'It's great fun to play. Not least because I get to share a studio with actors I've been listening to for years.' And in the case of Terry Molloy (Mike Tucker) sharing a bed in only her third episode. Was it just Rachel, Terry and the spot effects engineer shaking the duvet? 'I shake my own duvet if you don't mind,' she says, slipping into Vicky mode for a moment.'

As a character, she's certainly made an impact, dividing villagers and listeners into pro and anti factions. 'I was brought in and asked to be a Heather Mills-type character,' she says. Now it so happens that Terry Molloy has performed at the Cavern Club in Liverpool, but Mike Tucker is hardly Paul McCartney. He's a village milkman with a limited income. Then again, he did marry again fairly soon after being widowed and that made his new bride deeply unpopular with at least one of his children. Now that 'the cracks are beginning to show', as Rachel puts it, could it be that Brenda might be proved right after all about her father's new-found happiness with a woman who was naked but for his dressing gown when she first met her?

All the actress knows is that lunchtime doesn't last for ever. It's time to get back to the microphone and revive that Brummie accent.

SOUND EFFECTS

HOW IS THE ATMOSPHERE of The Bull conveyed through the sealed and rather soulless medium of a radio studio? Answer: you blend your 'spot' effects and your 'gram' effects through a mixing desk that looks as fiendishly complicated as a control panel at the Kennedy Space Center. The spot effects studio manager Lisa Wallace is out there with the actors, rattling loose change, opening bottles, ringing tills and whatever else is required to make listeners feel that they're eavesdropping on a conversation in a proper village pub. Her equivalent on the gram is Kath Shuttleworth, who is sitting at a computer on the other side of the glass, feeding in the gentle hum of conversation, the clink of glasses, the thud of darts and the sound of beer making progress from cellar to glass.

Sitting just in front of Kath is today's producer, Kate Oates, ears attuned to the fine details of the actors' interpretation of the script. She is dealing with professionals who know their craft, so she's relentlessly encouraging – 'well done, guys, that's great' – while also expecting retakes should there be a pause in the wrong place, an emphasis on the wrong word or a tiny verbal fluff.

Manning the mixing desk is studio manager Michael Harrison, responsible for blending all these sounds together in a way that is convincing but not intrusive. 'Our aim is always to be there but never noticed,' he says. He wants listeners to concentrate on the drama in those voices, in other words, without being distracted by the wrong doorbell at Glebe Cottage; a door slamming too softly for a stroppy teenager or too loudly for a nursing mother; a migratory willow warbler warbling out of season; or even Robert Snell being served the wrong kind of pint on those occasions when he slips off Lynda's leash.

'Sorry. Not quite the right beer,' says Kath, having played in a lager tap by mistake. It has been decided that Robert, a man of discernment who likes a decent Armagnac when he's not slumming it on the Grundys' cider, would be a real ale drinker. Cue a pint of Shires being pulled by a traditional hand pump. That was a gram effect, recorded on location and played through the computer. The studio spot effects are quite ingenious and usually the results of much trial and error. Here are a few examples:

'Our aim is always to be there but never noticed…'

- Brian opening a bottle of champagne – that's a cork on a string flying out of a bicycle pump. And being poured? That's an Alka-Seltzer being tossed into a glass of water.
- Brian being kicked by a mad cow, as he was some years ago? That was a water melon being struck by a hammer. 'It was very messy, but Charles [Collingwood, the actor] wouldn't let us do it to him,' Michael points out.
- A calf being born involves plenty of yoghurt, a wet tea towel and a pile of old recording tape. 'Sounds fantastic.'
- A rustling in the grass? More tape.
- Artificial insemination? More yoghurt, only this time with a metal pole sliding in and out.

The studio is ingeniously designed. Different surfaces convey changes in location. There's a 'hard area' for milking parlours, bathrooms and church halls. And there's a 'dead room' lined with a curiously spongy-looking substance that thins the voice – ideal for a couple chatting while striding out over Lakey Hill. There's a kitchen area with a sink and a living room with a bottle of gin on a table, as though waiting for Lilian to pour herself a large one. 'It's radio gin,' says Michael. Water, in other words.

Gram effects are recorded on location and Michael is only too well aware of the twitchers and trainspotters out there, just waiting for him to get it wrong. 'We had all our bird songs checked by the RSPB ten years ago,' he confides. 'But the changing nature of the seasons is leading to different migratory habits.' So he's been out to record them again near his home in Malvern.

And the trainspotters? Well, years ago, a producer took a call from a man who had clearly not been impressed by a poignant Brief Encounterish scene played out at Hollerton Junction. 'The doors on Midland services do not slam,' he pointed out. 'They are electric and they close with a sort of whooshing sound,' he added in a voice that was rather muffled – possibly by the hood of an anorak.

ATTITUDES

WHAT'S IN A NAME? Enough to require subtle changes in the way that a long-running drama reflects the evolution of English village life. Twenty years ago, Eddie Grundy might have had one or two choice names for Brian Aldridge behind his back, but to his face he would always be 'Mr Aldridge'. Apart from anything else, Brian was a potential source of work. He still is for Eddie's sons. As chairman of Borchester Land, he leases Ed somewhere to graze his cows, and he is the direct employer of Ed's brother Will. 'But the Grundy brothers wouldn't dream of calling him anything but Brian,' says *Archers* editor Vanessa Whitburn. 'And that has happened organically as society has become more informal. Eddie, too, calls him 'Brian' these days.'

Sometimes it seems a very long time since Caroline Bone, as she then was (descended from the de Bohns), addressed her boss as 'Mr Woolley', descended from the Woolleys of workaday Stirchley, Birmingham. Now that she's running Grey Gables, however, her manager Roy Tucker calls her 'Caroline'. Bert Fry, meanwhile, had three different names for his former bosses – 'Mr Archer' for Dan, 'Boss' for Phil and a matey 'David' for the third generation.

Drama has always explored the sometimes baffling subtleties of the English class system and *The Archers* is no exception. 'But the younger generation is less aware of class distinctions,' the editor points out. Alice Aldridge's mother disapproved of her relationship with farrier Christopher Carter even before their spur-of-the-moment wedding in Las Vegas. Jennifer Aldridge appears to have forgotten that she came from fairly humble origins before marrying into money – 'new money' in the form of the self-made Brian rather than the 'old money' that her sister Lilian inherited as the widow of Ralph Bellamy. (That was long before she met freshly minted Matt Crawford, whose money turned out to be distinctly dodgy.)

Older listeners may also remember the outcry that greeted Jennifer's pregnancy back in the not-so-swinging 1960s. In 1967, a single mother could be roundly denounced, threatened with eviction and urged to marry the father, whoever he was. Over 40 years on and *The Archers* reflects a very different society – one where the 'illegitimate' product of Jennifer's pregnancy is involved in a civil partnership with another man and Jennifer's niece is actively seeking single motherhood through insemination by a sperm donor.

'Controversial storylines attract far fewer complaints from listeners than they did twenty years ago,' says Vanessa. One of her predecessors, Liz Rigbey, the programme's first female editor, remembers vitriolic press comment about feminist tendencies in *The Archers*. 'I think some columnists expected Shula and Caroline to stay at home sewing their samplers,' she reflects drily. Liz was also surprised by the volume of letters she received after a scene in a London hotel bedroom in 1987. 'It was when Alice was conceived,' she says. Brian and Jennifer, then – a married couple? 'Yes, and not exactly newly-weds! All the listeners heard was some heavy breathing.' Similar sounds had been emitted some thirty years earlier when Carol Grey and Tony Stobeman shared a sofa, leading a BBC executive to send a stiff memo to *The*

Archers complaining that 'Miss Grey had forgotten her mother's good advice.'

In other respects, the 1950s were rather more liberal. Thumbing through a photo album with her grandmother Peggy, Helen Archer pointed out a picture of her Auntie Jennifer behind the bar of The Bull as a child. 'You wouldn't get away with that now, would you?' Helen pointed out. 'And Grandpa with a fag in his mouth too!' Peggy concurred before reflecting: 'They were very different times.'

'You wouldn't get away with that now, would you?'

Uniquely among drama series, *The Archers* has charted the transition from those times to these. On the way it has covered everything from racist attacks to drug-taking and binge-drinking. But the high drama has always been interspersed with lengthier periods reflecting the quieter rhythms of rural life. When those rhythms are rudely interrupted – as they were, for instance, in 1993 when Clive Horrobin led an armed raid on the village shop – there is a tendency for city folk to query whether such things really happen in the countryside. Unfortunately they do, as more than one real-life raid on Worcestershire sub-post offices has shown with tragic consequences.

Nor is there anything new about rural crime being featured in *The Archers*. 'Back in the 1950s, Walter Gabriel's bus was held up by raiders wielding iron bars,' Vanessa points out, 'which makes Jamie and Josh's graffiti exploits pale into insignificance.'

2010... and Beyond

Helen's Baby

The new decade began with Annette still hiding the truth about the father of her child from Helen, whose own maternal instincts went into overdrive when she learnt that her friend was pregnant – and planning an abortion. In spite of Helen's pleas and pressure for her to keep the baby, Annette went ahead, and soon after decided it was time to leave Ambridge behind and move on to seek new horizons. Helen's deep emotional involvement in her friend's dilemma, perhaps abetted by her own continuing isolation after Greg's death, led her to take a momentous decision. Just a week or two after Annette's departure, she astonished her close family by announcing that she was planning to have a

Tony and Pat in the milking parlour at Bridge Farm

baby of her own. And no, she was not going to compromise her decision through any relationship with a man, but use donated sperm instead. In the face of strongly argued opposition from Tony, but with the general support of her mother, Helen pressed ahead resolutely – some might say obsessively – with her plan, and by May she was pregnant.

Although both Pat and Helen's close friend Ian shared in her delight at this news, it provoked just a hint of jealousy from Tom. Initially bemused by the whole affair, he now found his sister expecting a child, while Brenda was making it clear that she'd no wish to become a mother any time soon. But with ever-controlling Helen's baby due early next year, she still has plenty of emotional hurdles ahead of her, and many are wondering how she'll cope with the mixed joys and stresses of single motherhood.

Matt Returns

With Matt serving out his sentence at an open prison, Lilian found her first few visits very difficult, as she struggled to break through the defensive emotional shell into which he'd retreated. Meanwhile, she was contacted by Matt's half-brother Paul, with the news of the death of Matt's mother, Louise. Although Matt wanted nothing to do with his blood family, Lilian and Paul became close after she secretly went to Louise's funeral. For a while it looked as if their friendship might lead to something more intimate, but Lilian stayed loyal to her Tiger, and was there to pick him up on his release from prison in May. As he readjusted to home life on a curfew, Matt put aside any doubts he may have had about Lilian's friendship with Paul, and directed his energies into rebuilding his life. Although barred from running his own company, he and Lilian he set up a fledgling property business – 'Amside' – in Lilian's name. He then worried Tom by luring Brenda away from her new long-distance job in Leicester with the promise of a small raise and no commute.

One of the company's first successful projects was to buy and convert two small houses at Hillside. But soon after Matt crossed with his old sparring partner Brian, now firmly established as Borchester Land's new chairman, who outbid Amside on a pub for renovation near Borchester. Matt wasn't going to take this lying down and quietly plotted his revenge. His chance came when BL ran into trouble over their plans to develop Borchester's new cattle market. Objections from the local council had left them looking for a new access route from the main road, and Brian was dismayed to discover that Matt had slyly bought up the only suitable land, using money he'd secretly stashed away in an overseas account. Matt was willing to sell the land to BL, but asked a heavy price, one of his conditions being that Lilian should be installed as a director on the BL board. Brian's fellow directors drew the line at this, leaving Matt still holding his trump card: the market scheme won't go ahead unless 'Amside' has a share of the deal.

Although (for the time being, at least) careful to stay the right side of the law, Matt's time in prison seems to have done nothing to blunt his sharp eye for a lucrative deal, or mute his aggressive business instincts. His slow but steady rise from the humiliation of scandal and near-ruin promises interesting times ahead, not just for Brian and Borchester Land, but for the whole of Ambridge.

Sid's Farewell ⌘

In early June the whole village was shocked by the news that Sid Perks, while on a visit to his daughter Lucy in New Zealand, had died suddenly from a heart attack. Both Kathy and Fallon flew out to be with Jolene for the funeral. Jolene returned cocooned in her grief, and struggled to carry on running The Bull without Sid, as everything about the business only served to make her miss him all the more. Fallon, with help from Nic and Lilian, worked hard to support her, but by August Jolene was openly wondering about giving up the pub and starting a new life elsewhere. It was only after Fallon, who hated the thought of cutting her ties with Ambridge, had pleaded with her that Jolene gritted her teeth and decided to stay on for her daughter's sake.

Meanwhile, Sid's death had widened the cracks that were already beginning to show in Kathy's relationship with Kenton. Although she and Sid had now been divorced for many years, she was very upset by his death, and was correspondingly resentful when Kenton cried off coming with her to the funeral, preferring to stay on and see the newly reopened Jaxx Bar through its crucial early days. As Kenton's life became ever more devoted to the bar, it got to the point where she began to wonder if their relationship had a future at all. The breaking point came in August after a big row at the Golf Club dinner dance, and the couple finally went their separate ways; Kathy back to April Cottage, Kenton to seek refuge with his younger sister at Lower Loxley. To add to Kathy's problems, Jamie too had been deeply affected by Sid's death, and began to show worrying signs of anti-social behaviour. As the summer waned, he led his mate Josh into trouble after they were involved in the trashing of Kirsty's carefully planned and newly built hide at Arkwright Lake. Although Josh's parents were understandably furious with him, Jamie was clearly the ringleader. The incident left Kathy fearing that he was turning into a bit of a wild child, and might even end up going the way of the Grundy boys. Kenton, meanwhile, began to pass a little more time at The Bull, where he discovered something of a kindred spirit in lonely Jolene. He soon became her close confidant, able to sympathise with her doubts about staying on at The Bull. Although for the time being she's still hanging in there, many of the Bull regulars share Fallon's concern that it may not be for much longer.

Wedding Bells: Married Bliss?

In the summer Roy and Hayley weren't best pleased to learn that Kate planned to take some time away from her husband, Lucas, and kids Nolly and Sipho in South Africa to study for a Diploma in International Development at Felpersham University, starting in September. They were even more unsettled when informed that one of her motives was to spend more time with Phoebe, now approaching 12, and in her first year at Borchester Green. It looks like being a difficult year ahead for the Tuckers, and especially for Phoebe, as she tries to divide her time – and her loyalty – between her step and biological mothers.

*Tom with Gloucestershire
Old Spot pigs*

As Jennifer looked forward to Kate's return, her youngest daughter Alice was about to drop a bombshell on the whole family. In mid-August she and Christopher Carter returned from a road trip through the western United States as man and wife, after an off-the-peg impulse wedding in Las Vegas. While, from the start, Jennifer had quietly disapproved of Alice's ongoing relationship with farrier Christopher, nothing had prepared her for this startling turn of events. Alice, however, found it hard to understand what all the fuss was about. After all, they were in love, Christopher had a steady job with a good income, and being a married woman wouldn't stop her from returning to Southampton in September to finish her degree. Would-be social climber Susan was, of course, only too delighted to see her son become a part of the Aldridge family, but it's safe to say that Jennifer may not find it so easy to get used to her daughter now being Mrs Alice Carter.

There was also some happy news from Alice's new sister-in-law, Emma Grundy, who in August announced that she was pregnant again. Although husband Ed was thoroughly delighted, the prospect of a new half-sibling for George seems likely to reopen a few old wounds for Will. Already showing signs of unease at his partner Nic's part-time job at The Bull, neither Will's past form nor his jealous nature bode well for their future happiness.

There could also be some tricky times ahead for some other couples around the village. Still at Amside, Brenda managed some initial hostility from Lilian to establish herself as a valued assistant to Matt. Tom's doubts about her job remain, however, and she could find herself walking a narrow line if she's to continue to try and please everyone in her life. Last but by no means least, there's more than a hint of trouble ahead for her dad, Mike Tucker. After his wife Vicky put her heart and soul into 'saving' a few of Ed's bull calves and helping to raise them for veal, by the end of the summer she found herself struggling to sell them for anything like a profit. Forced to accept that in the end her courageous venture was a commercial failure, she didn't take it too well, and has become more than a little grumpy about the whole business. It could be that the gloss is finally starting to wear off her and Mike's shiny new marriage.

Passing On

Friday 12 February 2010 was a day of sadness for the whole Archer family. After a shopping trip with Peggy and Christine, Jill returned to Glebe Cottage to find that Phil had died peacefully in his chair, his favourite Elgar oratorio still playing on the stereo. Jill's grief was perhaps tempered by the knowledge that, at the age of 81, it was a fitting end to a long life in and around his beloved Brookfield, and then as head of a close and loving family. His death marked the gentle passing of the baton from one generation to the next. Among the many mourners at his funeral were the two remaining family members who'd shared Dan Archer's toast to the New Year in the first moments of 1951, almost sixty years ago: Peggy was now alone at the Lodge, after finally making the difficult decision to move Jack into the Laurels nursing home, while Chris was a widow and churchwarden living out a peaceful retirement. Among the younger generation, Ruth and David were continuing the young Phil's cutting-edge approach to farming, with a new rotational paddock system to graze their selectively cross-bred dairy herd.

Their three children, meanwhile, were probably giving them as much trouble as David and his siblings had caused their own parents before them. Over the spring, David in particular struggled to get his head around 17-year-old Pip's stubborn and tempestuous involvement with the 29-year-old Jude, while 12-year-old Josh upset both his mum and dad with his skillful but misguided use of a spray can around the village. But by the autumn, after a good deal of tears and heartbreak for Pip, Jude was already history. In September she

	7. GLEBE COTTAGE KITCHEN. FRIDAY 1.30PM. (MUSIC PLAYING ON STEREO OFF – ELGAR ORATORIO)
JILL	(EXT DOOR OPENED. APP) Here we are. Come on in.
PEGGY	(OFF A BIT) Thank you. Oh, what a lovely day we've had!
JILL	Phil's got his music on. What's the betting he's having a nap.
CHRIS	(OFF A BIT) Ooh, lovely and warm. (EXT DOOR CLOSED)
JILL	(MOVING AWAY) Put the kettle on, can you Chris?
CHRIS	Right.
PEGGY	Oh yes. A cup of tea would be lovely.
JILL	(GOING) I'll just see if Phil would like a cup.
	CROSS SLOWLY TO:-
	7A. INT. GLEBE COTTAGE SITTING ROOM. CONTINUOUS. (MUSIC CONTINUES)
JILL	(APP) There you are. You've already had a cuppa I see. Phil… (STOPS. BEAT. REALISES) Phil! Oh!
CHRIS	(OFF) What is it? (APP) Oh no…
JILL	(TEARS) Oh Phil… (FADE UP MUSIC, THEN SLOW FADE. NO SIG)

The next generation: David gives Pip (Helen Monks) some fatherly advice

returned to college, and was taking a renewed interest in the local Young Farmer's Club. It's likely that 8-year-old Ben is more concerned with competing for attention with his elder siblings; but with Josh's enthusiasm for the farming life never far below the surface, the way looks open for at least one more generation of Archers to work the land, milk the cows and fill in the DEFRA forms at Brookfield Farm.

Topical inserts don't come much more topical than the one inserted the day after a general election when hundreds of would-be voters found themselves turned away from polling stations. Jim Lloyd was heard pontificating about it in a scene written the morning after it happened and aired that very evening. He referred a rather baffled Susan Carter to the birthplace of democracy where ancient Greeks apparently packed the Athenian assembly several times a year. The democratically elected queen – of the community shop – a glowing example of the Tory leader's 'Big Society' if ever there was one – deftly dragged the conversation back from Athens to Ambridge before guiding the old classicist towards the teabags.

In the most dramatic night of 2010, Gordon Brown resigned and David Cameron became prime minister of the country's first coalition government since the war. Television cameras tracked their progress to and from Buckingham Palace as the Queen said farewell to one and hello to the other. *EastEnders* was postponed while, over on Radio 4, extended news coverage rolled over all other programmes. Bar one. The nation was not to be denied its nightly visit to Ambridge. While the new PM worked out what he was going to say to the waiting world on his way into Downing Street, Susan was updating Jill on progress at the community shop and reminding her of an imminent parish council committee meeting. Governments come and go but, like Old Man River, *The Archers* keeps rolling along.

An even faster insert came when Kenton updated Jamie on the England-Slovenia World Cup Match (including the score and Rooney hitting the post) just over two hours after full time. Jamie, alas, was not interested in events in South Africa, having just flown back from his father's funeral in New Zealand.